CHAMPAGNE AND SILVER BUCKLES

Champagne and Silver Buckles

The Viceregal Court at Dublin Castle 1700-1922

JOSEPH ROBINS

THE LILLIPUT PRESS
DUBLIN

First published 2001 by
THE LILLIPUT PRESS LTD
62–63 Sitric Road, Arbour Hill,
Dublin 7, Ireland

A CIP record for this title is available from
The British Library.

1 3 5 7 9 10 8 6 4 2

ISBN 1 901866 58 0

*The Lilliput Press is grateful to the Office of Public Works
for its support of this publication.*

Set in Georgia
Index by Helen Litton
Printed in England by MPG Books, Bodmin, Cornwall

Contents

Preface

For centuries Dublin Castle was the headquarters of British rule in Ireland. It was more than a mere building where the viceroy, chief representative of the British monarch, resided. If the viceregal throne was often occupied by vainglorious puppets with little political power or influence of their own, they were, for all that, the eyes, ears and mouthpieces of their British masters. And for a privileged and powerful minority of the population, the viceregal court also represented the apex of Irish high society.

The main focus of this book is on the social and ceremonial life of the viceregal court during the period 1700 to 1922. The year 1700 is chosen as the starting-point as it approximates to the beginning of a more sophisticated and formal court influenced by similar developments in England. The book ends with the withdrawal of the British administration from Ireland in 1922.

This is not a political history of Ireland, nor is it intended to look in depth at the role of the Irish ascendancy who dominated Irish affairs during most of the period, about whom much has already been written. But for an understanding of the influences and personalities that shaped the colourful life of the Irish viceregal court during these years, I have sketched in the wider political and social background.

I am grateful to the many archivists and librarians who helped my research. I wish to thank the staffs of the National Archives, Dublin; the National Library, Dublin; the libraries of Trinity College, University College Dublin and the Royal Irish Academy; and the Public Record Office of Northern Ireland. I thank Gregory O'Connor of the National Archives for directing me to relevant material; Fergus Mac Giolla Easpaig, Acting Keeper, Genealogical Office, for material on the Ulster kings-on-arms; and Freddie O'Dwyer for information about the architecture of Dublin Castle. I thank Barry Murphy, Chairman of the Commissioners of Public Works, and Commisioner Sean Benton for supporting my work, and Jacqui Moore and Patricia Wood in helping in my quest for illustrative material. The British Museum, the National Gallery of Ireland and the National Library were helpful in providing photographs. Dame Gillian Wagner kindly gave me access to parts of the diary of her kinswoman, Ellen Palmer. I thank Jim O'Donnell for his helpful advice; and I appreciate the interest and professional skills that Antony Farrell and Lilliput Press brought to the production of the book. I am grateful to my son, Killian, who read my typescript critically and made valuable suggestions, and to my daughter Keara, who steered me through the perils of word-processing. As always, I have been conscious of the burden that the demands of my writing imposes on my wife, and I appreciate her continuing tolerance.

CHAMPAGNE AND SILVER BUCKLES

ONE

The Irish Court

In 1204, thirty-five years after the Anglo-Normans arrived in Ireland, King John issued a mandate to Meiler Fitzhenry, his chief administrator, directing him to erect a strong fortress in Dublin, by now the headquarters of the country's new governors. By the fourteenth century Dublin Castle, as it had become known, had various roles. It was the seat of the king's chief representative, variously designated as justiciar, king's lieutenant, lord lieutenant or viceroy. The courts administering the Anglo-Norman law to the colonists and those of the native population who could be brought to book were also based there, as was a repository for the royal treasure under the control of a number of specially designated officials. There were also dungeons where troublesome Anglo-Norman lords and native chiefs might be lodged from time to time, quarters for the garrison, and a range of other buildings and activities that brought together within the walls the whole apparatus of English administration in Ireland.

By the end of the sixteenth century the Castle complex was taking on a character more akin to the court of a Renaissance viceroy than the quarters of the commander of a military outpost. Between 1556 and 1570 Sir Henry

Sidney, the first viceroy to reside there, converted it from a 'ruinous, foule, filthie and greatly decayed place' into a 'verie faire house for the lord deputie or the chiefe governor to reside and dwell in'. As well as providing a home for the viceroy and his entourage, the Castle became the seat of parliament from the early seventeenth century until it moved to its imposing new building in College Green in 1731. When the buildings housing the viceregal apartments were destroyed by accidental fires in 1671 and 1684, they were replaced by new and more sophisticated accommodation designed by the Surveyor-General, Sir William Robinson. During the subsequent century other buildings were added to complete what is now known as the Upper Yard.[1]

None of these changes altered the perception of the Castle among the bulk of the native population. From the beginning it was surrounded by strong outer walls and partially encircled by a moat. A drawbridge provided the chief communication with the surrounding city. In time the moat disappeared and the drawbridge was replaced by gates, but this didn't diminish the isolation of the building nor increase its accessibility to any but a privileged and trusted minority. To the native Irish it became more than a building housing their British governors. In an abstract sense 'the Castle' signified the power, authority and policies that determined how Ireland was ruled. Indeed, the drawbridge might serve as an apt symbol of the role of Dublin Castle during the whole subsequent history of the British administration in Ireland, a link between a beleaguered garrison and the hostile territory in which it was located. Over the centuries the Castle had to withstand not only occasional physical onslaught but continuing hostility in the hearts and minds of much of the population, who saw it as the seat of an oppressive and alien administration supporting, and supported by, a small, powerful elite: the Ascendancy.

THE ASCENDANCY

Irish Catholics had been subject to penal restrictions since the Reformation, long before the accession of King James II in 1685 and his attempts to remove the disabilities imposed on them. The defeat of James by William of Orange at the battle of the Boyne in 1690 copper-fastened Protestant dominance. It marked the beginning of the reign of a powerful ascendancy which would control the affairs of Ireland in England's interest until the union of the British and Irish parliaments in 1801. Its influence would remain in force, to a diminishing degree, until the withdrawal of the British administration in 1922.

The Ascendancy was not an ethnic grouping but an exclusive social class comprising Protestant families of Norman, Old English, Cromwellian and occasionally Gaelic origin. The foundation of ascendancy was the penalization of the majority Catholic population, which was assigned a subservient role in Irish society and denied the right to vote or to serve in parliament. Other religious, educational and economic restrictions ensured that they would remain a largely ignorant and impoverished population. The aim of the governing elite was to protect and advance their own social, economic and political interests and to guarantee that the governance of Ireland remained free from any threat to Protestant supremacy.

The development of a powerful Protestant ascendancy in Ireland had the effect of reducing the burden of responsibility on the shoulders of the viceroys, whose main task was to ensure that the will of the monarch was obeyed. The Ascendancy were in effect a garrison who could be trusted as long as they were kept in good humour with the largesse that successive lords lieutenant had at their disposal. They controlled a parliament from which the potentially troublesome papists and the dispossessed were excluded; even when discontented they were invariably loyal. The Irish parliament was a subordinate parliament in which no law could be introduced without prior consent of the English Privy Council acting through the lord lieutenant. And although many of the Ascendancy parliamentarians clamoured for legislative freedom towards the end of the eighteenth century, their acceptance of the British monarch was never at issue.

The wealth and privilege acquired by Ascendancy families encouraged many of them to lead an indulgent, even hedonistic, lifestyle. They built large, beautiful, richly furnished and decorated houses in the most attractive parts of the country, often with ornate gardens laid out by the leading designers. Some of the male members involved themselves seriously in political life. A minority took an interest in advancing the economic lot of their tenantry through agricultural improvements and the initiation of small industrial activities. But for many, and particularly for their women-folk, life was a constant round of pleasure.

It was important for them to have access to the centre of power and influence and to the more sophisticated and varied pleasures of high society integral to a metropolitan environment. Many among the Ascendancy had English family connections and, despite the hardships of cross-channel travel, journeyed frequently to London and to the Continent. To an increasing degree, however, the Irish Ascendancy sought their pleasures in Dublin, which was assuming the status of the second city of Britain and Ireland. And at the apex of the social ladder stood the viceregal court at Dublin Castle, and those accepted into its circle.

THE VICEREGAL COURT

Even before the outcome of the Williamite wars had strengthened the basis for Ascendancy and English control in Ireland, the apparatus of a viceregal court had been formed at Dublin Castle. Lady Essex, whose husband had been viceroy from 1672 to 1677, was the first vicereine to entertain lavishly as a great hostess. James, Duke of Ormond, who succeeded Lord Essex, served for several periods as lord lieutenant and created a brilliant court by the time he finally left office in 1685. His private and public apartments at the Castle were richly furnished and carpeted, and he had a personal entourage of over a hundred court officials and servants. He entertained sumptuously. According to the household records for the period from May 1682 to September 1683, six thousand gallons of French, Canary and Rhenish wines and large quantities of other forms of alcohol were consumed by his household and his guests. He set patterns of exclusivity and hospitality that were carried on by his successors. A proclamation of November 1678, for example, forbade Catholics to enter the Castle without a special order from the lord lieutenant himself.

Ormond's successor Richard Talbot, Earl of Tyrconnel, added to the pageantry of office. Tyrconnel commanded the English army in Ireland for King James and led Irish opposition to the Williamite forces. When James entered Dublin in March 1689, he rode to the Castle through streets lined with soldiery and cheering crowds beneath balconies hung with ornate tapestries. On the last stages of his journey he was preceded by forty beautiful maidens, dressed in white silk, strewing his path with flowers. The king's next entry to Dublin in July 1690 was somewhat different in character as he fled from the defeat of his forces at the battle of the Boyne.[2]

By the beginning of the eighteenth century the life of Dublin Castle had taken on many of the characteristics of the London court of St James, although on a more modest scale. It was clear, however, that the viceroys of the period saw themselves as surrogate monarchs and that the Ascendancy elite expected to have the trappings of a royal court with the power and privilege that it conferred. Since all the Irish viceroys were chosen from the English aristocracy, they were familiar with the style and protocol of the palace of St James. Some of them had held appointments there. The Duke of Grafton and the Duke of Carteret, for example, two early-eighteenth-century lords lieutenant, had both served at the court of George I and experienced its lavishness. The London court had swelled during the reign of William III (1689-1702), of whom it was said that one of his great qualifications as a king was his thorough understanding of patronage. By the reign of George I (1714-27) there were over one thousand people employed at huge expense at his court, absorbing about one third of the entire cost of civil government in Britain.[3]

To the extent that they could afford it, early-eighteenth-century Irish viceroys followed the rituals and extravagances of the London court. The Ascendancy elite gathered in great numbers at the Castle to celebrate and to enjoy themselves. Balls, banquets, drawing-rooms, levees and elaborate festivities to celebrate royal birthdays and other anniversaries were a regular feature of Castle life; they were splendid affairs, extravagant in dress and ritual, abundant in food and drink. But these activities were more than the colourful ephemera of aristocratic government. They had an underlying importance. An invitation to the Castle was seen as a recognition of loyalty and an acknowledgment of good standing. These social occasions gave the lord lieutenant and his officials an opportunity to gauge the opinions of influential members of Ascendancy society, and particularly to trawl the views and utterances of parliamentarians for early indications of political unrest. They also provided opportunities for supplications for a wide range of patronage – pensions, jobs, sinecures and promotions within the army, church, judiciary and government itself. For many, the attainment of nobility was the ultimate goal.

The careful manipulation of the social life, pageantry and privilege at Dublin Castle was an effective device for achieving political ends. The extent of its success tended to vary from lord lieutenant to lord lieutenant. It was said that during the tenure of the Duke of Rutland (1784-7), a period of calm descended on the hitherto troubled relations between the government supporters within the Irish House of Commons and those of the 'patriot' element seeking greater freedom for the Irish legislature. The extravagance and indulgence of the social life of the duke and his duchess and their beguiling personalities enmeshed all factions in a continuous round of pleasure which diverted them from political conflict. Later, as the Irish nobility demanded advancement within the peerage as the price of their loyalty, the creation by the then lord lieutenant, Earl Temple, of a new and exclusive Order, the Knights of St Patrick, served as a sop for influential senior peers whose loyalty was important but for whom further steps up the hierarchical ladder were not feasible.

Even with the dissolution of the Irish parliament by the 1801 Act of Union and the departure to Britain of many of the former ruling families, access to the pomp and pleasures of the viceregal court remained a hugely valued privilege. But social distinctions were becoming blurred. Purity of family origin counted for less; the *arriviste* found it easier to secure acceptance in the Castle circle. The remaining Ascendancy families were now joined by persons from the broader Anglo-Irish community and, increasingly, by members of the Catholic population as they moved into the professions and positions of influence previously denied them. The 'Castle Catholics' were a largely petit-bourgeois element who opted for a status as supporters of British rule in Ireland and of British culture rather than be

identified with the largely peasant and increasingly nationalistic population from which many of them had sprung. At all times, however, Catholics
remained a minority among those who frequented the viceregal court.

THE VICEROYS

During the earlier centuries of English rule in Ireland the post of the king's
principal governor was often held by a prominent member of resident
Anglo-Norman families. But after 1700 it became settled practice to give
the post of lord lieutenant to an English nobleman of wealth and high
standing. While the Irish nobility invariably gave their loyalty to the king,
prudence dictated that with the growth of a self-important and increasingly
assertive ascendancy with Irish 'attitudes', English aristocrats would be
likely to be more reliable in their governance of Ireland. The lord lieutenant's responsibility for securing the acceptance of British views by the
Irish parliament was considerably eased by the existence of a small group
of influential parliamentary members known as 'undertakers', who influenced and manipulated Irish affairs as best they could along the lines
desired by the government in London. In return, the undertakers and their
friends received the lion's share of patronage in the control of the lord lieutenant.

As long as the undertakers and the lords justices (consisting usually of
the Protestant primate, the lord chancellor and the speaker of the House of
Commons) succeeded in maintaining a reasonably smooth operation of
Irish affairs, it was considered unnecessary, prior to 1767, for the lord lieutenant to reside in Ireland except when parliament was actually sitting.
Previously the parliamentary session lasted from six to eight months in
every second year. The lord lieutenant usually arrived in Ireland for its
opening, gave the speeches, performed the functions associated with the
occasion, and remained in Dublin throughout the session. During his
sojourn in Ireland social life would reach its peak. He and his wife would
preside over a range of functions at Dublin Castle, accept the hospitality of
the lord mayor of Dublin and the provost of Trinity College and of a small

coterie of influential members of the Ascendancy, and return to England as soon as the sitting of parliament ended.

Early-eighteenth-century Ireland did not hold any great attraction for an English aristocrat. It was perceived as a somewhat distant outpost with a hostile population, lacking the sophisticated social life that was to evolve as the century wore on. Getting to Ireland and back involved an uncomfortable and sometimes hazardous sea journey. It took the Dorsets eight days in April 1752 to get from Dublin to a safe harbour on the other side. And, for those who were ambitious, acceptance of the post at Dublin Castle was more likely to be a step into the political wilderness than progress towards greater honours. Laurence Hyde, Earl of Rochester, an aspiring politician, regarded the post of lord lieutenant that he held nominally from 1701 to 1703 as a form of banishment. He was so enraged on being directed by Queen Anne to take up duty in Dublin rather than remain in London that he resigned.[4] The Earl of Onslow wrote of Charles Spencer, Earl of Sunderland, who served in the post from 1714 to 1715: 'He accepted the office but did not hold it long, taking it as it was intended, great in itself undoubtedly but often a step of disgrace to some men who have been or expect to be in the closer parts of the administration.'[5] Sunderland never visited Ireland during his term of office. Nor did Charles, 2nd Viscount Townshend, who accepted the post in February 1716 only on the understanding that it was a step to higher office. But proving to be only 'a languid supporter' of the government, he was dismissed from the post a few months later. The 2nd Duke of Bolton, who resided in Dublin for periods during his term of office from 1717 to 1719, was admired by his British friends for his pluck and fortitude in giving up the delights of London for Dublin.[6]

But there were lords lieutenant who enjoyed themselves in Dublin, particularly as the eighteenth century progressed. The apparatus of the Irish court at the Castle expanded, Irish Ascendancy society became wealthier and more sophisticated, and Georgian Dublin developed physically and socially into a more attractive city in which to live. It was a milieu that had attractions for viceroys and their consorts, particularly if they had regal pretensions and inclinations to grandeur. As far as their social position was concerned they literally reigned supreme, a status they could never have attained in England. To some, at least, it was more than adequate compensation for failing to make the political cut at Westminister.

POMP AND PAGEANTRY

The pomp and pageantry began as soon as the lord lieutenant stepped ashore in Ireland. The 'forms', the prescribed regulations for ceremonial occasions, were established early in the century but became more elaborate as the Irish court grew in self-importance. The basic details, however, changed little over the years. The lord lieutenant was formerly greeted by the lords justices at his point of disembarkation, usually Ringsend or Kingstown, and brought in a procession of carriages and mounted militia through decorated streets lined with footsoldiers and onlookers, whose mood varied between hostility, enthusiasm and indifference depending on the man concerned and the political atmosphere of the time. At Dublin Castle an elaborate ritual was performed, including the administration of an oath by the archbishop of Dublin, and the new viceroy took his place as chief governor of Ireland. Then, as he received the compliments of the assembled representatives of the nobility and gentry, trumpets were sounded, guns fired and bonfires lit outside in the Castle yard and in College Green and Phoenix Park. Subsequently, when the viceroy went to open parliament, to dine with the lord mayor or provost of Trinity of College, or to attend a charity function or any other function of significance, he travelled in a procession that varied in size and ostentation according to the importance of the event but that usually included contingents of horse guards, colourful foot-soldiers known as battleaxes, and a variety of uniformed court officials.

There were days that called for special celebrations or ceremonies such as the king's birthday, the queen's birthday, the coronation anniversary, the commemoration of the defeat of the Gunpowder Plot, royal births and weddings, the rebellion of 1641, the battle of the Boyne and the anniversary of the death of King William of Orange. Compared with the more lavish festivities that developed later, early-eighteenth-century ceremonies were simple. As the self-importance of successive lords lieutenant grew, the social and ceremonial programme of the Irish court expanded. During most of the eighteenth century, when the viceroy resided in Dublin during the 'parliamentary winter', there were many visitors to make up the brilliant social round. Later in the century, when the post of lord lieutenant required full-time residence in Ireland, Ascendancy social life intensified, reaching its apogee during the years before the insurrection of 1798 and the Act of Union. After the dissolution of the Irish parliament, the lord lieutenant and his court remained part of the apparatus of British government in Ireland and a sop to the Ascendancy community. Increasingly, the viceregal court became more a symbol of British authority than a centre of power, but until 1922 it remained the chief focus of high society in Ireland.

TWO

The Lords Lieutenant 1700–1767

The frequency and lavishness of Castle entertainment depended almost entirely upon the inclinations and the personal wealth of the incumbent viceroy. For much of the eighteenth century his annual salary was £12,000, with a small grant to cover equipment expenses. As the social obligations of the office grew, viceroys found it increasingly necessary to support the costs of their official entertainment from their private resources, particularly from 1767 when they were obliged to live in Ireland on a continuing basis. Lord Carlisle was 'about £10,000 poorer' after an eighteen-month residency in Dublin and a few years later Earl Temple claimed that the post required at least £15,000 per annum extra.[1]

In general, however, early-eighteenth-century lords lieutenant appeared to have had no difficulty in paying for their social programme during the short periods they spent in Ireland. They accepted that as long as they were resident in Dublin an important part of their official role was the provision of hospitality and ceremonials for the enjoyment of the gentry and nobility. Some of them needed little encouragement to do so, for pleasure and self-indulgence were central to their lifestyles.

James Butler, 2nd Earl of Ormond, held office twice, from 1703 to 1707 and from 1710 to 1713. It had been intended that he should live in Ireland throughout his period of office but, in the event, he spent only about one third of his time there. He was a licentious man, described by Lord Dunboyne in his 1966 Butler family history as 'rather an ass', but he had a strong personal following and maintained a busy programme of social events during his official visitations. He toured the southern counties for three weeks in July 1703 and later that year opened parliament in Dublin with 'much state and splendour'. During the following year he observed Queen Anne's birthday with celebrations of a splendour 'hitherto unknown in Dublin'. There was a programme of events at the Castle extending over two days including a ball and 'a very noble supper' at which Ormond was the only man seated. The famous alto John Abell was brought to Dublin to sing on the occasion.

Feasting and drinking on a grand scale was a feature of the viceregal regimen of the period. The Englishman John Cutts, one of the then lords justices in Ireland, wrote to his sister complaining of continuing colic because of the extent of the eating and drinking in which he had to participate. Robert Smith, who had served for a period as a cook on Ormond's staff, later published a book on court cookery that indicates the range and richness of food then in use in court circles. Ormond's wife was a popular hostess who sometimes remained in Ireland during her husband's absences, entertaining and promoting Irish industries, a practice followed by many subsequent vicereines. She is said to have appeared every week in 'a new stuff suit'. Although Ormond's period of office lacked any significant political achievement, it is remembered for adding to the pace of social life and for Jonathan Swift's incumbency as Dean of St Patrick's Cathedral.[2]

Swift's presence in Dublin helped to brighten the life of Ormond's successor, Thomas Herbert, Earl of Pembroke and Montgomery, appointed in April 1707. Swift became chaplain to Pembroke and his principal duty appeared to be amusing the earl during his brief sojourn.[3] Over the next few decades Swift would continue to amuse and enrage succeeding viceroys. As a pamphleteer and satirist, deeply aware of the subtleties of political society at the highest level, he was often a mocking commentator on what he regarded as the imbecilities of viceregal and parliamentary activities in Ireland.

Between Ormond's two periods of office, the post at Dublin Castle was held for a term by Thomas, Earl of Wharton, notorious for his profligacy even before he came to Ireland. In his youth he was popularly regarded as 'the greatest rake in England', a distinction that he found no difficulty in maintaining throughout the remainder of his lifetime. His first marriage, an arranged one, had brought him a large dowry, but his bride's person had not been 'so agreeable to the bridegroom as to secure his constancy'. Swift wrote to his friend Hester Johnson (Stella in his writings): 'I saw Lady Wharton as ugly as the Devil.' His wife's lack of attractions set Wharton on a career of horse-racing and general debauchery. Between the winter of 1708 and the summer of 1710, he lived in Dublin as he had lived in London. The Castle became the centre of drunken debauches where prostitutes, card-sharpers and members of his normal circle of friends and acquaintances forgathered for a continuous round of dissipation. At night he trawled the taverns of the city with wild companions, sometimes calling for a sword and bestowing titles indiscriminately upon tavern-keepers and waiters. Sheridan Le Fanu's 1845 novel *The Cock and Anchor* describes the atmosphere: 'There were coaches and four ... out-riders ... running footmen and hanging footmen ... crushing and rushing ... jostling and swearing ... and burly coachmen with inflamed visages, lashing one another's horses and their own.'

Wharton was virulently anti-Catholic but liked to deride all religion, treating with contempt the various Protestant churchmen who came to his court seeking advancements which were, ironically, within his gift. He once sought to make a bishop of the son of one of his own profligate companions, declaring that 'James was the most honourable man alive and possessed of a character practically faultless save for his damnable morals.' While he did not find it possible to have the individual concerned made a bishop, he had him compensated with a deanery. To Swift, who frequently met the lord lieutenant at the Castle where he served as one of the chaplains to the court, Wharton was 'the most universal Vilain I ever knew'. He excoriated him in a public attack: 'He is without the sense of shame or glory as some men are without the sense of smelling ... He goes constantly to prayers ... and will talk bawdy at the chapel door. He is a Presbyterian in politics and an atheist in religion; but he choseth at present to whore with a papist.'[4] Wharton's second wife Lucy, daughter of Viscount Lisburne, was said to be as abandoned and unscrupulous as her husband. But he had no problem in suffering her many infidelities for she had brought him a huge fortune which facilitated his unbridled indulgence. The historian Macaulay (quoted in the *Dictionary of National Biography*) wrote: 'to the end of his long life the wives and daughters of his nearest friends were not safe from his licentious plots'.

Following a change of government, Wharton was recalled from Dublin in May 1710. Ormond's second period of office was followed by Charles Talbot, 12th Earl and Duke of Shrewsbury, who was said to have been persuaded by his wife to accept the post so that she might play at being queen. The duke himself was familiar with court ceremonial, serving as lord chamberlain at the court of St James while simultaneously holding the post of Irish viceroy. The duchess, an Italian, was already a figure of fun in English society, uncouth and ridiculous in conversation, 'the constant plague' of her husband's life, unrelenting in pursuit of status in court circles, and a favoured courtesan of George I. Writing of a visit to the duchess, Lady Strafford described how she entertained her guests with a description of the peculiarities of her toes from which, she claimed, growths protruded resembling thumbs. The duke himself had only one eye, which was not a social obstacle for he had a very charming personality and was said to be most popular with the ladies of his time. The Shrewsburys stayed in the Castle whenever they visited Dublin for the parliamentary sessions, entertained expansively and celebrated the usual anniversaries and commemorations in style. The king's birthday was marked by the parade of a large contingent of troops to Oxmantown Green where rockets and gun salvoes were fired followed by a march to Stephen's Green as the bells of the city rang out. *Whalley's Newsletter* reported that when the duke commemorated King William on another occasion it was celebrated with such unusual magnificence and enthusiasm that it drew a public rebuke from the Bishop of Cork, who pronounced the drinking of toasts to the dead to be a wicked custom savouring of popery.[5]

Socially, at least, there appears to have been little said in favour of the personality of Charles Plowett, 2nd Duke of Bolton, during his periodical viceregal visits from 1717 to 1719. Swift said that he cut a poor figure in court circles and was perceived as 'a great booby', and Lady Cowper noticed that he was generally to be seen with his tongue lolling out of his mouth. There were other unflattering reports of his personality. Thomas Hearne, a contemporary chronicler, described him as 'a most lewd, vicious man, a great dissembler and a very hard drinker'. According to his biographical entry in *The Complete Peerage*, he joined Lord Santry and a number of other aristocrats in recommending the castration of unregistered priests as a measure for limiting the population of Irish Catholics.

SOCIAL LIFE QUICKENS

The pace of the social life at the Castle, and of the Dublin upper-class world in general, quickened from the 1720s onwards under a succession of viceroys inclined to regal living and to pomp and pleasure on a grand scale. A visitor to Dublin in 1739 wrote: 'Every entertainment which has the authority of fashion in England prevails here, and ... some it may be, in a greater degree.'[6]

In a thirty-year period, from the mid-1720s to the mid-1750s, the Duke of Grafton, Lord Carteret, the Duke of Dorset, the Duke of Devonshire, the Earl of Chesterfield and the Earl of Harrington provided Ascendancy society with lavish entertainment. The political impact of Charles Fitzroy, 2nd Duke of Grafton, during his periods of office from 1715 to 1717, and later from 1721 to 1724, was minimal. Grafton was imperious and distant, generally regarded as a fool and, according to Swift, 'almost a Slobberer without one good Quality'. He was clearly more at home in the social milieu of a viceregal court than in the rougher political arena. A gilded fop, before coming to Dublin he resided at the court of St James where he was court chamberlain. His contemporary, James, Earl of Waldegrave, regarded him as the ablest courtier of his time 'with the most perfect knowledge both of king and ministers'. At St James', Grafton made himself obnoxious to the queen, taunting her about past lovers, finally outraging her when, hunting with Princess Emily, one of the royal family, he contrived to lose their attendants and to spend the night with her in a private house in Windsor Forest. It probably hastened his assignment to Dublin. However, John, Lord Hervey, in satirical verses directed at Grafton, found him no threat to womankind since 'his body's as impotent as his mind'. He and his wife entertained well at the Castle and the duchess followed the pattern already set by encouraging the use of Irish fabrics. An adulatory poem of 1723, 'Irish Happiness Compleated ...', saluted her:

> His Duchess, too, whose Beauty would surprise
> And force ee'n Jove, a Captive to her Eyes.
> To show her Love to this now thriving Isle
> She deigns in woollen Stuff on us to smile
> Contemns Silk, Vanities and foreign Toys
> And will our Manufactures only Use.[7]

Eventually Grafton was found lacking by his English masters. According to the nineteenth-century historian Froude, a stronger hand and a stronger head than Grafton's were required to combat Irish problems, which could be best overcome by 'corruption and resolution, adroitness and good dinners, Burgundy, closeting and palaver'.

Grafton was replaced by a stronger representative in the person of John Carteret. Although only thirty-four, Carteret, baron, later Earl of Granville, was on the downward slope of his political career when appointed to Ireland in 1724 following an attempt to undermine Sir Robert Walpole, the prime minister. He was a handsome man, engaging, eloquent, a scholar and a friend of Swift's, who wrote of him that he had 'a genteeler manner of binding the chains of the kingdom than most of his successors'. Socially, his personal traits and hard drinking fitted easily into the lax Ascendancy milieu. Horace Walpole wrote that it was difficult to say whether 'he was oftener intoxicated by wine or ambition'. Lady Carteret played her part in easing her husband's political progress. Her wit and beauty helped to soften the attitude of the aged bachelor archbishop William King, main opponent of her husband's policies in Ireland. And she had a long and affectionate friendship with Swift, once, in a display of high spirits, flinging his hat out the window and impaling it on neighbouring railings.[8]

The social programme of the Carterets was a very full one: the duchess, relentlessly active, liked to hold a weekly ball at the Castle to which a large crowd was usually invited. The fact that the viceroy himself was affable, courteous and easily accessible created considerable demands on his time. Once, impatient at being kept waiting by Carteret, Swift sent him a couplet:

> My very good Lord 'tis a very hard task
> For a man to wait here who has nothing to ask

Carteret rejoined:

> My very good Dean, there are few who come here
> But have something to ask or something to fear.[9]

Carteret's scholarly interest in the Greek and Latin classics probably encouraged the king's birthday presentation in May at Dublin Castle of 'serenades' such as *A Contest between Marsyas and Apollo* ..., choral pieces with classical allusions lauding the monarch. These were composed by John Sigismund Cousser, Master of the Musick at the viceregal court as well as chapel master at Trinity College. The serenades had dramatic roles for several singers. These dramatized serenades were later replaced by odes, lengthy adulatory verses set to music by the incumbent Master of the Musick who, in the mid-century, was Matthew Dubourgh, friend and associate of Handel.[10]

THE DORSETS

Carteret was succeeded by Lionel Sackville, Duke of Dorset, who arrived to open parliament in 1731, stayed until early 1732, and returned again for the parliamentary sessions of 1733 and 1735. During some of his visits he lived in an earlier viceregal lodge built at Chapelizod towards the end of the previous century. Dorset enjoyed being viceroy. The salary at that time was regarded as attractive and he was able to add to his income by the sale of offices. He resented being replaced by William Cavendish, 3rd Duke of Devonshire, in 1736, but was reappointed for a further period of office from 1750 until 1755.

The court conducted by Dorset and his duchess at Dublin Castle was a brilliant one. They came to Ireland determined to make an impact with the splendour and elegance of their ceremonials and entertainments. Dorset's initial official function in October 1731, the opening of the first meeting of parliament in its striking new premises in College Green, provided an appropriate occasion for the launch of his viceroyalty. The intensity of the Dorsets' social programme was such that Walter Cary, chief secretary to the viceroy, complained to a friend that his back was almost broken from bowing and having his belly constantly stuffed from eating. The duke had a courtly style about him. Lord Shelburne described him as 'in all respects a perfect English courtier and nothing else', who preserved the good breeding and decency of manners and deportment of Queen Anne's time. The fact that he was a 'safe' man, never having an opinion of his own about any public issue, ensured him a continual succession of government appointments. But he had another side. Horace Walpole said that, in private, Dorset was the greatest lover of low humour and buffoonery. This combination of refinement and crudity did not put him at any disadvantage in Dublin society. Elegance and good manners were merely one aspect of Ascendancy lifestyle, contrasting with a cruder, hard-living ethos personified in the unrestrained roistering of young bucks such as Richard Parsons, 1st Earl of Rosse, who, at about this time, helped to establish the notorious 'Hell-fire Club' in a tavern close to the Castle walls.[11]

The duchess herself had experience of the court of St James which fitted her for the role of vicereine. She had been maid of honour to Queen Anne and first lady of the bedchamber to Queen Caroline. During the winter of 1733 and spring of 1734, with the duke in Dublin for the parliamentary session, various anniversaries provided excuses for elaborate celebrations. These included birthdays of the king, the queen and the

Prince of Wales, and anniversaries of the coronation and of King William. The programmes were by now following a pattern. During the day the nobility and gentry were received at the Castle by the duke and duchess, a commemorative ode set to music was sung, and gun salutes and fireworks followed. Later the duchess entertained the ladies to a play at the Theatre Royal and the day concluded with a ball at the Castle. A fountain was devised in the council chamber that flowed all night with wine for the guests. A separate conduit led from it to the courtyard below providing wine for the 'common people' gathered there. *Faulkner's Dublin Journal* reported that when Queen Caroline's birthday was celebrated in March 1734, the ode written for the occasion by William Dunkin and set to music by Mathew Dubourg was 'superior to Anything that was ever wrote in this Kingdom upon that or any the like Occasion'.[12]

Mrs Delany, the society hostess, often a guest at official events during the Dorset viceroyalty, describes the splendour of these occasions in her autobiography and correspondence. A highlight of the 1731 winter season was a military review in the Phoenix Park: 'The Duchess of Dorset was there in great state and all the beau monde of Dublin.' There were frequent events at the Castle, too, although the duchess disliked the great crowds. She would usually excuse herself after having made her compliments and retire to her private apartments to play basset – a popular card game among the upper set – with close friends. But balls were unavoidable even if the Dorsets were unhappy about the condition of the main hall (later improved as St Patrick's Hall), then 'very much out of repair' and lacking the setting for the creation of the brilliant spectacle to which they aspired. But one military officer attached to the court applied his creative imagination so successfully to decorating the hall to commemorate the king's coronation in October 1731 that Dorset wrote later, 'I never saw a more beautiful scene'. It made a great impact and brought 'a vast crowd ... so hot and over-crowded'. A few weeks later another ball, and a supper with a profusion of food and drink, was 'attended with great crowding and confusion'. By now the largesse of the Dorsets, and the lack of organization during their functions, were turning them into free-for-alls, not dissimilar to the scrambling for food and drink by the city poor admitted to the Castle when supplies

were handed out to mark special celebrations. Mrs Delany describes a ball
of March 1732:

> ... never did I behold a greater crowd. At eleven o'clock minuets were
> finished and the Duchess went to the basset table. After an hours
> playing the Duke, Duchess and nobility marched into the supper-
> room, which was the council chamber. In the midst of the room was
> placed a holly tree illuminated by a hundred wax tapers; round it was
> placed all sorts of meat fruit and sweetmeats ... the company came in
> turns to take what they wanted. When the doors were first opened
> the hurly burly is not to be described; squawking, shrieking, all sorts
> of noises; some ladies lost their lappets, others were trod upon. Lady
> Santry almost lost her breath in the scuffle and fanned herself two
> hours before she could recover herself enough to know if she was
> dead or alive.

It was a frenetic life. Mrs Sicon, a friend of Swift, noting the unrelenting
pursuit of pleasure among the ladies of Castle society and their utter
detachment from the harsh world outside, commented, '... nothing about
them Irish but their souls and bodies: I think they may be compared to a
city on fire which shines by that which destroys them.'[13]

The Duke of Dorset returned as viceroy in September 1751 and once
again was acclaimed for the panache of his court. It was an outstanding
autumn season, full of pageantry and excitement. Dorset's coach bearing
him to the opening of parliament was a dazzling spectacle of glass and gold,
drawn by six richly caparisoned horses, accompanied by six tiny pages
attired in crimson velvet and gold lace and feathered hats. Escorting the
coach and walking on either side were gentlemen of the viceroy's entourage
in full regalia, hats under their arms. The usual Castle social programme
was enhanced by the presence in Dublin of Peg Woffington, the famous
actress then playing at the Smock Alley playhouse, from whom a command
performance was ordered for Dorset. It was a pleasant period to hold office
as viceroy. In general, up to the mid-1750s Dorset and his viceregal predecessors had not been put under any great burden of official responsibility.

They were happy when the 'king's business', as it was called, was out of the way and the money bills had been passed without undue parliamentary friction. The social life of the Castle could then proceed and, as Archbishop George Stone observed sarcastically, the viceroy 'gave wine to the men and fiddles to the women, as usual'.

But Dorset's political fortunes plummeted as his second viceregency progressed. He allowed himself to be excessively influenced by his youngest son, Lord George Sackville, who served as his chief secretary, but particularly by George Stone, Archbishop of Armagh, privy councillor, an ambitious and determined opponent of the 'patriot' faction. Stone, in return for his political services, had been hurried through various bishoprics to the primacy 'without even the graver excuses of learning or sanctimony'. When, encouraged by Stone, Dorset insisted that the Irish parliament could not use surplus revenue without the consent of the Crown, popular feeling ran strongly against him. There were public demonstrations including a destructive riot in a Dublin theatre.

The lord lieutenant became anathema to the patriot supporters, who reviled him in newspaper notices and banned the usual drinking of toasts to his good health on festive occasions. The list of toasts drunk at a dinner of the Patriots Club of Newry in January 1755 reflects the feelings of the time. While Dorset's name would normally have been given precedence, there was no reference to him at all in the twenty-four resolutions proposed, which included some clearly directed barbs:

Disgrace and Disappointment to all such as would build their fortunes on the Country's Ruin
    and
May no Ecclesiastic acquire any Influence in the House of Commons.

Dorset was recalled by the British government in February 1755.[14]

THE CHESTERFIELD PERIOD

The interregnum between Dorset's periods of office had been filled for a thirteen-year period, 1737 to 1750, by William Cavendish, Duke of Devonshire; briefly and memorably, by Philip Dormer Stanhope, 4th Earl of Chesterfield; and then by his half-brother, William Stanhope, 1st Earl of Harrington.

Devonshire arrived in Dublin for his initial visit in September 1737 accompanied by his duchess, seven children and an entourage of servants. Fond of drinking and the social round, he was adjudged to have been a good host during his periodic visits to Dublin for the usual sessions of parliament. There were frequent balls and banquets and special entertainments for the ladies at the Castle. He was fond of the theatre, and the Theatre Royal in Aungier Street sometimes held command performances for him. Nevertheless, he found Irish affairs a bore and the Irish parliament 'impossible' although he was prepared to tolerate the fruits and status of office for seven years.[15] No more than any of his predecessors did he appear conscious of the privations suffered by the majority during his reign as viceroy.

While eighteenth-century viceroys could ignore the wretched conditions of the bulk of the population, these were highly visible in the streets of Dublin. The images of deprivation in the city mirrored the national scene. Even at the best of times much of the rural population was in dire poverty. The economy was stagnant, Irish exports were restricted and tenants of land were forbidden by their leases to break or plough the soil. Application of the penal laws, directed at ensuring the continuing subservience of a Catholic population, aggravated these conditions. Great numbers lived in compulsory idleness. Crop failures and recurring epidemics of contagion ensured that the population was kept down. The English Elizabethan Poor Law system based on parochial charity had not been applied to Ireland, so in time of want hordes of the rural poor trooped into the city streets hoping to find relief for their destitution, adding to the city's own burden of poverty. By the end of the previous century, alarmed citizens were complaining that 'beggars are seen in great numbers in all parts of the city to the great dishonour of the government thereof and the disturbance of all the inhabitants'. Some years later 'the most considerable persons' were being unsettled by starving pauper children, 'crying at their doors at unreasonable hours in the night to excite them to give relief'. A few, like Swift, were appalled by the indifference of those in authority. His famous satirical pamphlet of 1729, 'A Modest Proposal', sprang from his indignation, proposing that pauper children be fattened and reared at public expense to provide a delicacy for the jaded palates of gentlepersons of refined taste. The City Fathers established a large 'work house' at James's Street in 1703 for various categories of Dublin's paupers but this was less a manifestation of public charity than a measure to relieve the more fortunate and influential citizens of the nuisance of beggars. Later, separate accommodation was added for children, which would form the basis for the notorious Dublin Foundling Hospital of 1729.[16]

By Devonshire's time few measures had had any impact on the pattern of Dublin's poverty. In April 1737 *Faulkner's Journal* reported the finding of a dead child in a street not far from the Castle, 'turned green by lying too long without interment'. It was a common occurrence. The Foundling Hospital received large numbers of infants who survived abandonment in a basket attached to its gate. It was usually a brief respite from death; during Devonshire's time three quarters of all the children died within a short time of admission to the hospital.[17]

Chesterfield's reputation preceded him, and his appointment provoked excitement in Dublin society. A politician, wit and letter-writer, wealthy, handsome and refined in manners, with a reputation for womanizing, he was well equipped to ensure that social affairs at the viceregal court would be elegant and scandalous. His status gained immeasurably from the fact that his wife was a half-sister of the reigning monarch. She was Countess of Walsingham in her own right, and an illegitimate daughter of George I by the Duchess of Kendal.

Chesterfield's cultural interests and tolerance had a civilizing if passing influence on Ascendancy society. While he entertained freely and lavishly at the Castle, he had a passion for sobriety and set an example for the hard-drinking habitués of the court circle. He described the huge amount of claret imported annually into Ireland as a 'melancholy truth ... a sure but indecent proof of the excessive drinking of the gentry'. He prohibited gaming at the Castle, a hitherto normal feature of viceregal social gatherings. He was shocked by the poverty of Ireland and found it difficult to understand why so many were content to live in conditions worse than those of Negro slaves. He found it difficult to accept that Catholics were dangerous and potentially rebellious. After his initial perusal of the state of affairs in Ireland he reported to London that he had come across only one dangerous papist, Eleanor Ambrose, daughter of a Dublin brewer and the reigning beauty of the day. Chesterfield also disliked the constant importuning by prominent politicians and churchmen for jobs, pensions and other favours. He described Archbishop Hoadley of Armagh, who was demanding a revenue appointment for his son-in-law, as 'a dirty, troublesome person'.

Chesterfield's political performance was low-key for he refused to take too seriously the alarms normally associated with the life of an Irish viceroy. Once an excited official burst into his bedroom with rumours that the papists were rising. 'Rising!' said the nonchalant Chesterfield, 'It is time for every honest man to arise; it is past nine o'clock and I shall rise myself.' He preferred to remain politically detached and to put his energy and time into cultural and social activities. His choice of secretary illustrated his approach. John Addison, later the noted essayist, was chosen because he was genteel and good-looking rather than 'a man of business'. But while Chesterfield may have irritated some prominent politicians who would have preferred less of an aesthete and more of an intriguer, he was generally popular with all classes. His tolerance appealed to the masses. He did not believe in punishing Catholics, although he had no qualms about encouraging their children to seek the Protestant education and proselytism of the charter schools. He conscientiously drank tar water when Bishop Berkeley publicly recommended its benefits. On celebratory occasions there were usually fountains of wine in the lower Castle yard for the populace in general. He was accessible informally to traders and members of the professions although they were not allowed to participate in the formal social life of the Castle, which was restricted to the nobility and gentry. While Chesterfield disdained the 'silly forms and ceremonies' which were part of the ritual of his office, he believed in maintaining the exclusiveness and privileges of the ruling class, and etiquette and protocol appropriate to a royal court. Lady Chesterfield, a plain-looking woman but 'goodness itself', according to the Earl of Corke, presided over splendid balls where the wearing of gowns made from Irish fabrics was encouraged. The viceroy charmed his guests with his rakish limericks and his *bons mots*. But the centre of attraction, and generally acclaimed beauty of these balls, was Eleanor Ambrose, with whom Chesterfield conducted a very public affair tolerated by his duchess. This happy, exciting scene for those habitually welcome on such occasions at Dublin Castle epitomized the privilege, style, and manners of the eighteenth century, before the first rumblings of political and social unrest threatened its foundations in its latter decades.

Considerable imagination and expenditure ensured that the Castle's social programme consisted of dazzling events. To facilitate them, new rooms, including a ballroom, elegantly designed on the initiative of Chesterfield himself, were added to the existing accommodation although they had not all been completed before his return to England. For the more lavish functions the long gallery was laid out with a series of decorated stalls serving sweetmeats and rare wines, lit by concealed candles to give the illusion of moonlight. The guests circulated to the sound of soft music from flutes and other instruments played by concealed musicians, while at each end of the gallery fountains of scented lavender water plashed abundantly. When the king's birthday was celebrated in October 1745 the supper room was partially converted into an extravagantly decorated Temple of Minerva with several statues spouting a constant flow of wine, some of it piped to the expectant *hoi polloi* gathered in the Castle yard.[18]

Chesterfield's appointment in Ireland was cut short by ill-health and lasted only a year. Despite his short stay in office, his impact on the manners and the civility of Irish society was far greater than that of any of his predecessors. After his departure he said that he liked to think that he had reduced the extent of jobbery and discouraged 'the pernicious and beastly fashion of drinking'. And he hoped to be remembered as the Irish lord lieutenant rather than the lord lieutenant of Ireland. The Earl of Orrery wrote, 'Lord Chesterfield's influence, like the departing sun, has left a warm and serene sky behind it ... Duels are at an end. Politeness is making some progress. Literature ... is close behind.'[19]

Orrery exaggerated the extent to which the departing Chesterfield raised the tone of Irish society. It had been a pleasant and benign interlude, but it was followed by a gradual return to the old ways. Chesterfield was succeeded towards the end of 1746 by his half-brother, William Stanhope, Earl of Harrington. While Harrington lacked Chesterfield's talents and style, he settled easily into the established routine of the viceregal court. Lord Orrery, writing to a friend in November 1749, said of him: '... he is extremely acceptable by his politeness and affability to everybody here. We pay our court with a true duty and devotion as if we were Frenchmen and Lord Harrington the Grand Monarch of Versailles.'

His social programme was organized by his daughter-in law, Lady Caroline Petersham, as his wife had died before Harrington came to Dublin. The great attractions of Castle events at the time were the beautiful Gunning sisters, Maria and Elizabeth, who, with determination and the connivance of their mother, and despite a background of poverty, succeeded in insinuating themselves into the Castle circle. They had attended their first ball in borrowed theatrical costumes when the king's birthday was celebrated in October 1748. It was an immensely successful début. Impressed by their beauty and personalities, Lady Petersham and her father took a continuing interest in them which led to a pension for their mother, a brilliant theatrical career for the sisters themselves and, eventually, marriages to the Duke of Hamilton and the Earl of Coventry. Elizabeth's marriage to Hamilton ended in widowhood, but she was re-married to the Duke of Argyll. As Horace Walpole commented, she was 'double duchessed'.

Despite Harrington's initial acceptability to all classes, he gradually found himself in conflict with the patriot supporters. A political *enfant terrible* of the period, Dr Charles Lucas, had gathered popular support for his persistent attacks on the exclusivity and corruption of the political system, and on the constitutional constraints on the Irish parliament. Harrington had Lucas imprisoned and forced him to flee the country. By the time of Harrington's recall in 1750 he was one of the most resented viceroys of the century. Bonfires celebrated his departure, while mobs howled curses at his carriage as it bore him from the Castle to the point of embarkation at Kingstown.[20]

PLACATING THE PATRIOTS

Both Harrington and Dorset were anathema to the patriot politicians by the time they finally departed from viceregal office. In the circumstances, the British government decided to mollify the Irish parliamentarians by intro-ducting a 'safe' man, the thirty-five-year-old Lord Hartington, later 4th Duke of Devonshire. Hartington set out to make an impact on Dublin soci-ety assisted by his wife, heiress of Richard Boyle, Earl of Burlington and Cork, already a woman with important social and political connections. A ship sailed from Holyhead to Dublin loaded with provisions and household furniture for the new viceroy and his entourage. Improvements were made to the Castle, existing staff moved out to provide more space, and skilled tradesmen employed to enrich the quality of accommodation.

Rejecting the traditional cavalcade and ceremonials associated with the triumphal entry of a new viceroy, Hartington arrived unexpectedly in May 1755 on an ordinary packet boat at Skerries, north of Dublin. It was the first time a new chief governor had crossed the Irish Channel other than by royal craft and with accompanying panoply. A small number of nobility and gentry met Hartington and travelled with him to the Castle, where he was sworn in. The government in London were anxious to avoid the embar-rassment of protesting crowds during viceregal parades. A few days before Hartington's arrival James, 20th Earl of Kildare, had also arrived back in Ireland after an absence. As the senior Irish peer and acknowledged spokesman for the patriotic faction, he received a huge welcome. *Faulkner's Journal* reported 'great rejoicings in many parts of the city and suburbs and firing of guns, bonfires, illuminations etc. And on Thursday morning His Lordship received the compliments of many of the nobility and gentry on his arrival'.[21]

The simultaneous arrival of the new viceroy and of Lord Kildare was handled deftly. Kildare participated in all the introductory festivities organized by Hartington, a full programme of balls, banquets, levees and draw-ing-rooms as well as the usual peripheral excitements of bell-peals, bon-fires and illuminations. The grievances arising from the policies of previous viceroys rapidly faded. Kildare wrote to his wife: 'I dined at the Castle yes-terday where I stayed till past 12 o'clock. I don't think I ever drank so hard and fast in my life; every one of the company complain to-day. I could not write this morning to you for I was sick ...'

Hartington then embarked on a successful tour throughout Munster, staying with some of the most influential members of the nobility. There were popular celebrations. The inhabitants of Carrick-on-Suir 'dressed in their own manufactures with cockades and all the ensigns of their trade, colours flying and drums beating ...'. Sixty county gentlemen adjourned to a local tavern where they drank various toasts; other taverns were desig-nated for the entertainment of the workers at the expense of the masters. Both the gentry and the populace in general were impressed by the progress of the young viceroy. And as the centre of viceregal activity returned to Dublin Castle, the social tempo quickened. In November 1755, the birthday of the seventy-three-year-old George II was the occasion for particularly lavish celebrations and gathering of gentry and nobility, 'who all made a finer Appearance than ever was known, vying with the other in the Elegance and Richness of their Dress'. In all respects Hartington's period of office was very successful. According to a contemporary com-mentator, 'smiles and good humour resumed their influence in the draw-ing-room and levee'. He avoided political trouble, pleased all parties, and was acknowledged to have had a brilliant programme of social events. When summoned back to London in November 1756, he was appointed to the premiership.[22]

THE BEDFORDS

Hartington's successor John Russell, 4th Duke of Bedford, continued the policy of avoiding political controversy and made known before arriving in Ireland that he did not intend to govern 'on the narrow maxims of intolerance and exclusion which had hitherto prevailed'. Helped largely by the social skills of his duchess, he succeeded in keeping the various factions happy. The duchess welcomed the opportunity to play vicereine in the setting of the Dublin court. Walpole observed that 'she had all her life been practising the part of a queen: dignity and dissimulation were natural to her'. She pandered and flattered and pleased the throngs of the nobility and gentry who flocked to the ceremonials and entertainments.

By the latter part of the century official hospitality expected from lords lieutenant was costing far more than the government payments for the office of viceroy. In general, the incumbents were quite willing and able to support an extravagant regime. The Bedfords in particular were immensely wealthy and spent lavishly, ensuring an easy path for viceregal policy. The duke was not given to excessive roistering but the 'joviality' of his chief secretary, Richard Rigby, soon made him 'not only captivate so bacchanalian a capital but impress a very desirable memory of his festive sociability'. Rigby would sometimes voice political notions of his own, such as the creation of a legislative union of the two kingdoms, which might be discomforting to patriotic ears, and there was some concern in London about the extent of Rigby's conviviality, but it did not prove an obstacle to his holding further office. Bedford believed the key to being a successful Irish viceroy was to provide an abundance of 'douceurs', creating new members of the nobility, promoting others and awarding pensions to the potentially troublesome. And he also helped to keep the king himself happy by arranging an annual pension of £5000 from the Irish revenue for Mary, Princess of Hesse Cassel, George II's royal daughter. Viceregal hospitality was often generously reciprocated. In January 1758 a number of the nobility and gentry gave a ball for the Bedfords in honour of the birthday of the King of Prussia in the music hall in Fishamble Street.

While Bedford himself lacked social sparkle, being proud and ungracious, his wife brought discipline and civility to court proceedings. The duchess insisted on strict attendance at their posts by government officials and encouraged the viceregal entourage to hone their intellectual and social skills in keeping with the growing concept of nobility at European courts. The second part of the century saw a relentless pursuit of style and the cultivation of elegance and sophistication to a degree that would leave no doubt about the superiority of the breeding and manners of the aristocrat. If Anglo-Irish society was marginalized with a pinchbeck court of little consequence, its members, for all that, considered themselves no whit inferior to the wider brotherhood of European aristocracy.

A number of teachers were appointed to the staff of the court in November 1757, including a writing and mathematics master, a French master and a fencing master. Appropriate court dress became *de rigueur* on all official occasions. For example, ladies attending at the Castle on the death of Princess Caroline in December of that year were required to wear black bombazines, thick or thin Irish cambric or plain muslin, crepe hoods, shamoy shoes, gloves and crepe fans. Men had to don a black jacket without buttons on the sleeves or pockets, plain muslin or Irish cambric cravats, weepers, shamoy shoes and gloves, crepe hat-bands and black swords and buckles.

Insistence on proper court dress was just one aspect of the search for high standards. The quality of social life in all aspects was of importance. There were excellent theatres; the main streets and buildings of the metropolis were being improved under the aegis of the 1757 Wide Streets Commission. Under its guidance there were major changes in the physical appearance of the city. Dame Street and the central quays along the Liffey were widened, the old Essex Bridge (Capel Street Bridge) was replaced and Carlisle Bridge (O'Connell Bridge) was built. A grand design was applied to the interconnected Lower Sackville Street (Lower O'Connell Street), Westmoreland, D'Olier and Lower Abbey Streets. Private initiatives led to the emergence of residential areas of distinction such as Rutland Square, Merrion Square, Mountjoy Square and Fitzwilliam Square. The powerful families involved in these developments were also represented on the Commission, ensuring that fashionable areas of the city were linked to the broad thoroughfares. The centrally located Castle became more easily accessible to its habitués and their carriages; and the new streets offered a more pleasant vista for the travellers even if the teeming throngs of beggars remained an irremediable feature. A Norfolk gentleman visiting Dublin about this time, impressed by the manifestations of wealth and good living, wrote, 'it has vastly the air of London'. When Lady Sarah Lennox, sister of the Countess of Kildare, met the Prince of Wales at a court ball in London in 1760, she took the opportunity to tell him that the balls at Dublin Castle were far more enjoyable and frequent than those of St James'.[23]

Politically these were difficult times for the lords lieutenant. New voices of political opposition were emerging in conflict with the strongly established 'undertaker' families. Bedford tried to maintain neutrality, but riots in Dublin followed rumours that legislative union was to be introduced and he had to call out troops to quell them. Bedford eventually resigned the viceroyalty in March 1761.[24]

Bedford's successor, George Montague Dunk, 2nd Earl of Halifax, managed to maintain a high level of social activity during his brief stay in Dublin. He lived in Ireland only from March 1761 to May 1762, returning to England and leaving the conduct of the Irish administration to the lords justices. Halifax had been born into relative poverty but had the good fortune to marry Ann Dunk, a wealthy heiress, and in gratitude paid her the compliment of adopting her family name. When his wife died, Halifax brought his mistress, and governess of his two children, to Dublin. She was Mary Ann Faulkner, adopted daughter of George Faulkner, printer of Dublin's most prominent newspaper of the time. Halifax was a spendthrift who spent more than his official allowance but supplemented his income by selling offices within his patronage as lord lieutenant. The Irish parliament agreed to increase the viceregal allowance to Halifax because it regarded it as inadequate for the costs of his court, but he accepted the increase only for his successors. But the power behind the court was his mistress, who lived convenient to the Castle and closely scrutinized his spending and his place-mongering. Walpole called Halifax 'overbearing and ignorant of the world', and *The Complete Peerage* described him as 'of debauched character'. He would have preferred to have been appointed Secretary of State for the West Indies rather than to Dublin, but was eventually chosen to serve as first lord of the admiralty. He resigned as Irish viceroy in April 1763.[25]

Hugh Percy, Earl (later Duke) of Northumberland, had, like his predecessor, the driving force of a strong woman behind his tenancy of Dublin Castle. His wife had been a lady of the bedchamber to the queen before coming to Dublin, a post that gave her status and power. Northumberland, like many of his viceregal predecessors, had previous experience of the routine of the court of St James and served as lord of the bedchamber to both George II and George III. He was regarded as a master of court etiquette, helped by a striking presence and by being perceived as the most handsome man of his day. The Northumberlands lived regally and extravagantly during their Irish visits. The *Freeman's Journal* had some concern about the 'most awful condition' of their accommodation in the Castle compared with the opulent residences to which they were normally accustomed. The duchess maintained an ostentatious social programme, earning her the epithet 'junketaceous' from Walpole. Her correspondence showed a literary bent which included descriptions of incidents at the court of Versailles, where she met Louis XV. She was wont to find in the comments of others exaggerated approval of herself. When she accompanied the viceroy to the opening of parliament in 1763, encouraged by the flattery of Lord Drogheda, she interpreted a reference in her husband's formal speech as a public declaration of his love for her. Northumberland's speech contained the words 'domestic felicity', but this clearly referred to the king's ménage rather than to his own. And, departing Ireland, she believed that among her predecessors only the Dorsets and the Chesterfields had achieved equivalent heights of social brilliancy. The Northumberlands were abruptly replaced following the dismissal of Lord North's administration, but their disappointment was compensated by a dukedom to the satisfaction of both the new duke and his duchess.[26]

His successor, the Earl of Hertford, spent only a year in office. He too had experience as a courtier, being lord of the bedchamber to both George I and George II. He was, according Walpole, 'the most decent, cautious, discreet and submissive of courtiers' with a beautiful wife, Isabella, 'her mind uncultivated but full of strong sense', who came to Ireland accompanied by most of her thirteen children. He had an interest in playing loo, a card game, with 'unlimited half-guinea stakes' which often went on all night. One of his gambling companions was Richard Rigby, the former chief secretary, as well as a number of society ladies who habitually lost considerable sums, including 'Mrs Lomm ... who loses two or three hundred on a night'. But Hertford grew tired of the limited diversions in Dublin and, in any event, his wife wanted to go home. Given the growing power and influence of the undertakers, it was hardly desirable for the government to have an unhappy viceroy in Ireland. He was the last part-time viceroy to be appointed to Ireland. Succeeding viceroys were required to live full-time in Dublin, a constant reminder to Irish politicians that the seat of power lay in the Castle and not in College Green.[27]

THREE

The Lord-Lieutenant's Household: Dining, Wining, Ceremonials and Fashion

The process of refining the viceregal court, including its staff structure, manners, and ceremonial and social programmes, took place mainly before the 1760s although it didn't reach its peak of sophistication until the 1780s. The Duke of Shrewsbury was an important influence on its early formation. He'd served as court chamberlain to the court of St James while holding the post of viceroy to Ireland (1713–14). It was unusual to hold two such senior appointments simultaneously but, in keeping with the practice of the times, his visits to Dublin were periodic and his combined responsibilities were not overwhelming. Towards the end of 1713, not long after beginning his period of office at Dublin Castle, he had in place a detailed plan for the organization and operation of his household.[1] This remained the broad basis on which the households of subsequent lords lieutenant were organized during the eighteenth century, although their establishments tended to expand as the notions of an Irish court grew more grandiose.

It was obvious that Shrewsbury, a senior and long-standing courtier at St James', had applied his London experience to arrangements for the viceregal household, reflecting on a lesser scale all the main features of court of St James. There, as court chamberlain, he was in charge of the whole household above stairs and responsible for organizing the ceremonials, protocol, invitations and the entertainments. The lord steward, lower in status than the chamberlain but nevertheless important, was in charge of the household below stairs, supervising the domestic staff, planning meals, and ordering the food.[2] Dublin Castle was arranged on similar lines. The ceremonials and the court officialdom grew as above-stairs activities of the Castle expanded and as successive lords lieutenant sought to gild their court rituals and add to their entourage. But the below-stairs activities, and the large establishment of staff needed to maintain the domestic comforts of the lord lieutenant and his family, were most expensive. Records show that there were usually about one hundred people employed in cooking, serving and maintaining the personal apartments of the viceroy.

DOMESTIC ARRANGEMENTS

The personal status of each individual who worked downstairs was defined within the domestic hierarchy and was reflected in their pay and rations of food and drink. The highest-paid were the house steward, who received £150 annually, and the comptroller, who was paid £50. Clerks and ushers got from £10 to £50, cooks got from £25 to £40, and a large range of kitchen servants, porters and other menials received about £5 annually. On special occasions money 'presents' were distributed to various servants and suppliers of the household, graded in accordance with the status of the individuals concerned. For instance, bell-ringers from Christ Church and musicians involved with the ceremonial welcome of a new lord lieutenant received from ten shillings to a guinea each. To commemorate the new year the presents given included £1 9s 3d for park keepers bringing venison to the Castle, 5s 5p each to the milk woman and the herb woman, and 10s 3p for the verger of Christ Church.

The regulations for Shrewsbury's household also specified an allowance of food and drink per individual according to the classification of the table

at which they dined. At 'His Grace's Table' on normal, non-public occasions, dinner consisted of a course of sixteen dishes (items), four removes
and a dessert on Sundays, Wednesdays and Fridays. On the remaining days
there were fewer dishes. A 'remove' was a dish replaced and replenished
following removal. The steward's table was served with six dishes and he
was joined by the comptroller, gentlemen ushers and other senior personnel of the household totalling seventeen persons. The table of the clerk of
the kitchen was allocated five dishes where nineteen persons of similar status were accommodated; the 'gentlewoman's table', where the housekeeper
and three personal staff of the wife of the viceroy dined together, was
served four dishes; the 'maid's table', with ten housemaids and laundry
maids, was served two dishes; the 'footmen's table' seated twelve footmen
who were given two dishes; and the kitchen porter was given 'one dish of
meat'. Some servants of low status were not assigned to a place at a table
but were entitled to participate in the food left over by those who dined
before them. Depending on the status of the table, the leavings might be of
good quality. There were also specific rations of bread, butter and beer,
morning and night, for all staff. Even the foddering of the horses in the Castle's stables reflected their particular working role, with designated
amounts of oats, beans, bran and hay which varied between saddle and
coach horses.

There was a provision for a separate table known as the 'green cloth'
where important visitors to Dublin or relatives of the lord lieutenant or of
senior officials were invited to dine informally. In Buckingham's time
politicians supporting the government who were involved in 'managing'
parliamentary business were often invited to dine at the green cloth. It was
in effect the lord lieutenant's second table.[3]

PUBLIC DINING

Dining at the Castle on public occasions was on a substantially greater scale
than for private meals. By the time of the viceregency of the Duke of Devonshire in 1737, the amount of food served when the lord lieutenant dined in

state had increased enormously: a course of thirty-four dishes and six removes was accompanied by fourteen dishes of sweetmeats which stood throughout the dinner on a long middle table. There were fewer dishes served for lesser state occasions but even then huge amounts of food were provided for the guests. By Chesterfield's time all public dinners in the Castle consisted of two courses of twenty-one dishes each, not including removes and a generous provision of desserts.

All public dinners involved elements of ceremonial. They were usually served in the Old State Room, which towards the end of the century was improved and redesigned and became St Patrick's Hall. On more important occasions the battleaxes, the colourful ceremonial bodyguards of the lord lieutenant, carried up the dishes as each service began accompanied by a fanfare of trumpets. Other courtiers attended in various roles, and state musicians, the State Musick, played popular airs of the period throughout the meal. When the music ended the nineteen musicians and trumpeters dined together in a separate compartment on six dishes, thirteen bottles of wine and four gallons of ale; while the forty battleaxes were given two dishes of fowl and bacon, two venison pastries, two pieces of roast beef, twenty bottles of wine and six gallons of ale. Other members of the household also received generous quantities of food and drink; and the populace in general had hogsheads of wine set out for their enjoyment in the sentry boxes in the lower Castle yard.

Particular state dinners were designated 'largesse days', when the poor were admitted to take away what remained of the huge meals. On these occasions, after the battleaxes had placed the second course on the table, the Ulster king-at-arms, the chief herald, proclaimed the various titles of the king in Latin, French and English. Then, after his assistant, the pursuivant, had intoned loudly 'largesse, largesse, largesse', the doors were thrown open and a rabble of women of the town rushed in and took up position behind the lord lieutenant and his guests. The diners would pass sweetmeats back to those behind and watch as the shrieking women scrambled and fought with each other. It was part of the entertainment; the guests, already satiated with huge quantities of food and drink, found amusement in the free-for-all of the ragged, hungry mob. It was sometimes difficult to impose any degree of control and the women, becoming more unruly and impatient, tended to reach over the heads of the diners and grab plates from the table. When on one occasion a woman dropped a pie on the head of a bishop, and custard ran down his face and on to his fine ecclesiastical garb, it was decided that the lord lieutenant should thenceforth be spared such sights. By 1760 the mob (which now included men and women) was not admitted until after the lord lieutenant and his guests had risen from the table and had moved to one end of the chamber. After the glass and the ornaments had been taken away, the mob was allowed to enter and a wild melée developed for what remained of the food.[4] It had the character of a coarse medieval spectacle.

While it was usual for a huge quantity of alcohol to be consumed during banquets, the drinking might continue throughout the night depending on the inclinations of the lord lieutenant. When parliament was sitting, members who were in favour with the sitting administration were usually admitted to the lord lieutenant's cellars to drink their fill from hogsheads of their choice. Ormond had set an example for heavy drinking at the Castle but refused to have chairs provided in the cellars because he 'could not encourage any gentleman drinking longer than he could stand'. He appears also to have been the originator of a custom associated with the annual banquet given by the lord lieutenant to the lord mayor of Dublin, whereby after the lord lieutenant had withdrawn, the lord mayor and his entourage of aldermen and officials were conducted to the cellars. A large glass of wine was given to the mayor into which he placed a piece of gold and drank to the health of the lord lieutenant. The glass was passed around, constantly replenished, while all present each placed a piece of gold in it. The practice continued throughout the eighteenth century but when in 1762 the incumbent lord mayor asked the lord lieutenant, Halifax, to be excused the demands of the wine cellar, the lord lieutenant consented. The annual ritual was subsequently more honoured in the breach than in the observance.[5]

CEREMONIAL STAFF

The ceremonial staff of the household had clearly prescribed duties even if some roles required little more than having to stand around decorously in colourful regalia. Most senior courtiers were members of the nobility or of other influential families; some actually served as members of parliament or had close relations in the Castle. While the majority of the courtiers were paid, others served for the honour, usually with minimal duties and only during more elaborate ceremonial occasions.

Some courtiers organized minor perquisites for themselves. A Dublin lady not on the court's list recorded in her diary at the end of the 1750s how she'd managed to view a state ball from the gallery on paying 2s 8d to an official. Easy access to the court and to the person of the viceroy could help the ambitious along the path towards greater preferment. Appointment to the viceregal entourage not only conferred status but offered the prospect of further honour and profit. It also carried exemption from certain irksome and unprofitable public duties such as militia and jury service. All the posts were eagerly sought and were entirely within the patronage of the lord lieutenant. While change of lord lieutenant was accompanied by the turnover of most previously serving courtiers, incoming viceroys would occasionally condescend to retain some favoured staff of a former viceroy. The choice of courtiers, like other areas of viceregal patronage, usually depended on whether a lord lieutenant was anxious to direct his favours towards the 'government' or 'patriot' faction.

Court duties were usually prescribed anew by each lord lieutenant although they did not normally differ significantly from those of his predecessor. Thus, the Duke of Devonshire's (1737-44) arrangements were broadly similar to his predecessors', and were clearly influenced by what evolved at the early Georgian Court of St James.[7] In time, court rituals became more detailed and polished as the deeply rooted protocols of the past lent validity, authority and majesty to the royal power of the present. Between 1770 and the Union of 1801, court routines reached an apogee of sophistication thanks mainly to the work of Sir John Hasler, court chamberlain, and to his successor, Sir Charles Vernon. Each served under a number of lords lieutenant and were regarded as masters of the art of court regulation.

In the hierarchy of courtiers each had a detailed role. Those closest to the lord lieutenant when performing his official duties were the gentlemen of the bedchamber. They were a trusted inner circle and provided immediate attendance from the time he emerged from his private apartments until he had completed his participation in the levees, dinners and other official events. They introduced petitioners and other visitors, diverted the troublesome and dealt discreetly with situations likely to ruffle their master.

The gentleman usher walked in front of the lord lieutenant, guiding his path from his private chambers to where he was seeing company, walking before him as he moved from place to place. When the lord lieutenant went out, the gentleman usher travelled in advance and ushered him into any place he visited. However, when the lord lieutenant travelled by horse, the gentleman usher had to give place to the gentleman of the horse, who rode next to his master, while the yeoman of the stirrup and the gentleman usher followed behind, in that order. Their respective duties were clear. There were detailed instructions about the manner in which the lord lieutenant was to be helped to mount: '... if His Grace dines abroad, when he mounts, the Gentleman of the Horse holds the horse by the near cheek and the Yeoman of the Stirrup by the off cheek and holds the stirrup when the lord lieutenant is mounted.' Given the tendency of lords lieutenant of the period to over-indulge when dining, this particular duty was especially important.

The birthdays of the king and queen, the births and weddings of the royal family, the commemoration of William of Orange, and the anniversaries of famous victories, were always celebrated in the grand manner and included a day-long programme of events, usually culminating in a banquet or ball, or both. The king's birthday began with the recital of an especially written ode set to music by the Master of the Music. In 1755 George II was honoured thus:

> No tyrant Views t'oppress Mankind;
> No Ambition fires his Mind,
> To purchase Fame with Blood;

> Our Monarch glows with purer Heart,
>
> Convinced that to be truly Great
>
> Is only to be Good.[8]

The larger social functions at the Castle such as the levees, drawing-rooms and balls were brightened by liveried courtiers of various classes. The household of courtiers was required to attend on all major occasions, and otherwise on each alternate week. The steward and comptroller, having mainly below-stairs responsibilities, also had ceremonial roles. Each carried a white rod whenever the lord lieutenant received company, and was involved in the supervision of public dinners. Many attendant staff consisted of gentlemen-at-large who provided support for the more senior courtiers but took their directions from the gentleman usher. During 'State' dinners they waited at table throughout the meal with a napkin on their arms. At lesser public dinners they stayed until after the second course had been served and then were relieved by the lower-ranking yeoman ushers. John Blaquiere, chief secretary to Lord Harcourt, observed of gentlemen-at-large in 1772: '[They] have nothing to do nor a great deal to receive; they only wait behind you at table and have claim to a bellyful'.[9]

Others of subordinate rank dressed in colourful, distinctive uniforms, such as grooms of chambers, footmen, coachmen, postillions who rode on the backs of carriage horses to guide them, and pages. Bewigged young male pages were a particularly decorative feature of viceregal ceremonial, whether standing in the front part of the lord lieutenant's coach, leading the processions to church or parliament, or surrounding their master as he dined in state – baroque embellishments to the colourful scene. Peacockery was to the fore on these occasions. Lord Temple, parading to College Green to commemorate King William in November 1782, wore a coat 'of the finest gold tissue combining every idea of splendour of and elegance'. The Duke of Rutland presided over a ball in 1787 for the queen's birthday dressed in scarlet velvet. The succeeding lord lieutenant, the Duke of Buckingham, attended the same event in 1788 wearing a richly embroidered suit of white and lilac velvet.[10]

While there was emphasis on order and propriety above-stairs, it was not always thus below. There are frequent references in the records to drunkenness and theft, but it would have been impossible to divorce the behaviour of Castle servants from the normal life of the poverty-ridden populace from which they were drawn. Lord Nuneham, son-in-law of the lord lieutenant, Lord Harcourt, wrote in June 1772:

> All the lower people are idle, drunken, and universally thieves, but the Castle is where they shine in the most in their profession. There are four or five keys to every room and to every table and chest of drawers in these rooms, for which reason the locks are frequently obliged to be changed. The night we arrived the master of ceremonies was robbed of all his cloaths ... How shocking is the contrast between the royal pomp of the viceroy and the wretchedness of the people![11]

CARING FOR THE LADIES

As the eighteenth century proceeded, greater courtesy was extended to the ladies of the court, not only because they added to its culture and adornment but because the consorts of lords lieutenant themselves could be formidable and influential. In keeping with their station, the women of the Ascendancy gave much of their lives to pleasure and its pursuit. It could be said that the social programme of the court was directed for their benefit while they sought to exert some political influence on their menfolk.

By the 1770s the main responsibility for organizing and overseeing social affairs fell on the shoulders of the gentleman usher, whose title often carried the appendage of master of ceremonies. While the court chamberlain had overall responsibility, the more detailed arrangements for ensuring that pleasure and fun proceeded smoothly fell on the shoulders of the gentleman usher. Under some lords lieutenant the court chamberlain appeared to rank lower than the usher, but usually the chamberlain was clearly in charge. The chamberlain under successive lords lieutenant in the 1770s and 80s was the aforementioned Sir John Hasler, who had been continued in office because of his long service and accumulated skills; but the best-known, most popular courtier of the period was Sir Boyle Roche, gentleman usher and master of ceremonies. Roche was a member of the Irish House of Commons when appointed to the viceregal entourage. He was a noted wit and perpetrator of 'bulls' ('Why should we put ourselves out of the way to do anything for posterity,' he declaimed in a parliamentary debate, 'for what has posterity done for us?'). He was also a striking figure, urbane, polite, and hugely attractive as chaperon to women of the court circle, for whom as gentleman usher he had official duties to perform. 'His ideas were full of honour and etiquette,' wrote the contemporary memoirist Jonah Barrington. Before the 1770s there appears to have been only one gentleman usher, but subsequently there were two, one specifically responsible for the ladies.[12]

The presentations of all ladies to the lord lieutenant and his wife were made by the gentleman usher. When the vicereine walked in formal procession to banquets and drawing-rooms, the usher walked alongside her, supporting her arm while her pages carried her trail, smoothing her passage through the crowded corridors and guest rooms. He was responsible for the conduct of drawing-rooms and balls, and the direction of other court staff on duty. He opened and closed every ball. He was required to carry out 'visits of enquiry' to ladies of the nobility when they were indisposed or when a marriage had been announced, travelling by coach on such occasions with attendant servants provided by the lord lieutenant.

Sometimes the vicereine would partake in the visiting, particularly if the lady concerned had been presented at court for the first time. The visits were intended as a public indication of good standing and social importance. Some wives, notably Lady Carlisle, Lady Temple and the Duchess of Portland, liked to shake off formalities when socializing privately and dispense with accompanying ushers and pages. When Lady Carlisle gave a private dance and supper for a circle of her friends, an official diary kept by the court chamberlain noted disapprovingly, 'this gave great offence', though his disapproval on that occasion may have been largely due to Lady Carlisle's advanced state of pregnancy.[13]

DANCING AT THE CASTLE

By far the most popular occasions at the Castle were the balls. A state ball might have as many as a thousand participants. They were colourful, exciting events, eagerly awaited and much discussed. For centuries dancing had been a popular element of the festivities of all social classes. As the upper classes became more refined in their manners and enjoyments, the rumbustious dances of the lower orders were gradually replaced by less spontaneous, more affected movements. The French court led the way by introducing formal dances such as the minuet and gavotte. The minuet came to be seen as the peak of the court dance, fashioned by the dancing-masters of the period and, when performed with skill and sensitivity, a work of art in itself; but it also developed as a stilted affair, reflecting the exaggerated courtesies of aristocratic society and the often encumbering dress of the times. The increasing polish and precision of movement required considerable practice, and enjoyment diminished. By the early 1700s the folk-based English country dance, or *contre danse* as it was sometimes called, was the most popular choice at Dublin Castle, as at other European courts. And while dances such as the minuet and the gavotte continued, they tended to be performed only on formal occasions, or as a prelude to the less inhibited dance forms that usually developed during court revelries as the night progressed.[14]

As dancing became increasingly popular with the Irish gentry and aristocracy during the eighteenth century, balls, some masked, others with varying lavishness of theme, were frequent events in town houses and country seats. Some were charity affairs for fashionable causes such as the Rotunda Hospital or Charter Schools, but for women of fashion an invitation to Dublin Castle represented the zenith of social achievement. Castle balls attracted large numbers of guests, fuelling themselves with gossip that added to the excitement of the occasion.

To reduce the discomfort of extreme heat and large numbers, an arrangement was devised involving the seating of the ladies in tiered rows around the ballroom. The top tier almost touched the ceiling. Windows and doors were left open to assist circulation of air. Tiered seating was also used at some private balls of the period; Elizabeth, Countess of Moira, for example, was able to accommodate large numbers in tiered seating in her ballroom. A striking contemporary painting, usually attributed to Van der Hagen but which may be the work of the painter and scene designer Joseph Tudor, depicts a state ball at Dublin Castle when the Duke of Dorset was in office. Baron Willes, watching a similar scene at the time of Bedford, thought the spectacle of four hundred richly dressed ladies arranged in rows 'the finest sight I ever saw'.[15] Apart from the pressure of the crowd, stamina was needed for long nights of dancing. In May 1735 the Earl of Orrery danced so frenetically from eight o'clock until four in the morning that his life was in the balance for a week.[16]

While formal dances continued to be *de rigueur*, many Castle guests danced minuets only as a duty or when they could not otherwise be avoided. John Hasler in February 1772 introduced 'a very new and uncommon set of minuets, surprising to all then present, the like never having been heard before'. However, it didn't add to their popularity. Many participants did not have the grace and expertise to please the onlookers, and it became the practice, for those willing to subject themselves to the criticism of fellow guests, to dance minuets only at the start of an important ball. A small number of the Castle set were known for the degree of perfection they attained. Lady Louisa Conolly described the 2nd Duchess of Leinster's dancing in November 1775 as 'really the finest thing I ever saw. Tis the most perfect graceful minuet that a woman of fashion can dance.'[17]

The military aides-de-camp had been trained as good dancing partners and were much in demand. Non-military male dancers could also be spoken about with approbation, such as Sir George Macartney, often referred to as a 'very fine dancer'. Most of the males showed little inclination to develop their dancing technique although they were encouraged to polish their manners. During 1770 the Hibernian Academy in King Street offered training for young gentlemen in 'polite accomplishments', including dancing, but to many it was seen as unmanly. When John Hely-Hutchinson, provost of Trinity College, tried to improve his students' social skills by introducing a dancing and fencing school, he was laughed to scorn and lampooned in contemporary periodicals as Jack Prancer.[18]

By the turn of the century the quality of the dancing of Irish gentlemen left much to be desired. A self-styled Dublin professor of dancing, James P. Cassidy, published a critical analysis of 'this graceful accomplishment' and found two important personal defects in the gentlemen dancers: '... the first is that of being in-kneed, when the haunches are straight and incline inwardly, the thighs lie near and the knees are protuberant, the other bow-legged.' These blemishes, advised Cassidy, were serious obstacles in the way of achieving gentility and grace of movement. Being bow-legged was a common enough characteristic of the male gentry who would have been happier on horseback, but, counselled Cassidy, the problem could be over-come: 'The art [is] ... to bring together the parts that are so much separated, and lessening that vacancy which is particularly observable between the knees.' And there were other bits of advice. The movement of the hand when presenting a card to a lady should be graceful and genteel, and waved in a serpentine line accompanied by a gentle inflexion of the body. The most graceful bow was a gentle one, achieved by sliding the foot forward while allowing the arms to fall carelessly before. 'The clownish nod, in a sudden straight line' was to be avoided.[19]

INSISTENCE ON PROTOCOL

In the last quarter of the eighteenth century the process of removing the rough edges from those who were part of Dublin Castle society reached its apex. There was a proper way of participating in all Castle events; those who ignored the rules were not welcome and ran the risk of finding them-selves out of the circle. The incumbent lord lieutenant and his wife set the tone and, guided by the accumulated wisdom of successive court chamber-lains, presided over court protocol. Lady Nuneham, who acted as hostess to her widowed father-in-law, Lord Harcourt, when he was lord lieutenant, wrote in October 1773: 'My great oracle is Sir John Hasler, Gentleman Usher ... [he] would be miserable if anybody belonging to the Castle walked to the right when they ought to walk to the left.'

It was considered 'very improper' that a lady should partake in a court ball who had not been earlier presented at a drawing-room. Drawing-rooms were usually held weekly by the wife of the lord lieutenant for the wives and daughters of the gentry and nobility already approved, or who were being introduced for the first time. The gentleman usher to the lady lieutenant was responsible for assembling the list of those not previously presented and for making the introductions. On ball nights, no gentlemen were admitted into the ballroom until the lord lieutenant and his wife had taken their places, but 'Ladies of Quality' were admitted in advance and seated on specially assigned red benches. The subsequent 'form' prescribed by the court chamberlain provided:

> At eight o'clock the lord lieutenant preceded by his pages, gentlemen at large, gentleman usher, gentlemen of the bedchamber, aide de camps and officers of the battleaxe goes into the ballroom and is followed by the lady lieutenant handed by her gentleman usher, and her train supported by her pages. As soon as they enter the room the ladies stand up, the musick plays and the battleaxes who were placed at the red benches retire to the cross benches … who are not to admit any gentlemen within them but those who are called in to dance by the gentleman usher, and as soon as they have danced they are to retire without the bar where the lord and lady lieutenant are seated.[20]

The gentleman usher then began the ball by dancing with 'the first lady of quality' and subsequently taking out any others who chose to dance, except young ladies who did not wear lappets. Lappets were pendants of fabric attached to a lady's headgear which indicated that the wearer was willing and competent to dance a minuet. When the 'French' dances were over and one country dance performed, the lord lieutenant and his lady mixed with the company or joined card games in the drawing-rooms, usually withdrawing by midnight. The country dances became then general, a heavily laden sideboard was opened, formality disappeared and festivities went on until after dawn had broken and laden coaches of the gentry rattled homeward over the cobblestones of an awakening city.

When in February 1782 the Carlisles celebrated the queen's birthday with a ball, of 438 ladies present at the Castle, seventy were regarded as 'ladies of quality' and the remainder deemed 'to have no place, including baronets' and privy councillors' ladies and daughters'. Twenty-five ladies were listed for dancing minuets and twenty-five minuets were danced. But the dancing became general once the minuets ended, the hosts departed and 'the supper was uncommonly superb'. Over subsequent years minuets gradually fell out of fashion. None was danced when the Buckinghams held a St Patrick's Day ball in 1788; there were only *cotillons* and other country dances on the programme and the ladies had been advised not to wear hoops. By the time of the Hardwickes in 1803 only four introductory min-uets were danced at the queen's birthday ball. The eight participants were Sir Charles Vernon, the court chamberlain, some members of his family and two army officers. But the country dances that followed 'were kept up with great spirit until a late hour'.[21]

On the purely ceremonial side, as distinct from the social side, each organization wishing to present its compliments to the lord lieutenant or to formally petition him had a prescribed ritual appropriate to its status. Great significance was attached to the specific elements of the ritual. For example, when a compliment was paid to the lord lieutenant while receiv-ing an official address he was expected to 'move his hat a little from his head'. The grace and precision of his movement would say much about his breeding and manners. The protocol changed on occasions during the period from 1780 to the Union but not to any significant degree. The high-est status was accorded to the lord mayor of Dublin and his entourage of senior officials of the city's council. Stressing their importance, the lord lieutenant always received them while seated on the throne. A sideboard with wine and cakes was provided. Representatives of various religious denominations tended to be given diminishing recognition as their faiths diverged from the principles of the Established Church, and depending on the personal attitude of the incumbent lord lieutenant.

When Carlisle held office the Huguenots were received as true Protes-tants and met with pomp by the lord lieutenant while standing under the state canopy. The gentleman usher introduced them, the address was pre-sented and the lord lieutenant thanked them and returned to his dressing-room. But, noted the court chamberlain's diary, they were not attended by the steward and comptroller carrying their wands, a sign that they were given less than full honours. Representatives of Quakers and Presbyterians, perceived as somewhat less loyal, were introduced in the lord lieutenant's chamber by the gentleman usher without any ceremony. Nevertheless, the use of the chamber, referred to sometimes as the bedchamber, signified that they were being received as select visitors. At the bottom of the scale were Catholics, discriminated against and shorn of their basic freedoms. They received their first official recognition at the Castle when Bedford accepted their address of loyalty in 1759 and told them 'that as long as they conducted themselves with duty and affection they could not fail to receive His Majesty's protection'. Over subsequent years they were usually received in the confinement of the 'closet', the lord lieutenant's personal office, and introduced without ceremony by the gentleman usher. Historically, the closet in St James' Palace had a backstairs entrance where the monarch met selected visitors in private. It could also imply that the persons being received were not entitled to any particular degree of public recognition. The extent of Catholic participation in viceregal rituals of obeisance depended on the political climate and temper of the incumbent viceroy. When in 1790 the Catholic citizens of Cork presented an address of loyalty to Westmorland, it was rejected as it expressed a timid hope that by their loyalty they merited a further relaxation of the penal code.[22]

Where ceremonial processions were concerned, a strict order of precedence developed involving an awareness by all parties of their 'proper place'. This was particularly true of the ranking and seniority of the members of the peerage (including senior churchmen). When the Duke of Rutland was viceroy, the Primate of Ireland and Archbishop of Dublin disputed at length about their respective placing during state processions. The primate claimed the right to walk single. The archbishop insisted that he should walk alongside and to the left of the primate. Rutland wrote somewhat despairingly to Earl Temple: 'the matter seems trifling but the dispute is conducted with great heart'.[23]

FASHION

Given that the social events at Dublin Castle represented the pinnacle of high society, the clothes worn by participants, particularly the ladies, were the most fashionable and in keeping with the best intelligence from other centres of fashion. Styles were mainly influenced by court circles elsewhere and above all by the French. Fabrics and designs for women of the Castle circle were lavish, no expense was spared, and there was a constant quest for the most skilled, imaginative dressmakers. The Castle, in effect, was an elaborate shop-window where the latest styles were seen, appraised and copied. Dress was deemed not only an indication of family wealth but of good breeding and taste.

Eighteenth-century court fashion was concerned with status rather than comfort. The usual court costume worn by Irish ladies in the early eighteenth century was an open robe consisting of bodice and overskirt with a petticoat made of luxurious, heavily decorated fabric. The bodice was shaped by whalebones and the wide skirts were held on hoops, whose amplitude tended to cause a crush in the relatively restricted space of the Castle apartments. When, exceptionally, as for the St Patrick's Ball of 1788, the ladies were allowed to come without hoops, the rooms appeared less crowded than usual, although there was more company. A correspondent in the *Hibernian Magazine* poked fun at the varying fashions then seen in high society:

> To-day the ladies are naked almost to the waist; tomorrow they are muffled up to the chin; the next day it is fashionable to be en bon point before and like a hay-cock behind; then to be as flat as a pancake on the bosom and to be as rumpless as a half-starved hen on the opposite protuberance.[24]

Fashion was important also to gentlemen of the court circle, although their clothes tended to be less encumbering. The historian Mairead Dunlevy describes their appearance:

Men showed their wealth and status with equally rich, stiff and heavy fabrics: plain silk or satin, brocaded with gold or silver and heavily embroidered or trimmed with gold or silver lace. The male silhouette was vertical, although with a sinuosity which reflected the contemporary baroque and rococo styles.

By the beginning of the nineteenth century, male guests of the Irish court wore a modification of the English country suit, which consisted of a dark cut-away coat with tails, ornate waistcoat, breeches and riding boots. The breeches were secured below the knees with a buckle. As yet, loose-legged trousers were to be seen only on sailors and members of the lower orders.

Streets in the vicinity of the Castle became the locations of shops and artisans supplying the luxury goods sought by those taking part in the social life of the court. Throughout the eighteenth and nineteenth centuries fashionable commercial activities associated with the Castle were an important source of employment. Following the Union, when continuing political demands were made for the abolition of the office of lord lieutenant, one of the arguments made for its retention was that an entire industry had grown up around the social life of the Castle and that considerable hardship would be caused were it to end.

Various fashion shops were located in a narrow passage called Hell near Christ Church. Newspaper advertisements during the mid-eighteenth century and later are an indication of the services offered in other adjacent streets. Blackmore and Mohollan in Sycamore Alley, wig-makers and hairdressers to the gentry and nobility, sold Italian flowers 'for the Hair and the Bosom, French curls, faverets [curls or locks of hair hanging loose] and ruffs'. Andrew Finlay in Parliament Street had a range of 'flowered silks, flowered and plain negligee sattins, armageens [plain silk], bombazines [usually a cotton fabric], ruffles and callimancoes [woollen fabric]'. John Carmichael sold a wide variety of silks opposite the Tholsel; and Hannah Crage, a hoopmaker of some repute, was employed by Stephen Bacle, perfumer, in Dame Street. The shop of Mr and Mrs Harris on the corner of Liffey Street and Mary Street offered embroidered dresses, painted silks and specially designed waistcoats. Apart from fashion items, other luxury goods were on sale in the Castle vicinity. Philip Magawley at the Blue Door in Abbey Street exported exotic spices and foods including Bayonne hams, Parmesan cheese, peaches in brandy, West Indian sweetmeats, green ginger, truffles, olives, macaroni, anchovies, Muscatel raisins and Marseille figs.

From the seventeenth century, there was continuing resentment among Irish manufacturers about the importation of foreign fabrics. Traditionally the silk, wool and poplin weavers of Dublin tended to be concentrated in the Liberties area, where they produced a wide range of weaves including expensive designs directed at a fashionable clientele. Local artisans had difficulty competing with imported textiles and there were regular slumps in the market, inflicting hardship on the many weaving families of the area. When the public hangman rode by coach to the execution of a butcher named Monaghan in June 1731, the weavers of the city dressed him in a colourful suit of imported fustian to bring into contempt the wearing of foreign manufactures. It became the practice of successive lords lieutenant and their wives to appeal to the gentry and nobility to wear Irish fabrics on social occasions. Chesterfield particularly had been successful in popularizing local products and on the day of his departure was accompanied to the waterside by an escort of grateful weavers.

The extent to which the Irish products were promoted depended on whether influential personalities from the court were prepared to set an example by choosing fabrics of local origin on major occasions. In 1765 'a vast concourse of ladies' attended the opening of a silk warehouse to promote the sale of local goods: the manufacturers celebrated the occasion at the Phoenix Tavern in Werburgh Street with twenty-nine toasts which included one in honour of the lord lieutenant, Northumberland, and his countess. In June 1778, at a time of distress in the weaving industry, a meeting of gentlemen and ladies undertook to be seen on a particular day in public gardens wearing Irish fabrics so that the *hoi polloi* might note that the gentry were inclined to favour Irish manufactures. At the queen's birthday ball in February 1782 the ladies present, encouraged by the Duchess of Leinster, made a special effort to wear clothes of Irish manufacture. The duchess wore 'mulberry sattin and ciel de empereur petticoats trimmed with gauze. She had a perfect blaze of diamonds.' Lady Antrim was 'in buff sattin with flowers ... and for elegance of person and stile of dress was universally admired'. And the men appeared mostly dressed in 'rabbinet coats with tissue waistcoats' of Irish manufacture. When the Rutlands were in office the vicereine energetically promoted Irish manufactures and, according to the *Freeman's Journal*, 'her mornings were chiefly spent in visiting the shops'.[25]

Champagne and Silver Buckles 1768–1800

In Ireland, by the latter half of the eighteenth century, all the trappings of a self-contained monarchy were in place. There was a bicameral parliament of lords and commons located in a magnificent, specially designed building in College Green. A facsimile royal court at Dublin Castle existed as a focus for power and privilege. A firmly ensconced and exclusive governing elite, by conquest and statute, had reduced the bulk of the population to impotent subservience. In the circumstances, it became increasingly necessary for the Irish Ascendancy to be reminded by their British masters that the kingdom of Ireland was a subordinate one, subject in all its major aspects to the overlordship of the king and parliament of Great Britain.

From the British perspective, a major weakness in their administration of Ireland was that the post of lord lieutenant required only part-time residence, so that the government of the country was in the hands of officials and parliamentary undertakers for long periods. To protect and fortify their constitutional position, the British decided in 1765 that henceforward lords lieutenant should reside continuously in Ireland, keeping a closer watch on

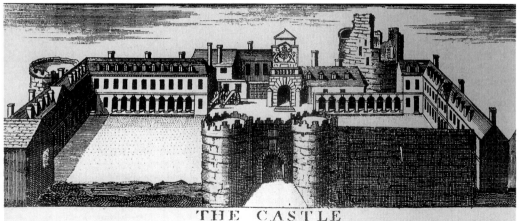

THE CASTLE

Brooking's drawing of 1723 (*top*) shows an early stage of the gradual transition of the Castle from medieval fortress to viceregal court. As the administrative, ceremonial and social roles of the viceroys expanded, the Upper Court Yard was surrounded by buildings designed to accommodate the activities of the Court and the living quarters of the viceregal household. The drawing by Tudor (c. 1750) shows the changes that took place, illustrating the emphasis on graceful architectural composition at a time when fine squares and wide city streets were adding to Dublin's attractions as a European city. (*Both images courtesy The Irish Architectural Archive*)

To make a Surtourte with Snipes.

TAKE the Breaft of Fowls, with fome blanch-
ed Bacon, and fome Veal Sweetbreads, two
or three Mufhrooms and Truffels, the Crum of
a Penny white Loaf foaked in Milk, all forts of
fweet Herbs, and a few Cives, and beat it well
together; feafon it with Pepper, Mace, and Salt,
and put in the Yolks of three or four raw
Eggs, and beat it well again; and if you find it
too thick, put in fome Cream; and if too thin,
fome grated Bread; then make a Rim round the
Difh you defign to ferve it on, with fome of
the Forc'd-Meat, and your Snipes muft be roa-
fted off, and cold; then you muft cut them in
long thin flices, with fome boned Anchovies,
fome hard Eggs mingled, fhred Parfly, and a
Lemon cut in Dice, and fome Cabbage Lettuce
cut fine, and well dried, and a few young Oni-
ons, all minced together; make a dozen Balls
of fome of the Forc'd-Meat, the bignefs of Chef-
nuts, and roll them in beaten Yolks of Eggs,
then in Crumbs of Bread; put them into a Difh
among the other Things, and cover it all over
with the reft of the Forc'd-Meat, and then gild
it over with Yolks of Eggs, and crumbed Bread,
and bake it till of a good brown Colour, then
ferve it for the firft Courfe.

Recipe used by a viceregal cook, from *Court Cookery or the Compleat English Cook* by Robert Smith (Dublin, 1724)

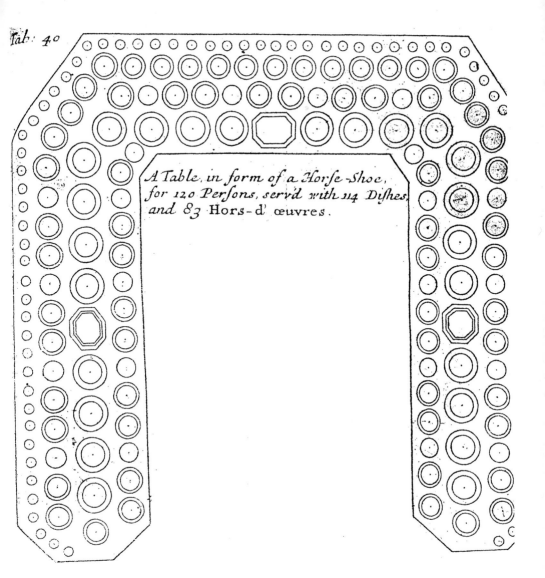

Tab: 40

A Table, in form of a Horse-Shoe, for 120 Persons, serv'd with 114 Dishes, and 83 Hors-d' œuvres.

Plan for the arrangement of dishes at a court dinner: '114 Dishes and 83 Hors-d'oeuvres' for 120 guests, from *Royal Cookery* by Patrick Lambe (London, 1726)

Maria, wife of the 2nd Earl Temple (later Marquis of Buckingham), from the *Hibernian Magazine*, April 1783. During their office the splendour of the Irish court reached new heights.

The Gunning sisters from Roscommon, supervised by their mother, successfully trawled the viceregal court for aristocratic husbands. Maria (*right*) became the Countess of Coventry; Elizabeth became the Duchess of Hamilton then, after widowhood, the Duchess of Argyll. (*National Gallery of Ireland*)

Above: Charles Manners, 4th Duke of Rutland (*left*) and his wife, Mary, 'This superb production of nature'
Below: 'Representation of the Body of His Grace the late Duke of Rutland lying in STATE in the [Irish] HOUSE OF LORDS', *Hibernian Magazine*, November 1787

Above: Richard Whately (*left*), Protestant Archbishop of Dublin, who protested to Queen Victoria over the excessive use of oaths at Irish viceregal ceremonials (*National Library of Ireland*); and William Henry Paget, Marquess of Anglesey, lord lieutenant from February 1828 to January 1829
Below: The Duke and Duchess of Richmond roistering at a viceregal party, from the *Dublin Satirist*, February 1810

The Carnival of FOLLY or FUN for the RICH and FOOD for the POOR!

Georgy loves good Ale and Wine
And Georgy loves good Brandy
And Georgy loves his C..n..g..m
..As sweet as Sugar Candy"

GEORGY'S·DELIGHT·
Or more Cunning than cautious"

George IV and his last mistress, Lady Conyngham. She was specially conveyed to Dublin to be with him during his Irish visit in 1821. (*British Museum*) political affairs. It was also decided that the undertaker system should be dropped and that the lord lieutenant should develop a 'Castle' party as a medium through which his policies would be presented and defended in parliament. They did not have people of high calibre in mind. North, the prime minister, expressed the view 'that it was not to be expected that men of the first rank in this country should chose to pass their lives in Ireland'. At the end of 1767 George, 1st Marquis of Townshend, arrived as lord lieutenant to implement this policy.[1]

Regardless of the political implications of this change, the social impact was immediate. In the past the intense programme of ceremonials and entertainments revolving around the presence of the lord lieutenant in the Castle had to be concentrated into his periodic visits. In his absence there was still a full programme of royal birthdays, anniversaries and other state feast-days to be commemorated, but they were usually formal events shorn of balls and banquets, in which the lords justices received guests at the Castle. Full-time residency for the lord lieutenant gave a huge fillip to social life of the Ascendancy, and during the last three decades of the century the Irish court reached its peak of brilliance and extravagance.

TOWNSHEND

The system of full-time residency, however, initially passed through a period when the standards and behaviour of the Irish court descended into indiscipline and profligacy. On arrival in Ireland, Townshend found himself immediately faced with the hostility of undertakers and their supporters, determined to defend their power and privileges. In London it was naïvely believed that he would find it possible to remove the corruption and patronage that had become such an endemic part of the Irish scene and to establish a greater degree of control and discipline in Dublin. It took Townshend until February 1771 to create a majority parliamentary group in support of his administration, assisted by the very corruption and abject patronage he'd set out to remove. The Octennial Act requiring elections every eight years (previously they expired only with the death of the monarch), and the dismissal of leading undertakers, came at a price. Froude wrote: 'Viscounts who had sons and nephews in the lower house wanted earldoms. Barons wanted to be viscounts, commoners to be barons. Patrons of boroughs required promotions in the army for their friends; sinecures and offices in remainder for themselves and their families.'[2]

The demands of some leading personalities of the period, such as the Earl of Ely, were insatiable. Ely, who received his earldom from Townshend, was also appointed privy councillor. Several of his friends were given appointments in the Revenue, valuable livings were provided for a number of clerics, a friend was appointed commissioner of customs, another made commissioner of accounts; pensions were provided for a number of Lady Ely's relations, others were given appointments in the public service including aide-de-camp on the lord lieutenant's entourage. The earl also asked for, and was refused, a bishopric and a deanery, as well as pensions for his wife's nieces. Townshend made parliamentarian John Beresford a privy councillor and commissioner of customs and gave a large living to his brother. When Beresford expressed displeasure at his brother being refused a bishopric because he was under-age, Townshend compensated him with the sinecure of Taster of Wines at £1000 a year. John Hely-Hutchinson, previously a supporter of the opposition, was lured to Townshend's side with the sinecure post of alnager, nominally responsible for attesting the quality of woollen goods, also worth £1000 annually. Later, despite his lack of scholarship, he was appointed provost of Trinity College.[3]

Townshend's own personality and conduct were deeply affected by the constant hostility his policies engendered. In the view of Lord Charlemont, 'his conviviality rendered him ... a not unpleasant governor', but his irregular behaviour 'was uncurbed by either principle or prudence'. Thirsting for what Walpole referred to as 'low popularity', he walked the streets of Dublin contemptuous of the decorum of high office, addressing strangers, indiscriminate in his choice of friends and drinking companions, and increasingly noted for buffoonery, profligacy and a fondness for drink and disreputable women. He was a welcome visitor to Mrs Leeson's high-class brothel but, as in other matters, he did not disdain less reputable dives.

Nevertheless, Thomas Waite, his under-secretary, wrote that 'with all his Oddities and Irregularities he is as a honest a Man as ever existed ...'[4]

Contemplating the plunging morals of the Townshend circle through the diary of a future lord lieutenant, a Dublin satirist wrote:

> Five o'clock. Finding myself inclinable to doze sent to the seraglio for six of my most favourable women ...

> Seven o'clock. Read the new treatise on the defence of sensuality, written by the Bishop of ------; an exquisite performance; the Christian heaven, like the Mahometan, incontestibly proved to exist in women and wine.

> Nine o'clock. Remember ... to order the pensions of a thousand a year for my favourite women, and to give Billy Sleek, my chaplain, the first bishoprick for his care in teaching my sons the art of marking a card without hazard of detection.[5]

Townshend found the levees held on Sundays, Tuesdays and Fridays, in accordance with previous practice, distasteful, since many of the nobility and gentlemen who attended were suspicious of his intentions or downright hostile. He changed levee days to Sundays only. His political enemies often showed their disdain for him by absenting themselves. Sir Edward Newenham warned Macartney, chief secretary in January 1770, that 'a certain set of men' were determined to ignore the levee on the king's birthday. Newenham himself would not be present due to 'violent erysipelas and no other reason'. Eventually fewer levees were held, but for most of the court habitués, particularly the ladies, other social events of Dublin Castle, especially the balls and banquets, were spiced by the behaviour of the lord lieutenant and the whiff of wickedness associated with his immediate coterie. A hostile political climate and an undercurrent of dissipation did little to diminish the attractions of the viceregal court.[6]

When Lady Townshend died in 1770, one of the beauties of the period, Dolly Monroe, adopted niece of Lady Loftus, chatelaine of Rathfarnham

Castle, competed unashamedly for Townshend's favours whenever the opportunity presented, encouraged and shepherded by her aunt. While fashionable Dublin looked on in amusement, Townshend chose to reject Dolly and to marry Anne Montgomery, one of three beautiful Dublin sisters portrayed in Gainsborough's painting popularly known as 'The Three Graces'. Elizabeth, one of the other sisters, married Luke Gardiner, later Lord Mountjoy; a third, Barbara, married John Beresford, who became chief commissioner of revenue. Townshend's choice of Anne wasn't entirely voluntary. He'd returned to England from his Dublin assignment without her, marrying only after being pursued by her brother, a noted duellist.[7]

Townshend was recalled to England in September 1772 when sixteen Irish peers presented a petition to George III seeking his withdrawal. He embarked in December with the usual attendant ceremonials. One of his parliamentary supporters viewing his departure wrote that the plaudits of the onlookers were as great 'as I have ever known given to any man of station', while his opponents claimed that the cheers accompanying him were those of a hired mob. Valedictories in the contemporary press and journals were entirely hostile. The *Freeman's Journal* saluted his departure thus:

> Drunkards, pimps and whores go mourn
> Townshend never shall return.[8]

HARCOURT

Simon Harcourt, 1st Earl of Harcourt and Townshend's successor, landed unexpectedly at the Pigeon House in the dead of night. In the absence of the usual welcoming personalities and ceremonials, he walked to Dublin Castle where he found Townshend, who'd remained in Ireland to greet him, drinking with a half-dozen convivial friends. The sudden appearance of Harcourt caused some confusion, but Townshend himself welcomed the new viceroy, assuring him that 'though he did come at the twelfth hour he had not found him [Townshend] napping'. It is unlikely that Harcourt himself would have been discomfited. Charlemont observed that although a stranger to the country, he was quick to catch its manners: 'he knew the importance of a table ... and distributed his Margaux with a very becoming profusion'. Walpole wrote of Harcourt that the only arts in which he was proficient were hunting and drinking; and his viceregal career, which lasted until January 1777, became known for the lavish social activities over which he presided at the Castle.[9]

Harcourt's personality was more attractive than his predecessor's and, allied with his acceptance of corruption as a way of life, ensured him great popularity. He was decorous, dignified and, according to Froude, 'inured by habit to the inanities of courts, with views generally honourable but pursuing them with languor, with the smallest imaginable insight into Ireland and its conditions and with an indolent cunning in the place of statesmanship.'[10]

There was some concern about his leniency towards criminals, critics asserting that 'he pardoned almost every street robber, housebreaker and thief ... to the great hurt of society'. But in other respects Harcourt pleased the ruling classes. He bought support for his administration by a plethora of appointments of new peers, additional offices and sinecures, and an extended pension list. Writing to the Earl of Darnley, Lady Clanwilliam said that Harcourt had offered her husband a totally unsolicited earldom. In May 1776 Harcourt sent a list of proposed creations and promotions to North, naming two new earls, four viscounts, eight barons and two baronets. In an accompanying secret list he sought agreement to promotions for six or seven further names. With few exceptions, the king accepted his recommendations.[11]

An additional sop for those wavering in their loyalty was the magnificence of the ceremonials at Dublin Castle under Harcourt. A man of immense personal wealth, Harcourt gave and expected extravagant hospitality. During his early days in Ireland he was unimpressed by what he was offered. Writing to his daughter-in-law Lady Nuneham, he complained 'there were few dinners worth going to'. Costly entertainment became the order of the day and many families of note beggared themselves in trying to attract him as a guest. He liked to be accompanied by the full panoply of state when attending dinners or other social functions outside the Castle, a

squadron of mounted militia leading the way with brightly garbed battleaxes walking on each side of the carriage. Even going to chapel required
a ceremonial procession of pages, gentlemen of the bedchamber, gentlemen-at-large and other officials.

He was more at home in court than the political arena, having served as
court chamberlain at St James and as ambassador in Paris, where he
delighted in the ostentation: '... this is the place for a person who loves La
Representation ... I could very willingly dispense with some of this state on
my account but that would be improper'. Lady Nuneham, who acted as his
hostess (he'd been widowed before coming to Dublin), wrote to a friend following a ball at the Castle: 'the lord lieutenant comes in much greater state
than the king'. And her husband Lord Nuneham, describing the scene on
the occasion of Harcourt's inaugural ball,

> saw ... His Excellency's royal march into the ballroom and I saw him
> mount his chair of state and stand until the first minuet was con-
> cluded which was performed with all the humiliating forms that are
> produced at St James' and it did not please me enough to make me
> desirous of seeing them twenty or thirty times repeated ...

And as Nuneham watched during ensuing days the splendour and
pageantry of Harcourt's initiation as viceroy, particularly the ceremonial
procession to the opening parliament through streets lined with soldiers,
he was increasingly disturbed:

> [The scene] had an air of absolute monarchy and of military force to
> support it and had I been an Irishman I would not have endured the
> sight ... How shocking is the contrast between the royal pomp of the
> viceroy and the wretchedness of the people! Were they less
> oppressed they should be more virtuous and industrious.[12]

This was a rare sentiment for the times from someone within the court circle.

Many resented the extent of the influence on Harcourt of his mistress,

Alicia McCartney, particularly where the social life of the Castle was concerned. She was variously described as an elderly unmarried woman 'of suspected reputation' and as the wife of Francis McCartney. Lady Louisa Conolly, writing to her sister the Duchess of Leinster, described her as 'a most hateful creature ... There are various conjectures about the connection ... She is absolutely on the footing of Lady Pompadour'. But Hugh Howard, a contemporary parliamentarian, suggested sardonically that 'as he [Harcourt] was a lone man it was probably the charms of her conversation alone fixed his attention to her'.[13]

Harcourt resigned as viceroy in January 1777 after a dispute with the commander-in-chief in Ireland. He returned to his English estate and in September of that year drowned in a well trying to rescue his favourite dog.[14]

BUCKINGHAMSHIRE

John Hobart, 2nd Earl of Buckinghamshire, who succeeded Harcourt, found certain deficiencies in the standards of his predecessor's court. When Mrs Waite, housekeeper at the Castle and wife of the serving under-secretary, Thomas Waite, visited the lord lieutenant's apartments in the Castle in anticipation of Buckinghamshire's arrival, she found them 'in woeful plight and most exceptionally dirty'. Buckingham also found shortcomings in the standards of behaviour and etiquette of guests at Castle functions. Some officials were lackadaisical in their duties and did not always insist on visitors to the court being appropriately clothed. Satirical verses of the period suggest that some guests, especially the higher clergy, were indifferent about their appearance and personal hygiene:

> But if you spy a rusty Gown
> Daggled by trudging through the Town
> And neither Shoes nor Linen clean
> His Reverence is some wealthy Dean.
> In Him, I own, it is no Hurt

He's privileged to bring Dirt
For filthy Clouts lose all their Stink
When found to be well-lined with Chink.

Buckinghamshire designated a courtier to scrutinize gentlemen coming on business to ensure that they were properly dressed. When Lord Clanbrassil presented himself improperly garbed he was encouraged to go away and to return in more presentable condition. Buckinghamshire reported that 'he took it in good humour … this decent regulation is generally approved of'. The Duke of Leinster, welcoming the changes to the court brought about by the new viceroy, wrote to his mother, 'he has discarded that banditti that infested his two predecessors'.[15]

Buckinghamshire pursued the policy of his predecessors in the distribution of patronage although he was concerned about the extent to which it had developed. Writing to the prime minister in February 1777 he set out his view about a more disciplined approach:

> My general plan is to give a degree of preference and to show a becoming distinction to the men of the first character and influence but not to depend so far upon them or their connections as to disgust detached individuals and above all things to spare the public purse …

But for all his assertions about discipline and quality of choice, he distributed peerages recklessly. In a single day in July 1777 he advanced five viscounts to earldom, seven barons to viscounts and created eighteen new barons.

The Buckinghamshires maintained a court of considerable style. The Earl of Huntingdon congratulated the viceroy in August 1778 on the excellence of the Castle social programme: 'I hear from every quarter that the prediction I made to Lady Buckinghamshire and to everyone else that she would play the part of a queen better than any is fully verified.'[16] It helped that she had Irish connections; her father William Conolly had been one of the great parliamentary managers of 'the Irish interest'. But not everyone was impressed by her social demeanour. Lady Charlotte Fitzgerald, watching her at a ball, wrote to her mother the Duchess of Leinster in July 1778: 'her loud voice, the quantity of rouge on ... she quite overpowered one, she is so very loud'. But the political climate of the period required more than Buckinghamshire's amiability, pleasing manners and social graces. In the absence of any other political stratagems or skills, his wholesale distribution of patronage and other favours could have only a limited influence on the great issues of the day, such as the introduction of free trade, the relief of Catholics and Dissenters, and the growth of the Volunteer movement. Describing himself as 'a man whose mind has been ulcerated with a variety of embarrassments' and lacking the ability to cope with the mounting problems of his post, he was recalled at the end of 1780.[17]

CARLISLE

Frederick Howard, 5th Earl of Carlisle, who took up duty at the end of 1780, was well-fitted to preside over the social demands of the Castle. A fashionably dissipated person of pleasure, he was acknowledged to be one of the best-dressed men in British society. One of his earlier affectations was the wearing of red shoes. While he was 'very slack in conversation' he had a cultivated mind, polished manners, an interest in the arts and some skill in writing poetry. It helped, too, that he had a strong chief secretary, William Eden (later Lord Auckland), who carried most of the political burden of his viceregency thus leaving him and his wife, Margaret Caroline, daughter of the 1st Marquis of Stafford, greater time for social affairs. There was a levee every Sunday, a drawing-room at least once a week, a ball every fortnight, and frequent dinners. The drawing-rooms at which both Carlisles were usually present were especially popular because of the mild gambling involved in cribbage, a popular card game of the time.

The Castle programme was interspersed with a constant round of private parties, balls and banquets. Lady Carlisle preferred to go unaccompanied by her entourage. A note in the court chamberlain's diary conveys a hint of disapproval: 'Her Ladyship chose to go to all parties in private although it was not usual.' She also flouted the established court rules for

Castle balls, on one occasion confining a ball to a small coterie of young dancers. Carlisle, writing to a friend, said that it was possible for his wife to organize such 'a very bold thing' without offence only because of the strength of his administration.[18]

This was a valid comment. Carlisle was very popular among the Ascendancy elite not just for his social acceptability but because he shared their view that Ireland could be better and more happily governed by an independent parliament. Furthermore, he'd won considerable respect without resorting to large-scale corruption. But a year after taking office he was tiring:

> ... two great dinners coming together (for almost before I have lost sight of the knives and forks of one, the soup of the other makes its appearance) fatigue me very much ... I feel such is the force of habit that I have this day nothing upon my hands only an audience, a dinner at the Archbishop of Cashel's and the ball at night. My levee on Sundays is a consumptive business; the insulting myself and every gentleman in Dublin with some nonsensical question for two hours makes me feel very thin and bilious indeed.[19]

In 1781 Carlisle acquired the former home of the ranger of the Phoenix Park and it became known as the Viceregal Lodge, but it was little used before the 1820s when it was refurbished and made more attractive as a residence. Prior to this a number of lords lieutenant used St Wolfstan's near Lucan as a summer residence.[20]

When political changes in Britain led to Carlisle's resignation in April 1782, a procession of at least of one hundred and fifty coaches bearing the most distinguished members of the nobility and gentry accompanied him to his embarkation at Ringsend.[21]

THE GOLDEN AGE

During 1782 the Irish parliament was granted a degree of legislative independence with the repeal of Poyning's Law and of other curbs on its powers. Irish legislation could no longer be altered by the Irish privy council. The years 1782 to 1800 became known as the years of Grattan's Parliament after Henry Grattan, the leading champion of Irish legislative independence. The introduction of parliamentary independence was largely cosmetic, the Castle continuing to have its policies implemented through parliamentary management. But there was, at least, an illusion of independence. The Ascendancy's sense that they'd made a political gain of consequence gave further impetus to the prevailing grandiosity and extravagance of the viceregal court. By now viceroys were receiving an annual salary of £20,000, but the level of entertainment expected of them required substantial private spending. Throughout the 1780s the tempo of social life of the Castle quickened and reached new peaks. It was the golden age of Ascendancy society. There was a huge appetite for dancing, dining and luxury, as the women aped the pre-revolutionary fashions of Paris salons and the French royal court, broadly indifferent to the prevailing intellectual ferment among French feminists. Extant diaries and correspondence of educated Irish Ascendancy women of the late eighteenth century, such as the Fitzgerald (Leinster) family's, are more concerned with family gossip and the social round than with politics.[22]

Between Carlisle's departure in April 1782 and the arrival of the Rutlands in early 1784, three different lords lieutenant served in Dublin Castle: the Duke of Portland, Earl Temple and the Earl of Northington. Portland (William Henry Cavendish-Bentinck) arrived with a large entourage and initiated his regime with a grand levee, 'the most crowded that was ever known', according to the court chamberlain, followed by a magnificent ball. According to the Charlemont memoirs, Portland was inclined to sit at ease at the Castle presiding over its social events while affairs of state were carried on by his officials, many of them his relatives who'd benefited from his patronage. It had the makings of an exciting season, but the duke fell from his horse in the Phoenix Park and broke some of his bones and was then recalled to London after five months to become prime minister following the sudden death of his predecessor Rockingham.

The 2nd Earl Temple (later created Marquis of Buckingham), who followed Portland, was an arrogant man with what Walpole described as 'many disgusting qualities, as pride, obstinacy, and want of truth with a natural propensity to avarice'. The splendour of the Irish court reached new heights of ostentation during his term of office. The balls, in particular, were hugely successful affairs, mixing feminine grace and military dash in an opulent setting verging on the vulgar. Writing to his brother W.W. Grenville, who was also his chief secretary, he boasted, 'our ball was the fullest and most splendid ever seen ... hardly a lady of quality absent'. But Temple's major contribution to court grandiosity was the establishment of the Order of the Knights of St Patrick with its extravagant ceremonies necessitating the refurbishment of the main hall of the viceregal apartments. (The background to the Order is dealt with in the next chapter.) The Temples chose to eat and sleep at the Viceregal Lodge: the earl came to the Castle each morning, gave audience and presided over social events of the day. The programme of entertainment and established ceremonials and commemorations were carried out with style. The *Freeman's Journal* reported in November 1782 that Temple, 'attended by the state regalia and a most brilliant retinue', took part in a parade from the Castle to St Stephen's Green and thence to College Green, where it paraded around the statue of King William to commemorate the day. The lord lieutenant was resplendent in a coat 'of the finest gold tissue, combining every idea of splendour and elegance'. On a later occasion the Temples had a new box erected in their honour in the Royal Theatre, Smock Alley, which was 'the most perfect and most elegant seen in this kingdom'.

Despite his own lifestyle, Temple was determined to root out overspending and peculation among his officials. Charlemont noted, 'The dismay was terrible. Clerks, treasurers and secretaries fled in all quarters.' Senior officials feared his intrusions. All were relieved, however, when changes in England following the appointment of the Fox-North coalition required Temple's removal from office. He departed from Ireland in June 1783. Patriot supporters regretted his departure and the ceremonial procession of carriages to his point of debarkation was several miles long.[23]

Northington's brief stay in Ireland from June 1783 to February 1784 made little political or social impact. Walpole wrote of him, 'In point of interest, connections or wealth, nobody was less distinguished, nor could he afford the expense.' The Earl of Charlemont said that although Northington ranked as an earl, he 'was not accompanied by sufficient splendour to give him that importance so necessary in the eyes of the people'. Socially, he was disadvantaged by being unmarried and afflicted by gout. But he had the reputation for being a bon-viveur and according to the *Freeman's Journal* was likely to obey the abstemious Duke of Portland in all things except living on vegetables and water. With the support of a competent court chamberlain, Hasler, and the ebullient master of ceremonies, Boyle Roche, he managed to have four balls and twelve drawing-rooms during the few weeks leading up to Christmas 1783. He celebrated the king's birthday with style the following February when there was an ode, a ball and a supper in which 253 ladies participated. Twenty-five minuets were performed, followed by more boisterous dancing that continued until dawn. But he quickly realized his inadequacies. Writing to Fox, the prime minister, he said that he'd come to the conclusion that the posts of Irish lord lieutenant and chief secretary required persons of ability and experience, 'not gentlemen taken wild from Brookes [the club] to make their Denouement in public life'. He added, 'I feel very forcibly the Truth of the Observation in my own instance.' He resigned with a change of government in 1784.[24]

THE RUTLANDS

Charles Manners, 4th Duke of Rutland, was induced by his friend Pitt the prime minister, with whom he had a close friendship, to accept the post of lord lieutenant in February 1784. His wife, Mary Isabella, was daughter of the Duke of Beaufort. Neither of them had come to Ireland with any particular talent other than social, but Rutland's political views were valued by Pitt, who on his advice decided not to pursue the Irish parliamentary reform then being sought by some powerful political interests.[25]

Ascendancy society was entranced by the viceregal couple and the hedonism they generated. They both lived life to the full, encouraged by having a regal court at their disposal. 'It was', according to the Earl of Charlemont, 'a season of much indulgence.' For the time being, at least, political tensions faded as the powerful and dissident were drawn into the court's never-ending round of eating, dancing and unfettered living. Earlier standards of decorum were overturned. The *Freeman's Journal* welcomed the changed atmosphere: '... the cumbrous reserve and sullen pride of the former times no more reign at the Castle'. The duchess's liberal use of oaths in conversation gave countenance to similar behaviour by other ladies of the court. Her beauty and charms had a disabling influence on many politicians. Henry Grattan wrote that both government and opposition members 'seemed to have laid down their arms at the feet of beauty'. On the occasion of the first visit by the duchess to the Houses of Commons and Lords in May 1784 the *Freeman's Journal* reported: 'She was dressed in magnificent style, her head powdered with diamonds and her sleeves adorned with finely composed knots of the same. A great number of people crowded on every side to view a face which must disarm faction and seemed created to command the admiration of mankind.' The contemporary historian N.W. Wraxall was told by a lady of his acquaintance who had seen the duchess in a state of undress that no words could convey an adequate idea of her 'formation'. But, wrote Wraxall, 'I never contemplated her except as an enchanting statue, formed to excite admiration rather than to awaken love: this superb production of nature not being lighted up by corresponding mental attractions.' Other male admirers were less restrained: '... they sprang up ... whenever she turned her eyes'. Some made fools of themselves. At a party given at the home of Dean Marlay in Celbridge, Sir Hercules Langrishe, prominent parliamentarian and a commissioner of revenue, dressed as a labouring man and read a long adulatory poem to her. According to a popular story, when Colonel St Leger, a handsome 'buck' from the Castle circle, observed the duchess wash her hands and mouth after dinner, he demonstrated his gallantry by calling for her bowl and consuming its contents. The duke witnessed the incident. 'St Leger,' he said, 'you are in luck. Her Grace washes Her feet tonight and you shall have another goblet for supper.'[26]

The social programme at the Castle for St Patrick's Day 1784 was an example of the ritualistic splendour of Rutland's court. It was the first social event of his reign as viceroy and he was determined it should make an impact. The day started with the knighting and investiture of Lord Carysfort as a member of the Illustrious Order of St Patrick. During the colourful ceremonial Rutland knighted Carysfort 'by the grand manner' with the Sword of State. After 'proofs of blood' were delivered in accordance with the statutes of the Order, Carysfort was invested with the riband and badge of the Order. A lavish banquet followed at which Rutland presided and where was put on display a sideboard of gold and silver plate which, according to *The Hibernian Magazine*, '… for quantity, fashion and richness vastly exceeded anything of late years seen within these walls'. Hasler noted in his household diary: 'This entertainment was superb beyond expression.' The splendidly attired Rutland entered St Patrick's Hall at about ten o'clock attended by the Knights with their ceremonial collars and, after he had been seated, the ball began. All the apartments had been illuminated and thrown open: country dances commenced in St Patrick's Hall, cotillions began in the Battle-axe Hall where an orchestra played, and supper was provided in the council chamber and other areas. Dancing continued until nearly three o'clock when supper started. *The Hibernian Magazine* reported that the food 'consisted of every curiosity that art could procure, imagination suggest or the season procure'.

The guests devised imaginative displays of fancy dress. *The Hibernian Magazine* wrote: '… the display of taste, elegance and fancy, represented an assemblage of beauty that realized all that fable ever fancied to have been found in the courts of a Venus or the temple of a Diana.' An 'enchanting' group of chained Circassian slaves included Lady Butler. Lady Crofton was 'superbly dressed as Night'. Lord Valentia came as a Turk accompanied by Lady Valentia as a flower girl, and Lady Muskerry arrived as Diana accompanied by one of her friends as a nymph. Captain Vernon was dressed as a Shepherd of the Plains of Boyle. Various gentlemen came as Paddies: by now paddywhackery was becoming part of the repertoire of Castle entertainments as the gentry and nobility found increasing amusement in the images of deprived and unsophisticated Irish peasant society. The fun went on throughout the night: some of the guests remained until seven, long after dawn had broken. Hasler, who would have been present at many previous festive occasions in the Castle, summed it up: '... every individual who was present appeared enraptured with the elegance and magnificence of that superb entertainment'.[27]

As his viceregency progressed, Rutland grew more eager in his quest for perfection of style. He bestowed on Margaret Leeson the accolade of running the best brothel in Dublin, being so taken by 'her art of pleasing' that he had her included on the pension list for £300 a year under an assumed name. On one visit to her place in Pitt Street, Rutland was accompanied by two aides-de-camp and an escort of cavalry who remained on duty at the brothel from one in the morning until five in the afternoon.[28]

Food was another of his enthusiasms. Throughout his term of office batches of fruit and expensive delicacies were shipped weekly from England. Talented cooks had been in short supply in Dublin for some time. Harcourt had had four competent cooks at the Castle but his successor Buckinghamshire had great difficulty in finding one of acceptable standard. During 1785 and 1786, Rutland sent George Kendall, a member of his military staff, on various trips to France to identify and supply the best foods and wines and the most attractive *objets d'art* in vogue in French society. Kendall also arranged for Jones, the principal cook at Dublin Castle, to spend periods acquiring new culinary skills working with the best kitchens in France, at the royal court at Fontainebleu and those of the Duke of Orleans and the Archbishop of Narbonne, both notable gourmets. In December 1786 Kendall reported to Rutland that he'd dispatched a consignment of wines to the Castle. It consisted of:

> 500 bottles of Sillery champagne of the very best quality in the proprietor's possession. 300 bottles of Hautevillers champagne, the growth preferred in Paris to any other: I had it directly from the prior of that convent by the Archbishop of Narbonne's intercession. If it is not perfect of its kind, the prior must be damned for perjury, for he has solemnly declared it to be so. 100 bottles of Chambertin from le President de Grosbois's own cellar; 300 bottles of St George from the very cellars of the Chapter of Nuits; and some bottles of Morachais, the very first growth of white wine in Burgundy.

There were other potential pleasures that Kendall investigated in France on Rutland's behalf. He visited Sevres to see whether he might find there some delicate pieces of porcelain which might be to the liking of the duchess, but met with nothing that pleased. Later, when the fawning Bishop of Killala arranged with Kendall for a present of some ornaments to be sent to her from the manufactory, they were broken on the journey. But Kendall was more successful in other quests. He reported on the purchase of snuff-boxes, paintings (including a Velazquez) and a specially made sporting gun. Rutland had expressed a particular interest in shoe buckles. Kendall wrote assuring him that 'the handsomest shoe buckles possible to be had in Paris shall be sent by the cook (diamonds apart)'. The choice of buckles had been made by Kendall after he'd looked at the most fashionable ones worn at Fontainebleu and after advice from a member of the French aristocracy. Diamond-encrusted buckles were then a feature of male fashion among those of wealth and status. The Bishop of Derry, a prominent supporter of the Volunteer movement, wore them on his shoes and his knees.[29]

The extravagant life style of the Rutlands was such that there were few among the gentry and nobility who would have felt at ease in offering them hospitality. When the duke and duchess made it known in October 1785 that they would like to visit Cork only on the condition that they were invited, it caused consternation among the members of the city council. An alarmed member wrote to the parliamentarian John Hely Hutchinson:

> ... for this city to entertain Her Grace would be ridiculous in the extreme. You know this city. What ladies have we here calculated for such an employment? Her Grace must fix her residence at Castle-martyr [home of Lord Shannon], or at some of the great houses in the neighbourhood, for there is neither place or person here fit to entertain her, nor even to invite her, for the mayor has no wife, and if we had, I would not wish to place our women in so ridiculous a situation.

In the event, the Rutlands were accommodated by Lord Shannon and later by Lord Mountcharles; a programme of entertainment for them was arranged by local merchants; and knighthoods were bestowed on two local personalities. The Rutlands went on to visit Killarney, where the local garrison arranged a grand ball; the duchess danced all night with all the officers present. The viceregal couple liked unrestrained and uninhibited merrymaking. Some of the Castle circle tried to facilitate it. Colonel St George, an inveterate roisterer himself, borrowed the seat of Lord Mornington at Dangan to provide a fitting setting for a party for the Rutlands. St George's newly married nineteen-year-old wife, Melesina, a reluctant participant in the protracted revels, wrote in her memoirs of night being turned into day, and of the bawdy conversation of the women guests while they impatiently played cards as they awaited for the men who, eventually, joined them 'in a state very unfit for the conversation or even the presence of our sex'.[30]

Rutland's friends became increasingly concerned about his frenetic lifestyle. The Earl of Mansfield, then Lord Chief Justice of England, warned him about his hard drinking and irregularity of hours at the Castle. 'I am the only man who will venture to give you hint,' he wrote. His sister Anne, deeply concerned about his deteriorating health, pleaded with him to change his behaviour. 'Health takes a sudden flight, and death happens as unexpectedly,' she warned.

During 1787 he set out on a punishing three-month tour of the country, being entertained lavishly by those who feared a loss of prestige if they failed to provide hospitality to such a distinguished guest. Rutland's capacity for food and drink and sheer exertion were huge. He would eat six or seven turkey eggs for breakfast, then ride for up to seventy miles, eat and drink copiously at six or seven o'clock in the evening, then sit up to a late hour and eat again before retiring for the night. Sometimes he broke his journeys between the seats of the nobility by staying in more humble abodes. As he travelled the land, often in a drunken state, he bestowed knighthoods liberally. Many of the recipients were innkeepers and tavern owners whose hospitality pleased him but who, receiving no subsequent official recognition for the honours bestowed, became subjects of derision. According to popular story, when the duke spent a night at a Kilbeggan inn, he was so entertained by the tales of the landlord Thomas Cuffe that he went through the ritual of knighting him on the spot. In the morning, when a more sober lord lieutenant offered a financial gift instead of the title bestowed, Cuffe replied that although he was willing to accept the offer, 'Her Ladyship says no!'[31]

A day or two after his long sojourn Rutland became suddenly ill and died at the viceregal lodge. He was thirty-three years old. His officials initially said that he'd died from 'a putrid fever' and that his physicians had tried bloodletting without avail, but everyone knew that he drank himself to death. When his body was opened his liver was found to be decayed. The duchess had been in England on a visit to her mother, the Duchess of Beaufort, and was unable to get back to Dublin before her husband's death. As he lay dying he told his physician, 'I must be content to die with her image before my mind's eye.'

His leaving of life, like his pursuit of it, was carried out in style. His embalmed body was conveyed in a mourning cavalcade to the great committee room of the House of Lords in College Green. There, under a catafalque, he lay in state on an elevated platform in a cedar coffin set in an outer leaden one, his elegant ducal coronet resting on a cushion close to his head. Huge numbers went to view the dead viceroy. Four days later his body started its final journey to England as his coffin was borne under the high portico of the building out into the streets while choirs of the two Dublin cathedrals chanted a funeral dirge. Then the procession of carriages began, accompanying the chariot bearing his body with the dignitaries of church and state, the officials of the court and accompanying troops and bands moving slowly through the streets of Dublin to the point of embarkation. The Earl of Charlemont described the scene: 'As a procession it was, perhaps, unrivalled: but the silent and decorous sorrow of the multitudes that witnessed it diffused an affecting grace and soothing solemnity over every object, beyond the reach of the most refined pageantry.'[32]

BUCKINGHAM (TEMPLE) RETURNS

Buckingham's return as viceroy following the death of Rutland was, initially at least, a popular appointment, and he arrived to a great welcome in December 1787. Units of Volunteers were drawn up to greet him at the quayside in Kingstown. When the procession reached Ballsbridge it was met by about four hundred members of the silk and woollen weavers' association wearing orange and blue cockades in their hats, who took the horses from his carriage and insisted on drawing him to town. 'More brilliant or general illuminations we never remember,' reported the *Freeman's Journal.* Banners proclaimed the right to an independent parliament and support for 'common rights, common friends, common foes and common king'.

Buckingham resumed the grand style he had adopted during his earlier period of office, but set out to curb certain excesses of the Rutland regime. He found distasteful the long nights of eating and drinking which had become common practice in upper-class society, and made it known that it was his intention to encourage dining before five o'clock, 'a custom much wanting in the city'. He set an example for hard work by remaining busy in his closet from early morning until five or six o'clock, declaring his determination to reduce the shortcomings and peculations of many of his officials who hitherto lacked supervision. In September 1788 he launched an initiative aimed at rooting out fraud and corruption by directing that every office and store of the ordnance service be sealed up and locked while all accounts were checked. The comptroller of the laboratory attached to the ordnance cut his throat in the Castle garden, a senior official of the bullion ended his life by similar means, and one of the commissioners for the imprest office shot himself. Jephson, a salaried ode-writer to the viceregal court, was dismissed from office when detected in a mirror mimicking the viceroy behind his back.[33]

But if there were stricter controls on expenditure and behaviour, there were no curbs on the resplendence of his court. Buckingham was anxious to make a dramatic impact, not just to impress the local population but to emphasize the depth of his loyalty to England. When he celebrated the queen's birthday all male guests were required to attend dressed entirely in green, the colour of the livery of his own household. He wrote in May 1789 to his brother and chief secretary, W.W. Grenville, resident in London much of the time, describing 'a most magnificent fete' that he'd arranged for the queen's birthday when 560 guests were provided for in St Patrick's Hall. He told him: 'I am anxious to establish the reputation of the three most splendid entertainments which I shall have given this winter.' And making sure that his celebrations would come to the attention of the queen, he hinted, 'pray take care that the compliment is not lost'. It was also important to him that the viceregal apartments at the Castle should reflect the opulence of the court's regime. Wall and ceiling paintings in St Patrick's Hall were commissioned from the Italian painter Vincent Waldre, brought specially to Ireland for the work. Inside and outside the Castle there were displays of flamboyance. In June 1788 the Buckinghams embarked on a new boat on the Grand Canal at Ballyfermot on Dublin's outskirts whence, with banners flying and a band playing on an accompanying boat, they sailed to the Bog of Allen where they dined.[34]

During the regency crisis of 1788–9, when George III was incapacitated, the Irish opposition supported the move to have the Prince of Wales given power on his own account, against the wishes of the government. When the issue was resolved with the recovery of the king, Buckingham dismissed from office those who'd taken this stance and attempted to shore up his administration with large-scale corruption and the liberal distribution of honours; but by now he was hugely unpopular, and with his health failing, he resigned his post in September 1789.

END OF A GOLDEN AGE

In an atmosphere of increasing tension and dissent, the English government hoped that Temple's resignation and his replacement by the Earl of Westmorland would ease public feeling. John Fane, 10th Earl of Westmorland, wealthy, convivial and with a penchant for entertaining on the grand scale, fitted easily into the mould of his predecessors. He was an open friend of the Protestant minority and opposed to any further relief for the Catholics. Eight years earlier he'd scandalized British society by running away with the daughter of a banker believed to be one of the wealthiest heiresses of the period. Jonah Barrington wrote that 'his splendid conviviality' procured him many friends in Ireland, at least temporarily. One of his young aides-de-camp, Arthur Wellesley, found the pace of social life at the Castle so hectic and expensive that he had to borrow from a local draper and from his bootmaker with whom he lodged. (Later, when Wellesley sought the hand in marriage of one of the Castle circle, Catherine Pakenham, daughter of Lord Longford, her family rejected him as unsuitable. They married despite opposition and Arthur eventually became the Duke of Wellington.) But splendid conviviality was no longer the answer to Ireland's problems, political or social. In an atmosphere of growing violence and threats to the old order, the death of Lady Westmorland towards the end of 1793, the removal of her husband at the end of 1794, and his replacement by Fitzwilliam, the golden age of Ascendancy society had come to an end.[35]

The golden age never embraced those outside the privileged ruling class. Alongside the richness of the life of Dublin Castle was a contrasting picture. For generations, the majority of the Irish population had lived for most of the time at subsistence level. R.B. McDowell has written: 'If fortunate they rose slightly above it; if unlucky they lapsed into destitution, joining the horde of beggars who drifted through the countryside or congregated in towns.' As it had been throughout the earlier decades of the century, nowhere was the misery of Irish conditions more manifest than in the streets of Dublin, where the city's paupers joined the teeming numbers of rural vagrants. Outside the walls of the Castle, the sights and sounds of absolute wretchedness were a constant feature. For a time at the end of the 1760s a lawless rabble gathered habitually at a ball alley in Aungier Street, close to the Castle, accompanied 'by breaking of windows, cursing, swearing and all manner of vice' until the alley was pulled down on the direction of the city magistrates. Later the lord mayor ordered the imprisonment of vagrants who had not returned to the country, and the lodging of their children in the workhouse 'to be bred up Protestants'. Similar directives had been issued in the past with little obvious impact. Parliamentarian Henry Grattan was conscious of both sides of the scene. He wrote, 'I am tired of Dublin and all its claret … swarming with poverty and idleness.' Lord Nuneham, writing when his father Harcourt was lord lieutenant, described his first visit to Dublin:

> This is the most dirty, the most gloomy, the most stinking and the
> ugliest city I was ever in ... every kind of filth is thrown into the deep
> stream of black mud that gently flows through the town ... half the
> inhabitants are in absolute rags and some of them ... almost naked ...
> you cannot stop in a carriage without being surrounded with crowds
> of importunate beggars.

And Lord Carlisle, quoting a visitor to the city in 1781, said that he never
knew what English beggars did with their old clothes until he came to
Dublin.[36]

From one aspect, at least, it summed up the golden age of Irish Ascendancy.

Interlude

As the 1790s progressed, political influences and events transformed Irish society in a way that was to have huge impact on the future path of Irish history. There is little to relate about the usual ceremonies and social life of the viceregal court for the period from the mid-1790s to the beginning of 1801 because the normal life of the court faded out. Lord Shannon, who held office in the Irish administration, writing to his son in October 1798, said, 'As to Castle, the doors are locked and the grass [is] growing in the yard.'¹ It was a time of repression, rebellion and slaughter. Hatred and terror dominated. The turmoil eventually culminated in the abolition of the Irish parliament.

When the American Declaration of Independence of 1776 led to the war between the colonists and England, troops were withdrawn from Ireland to bolster English forces in America. The 'patriot' members of the Irish Parliament formed the Volunteers, an armed movement to make up for the loss of the English troops. The new force was loyal to the Crown but not under its control. This gesture on the part of the patriots helped to secure the agreement of the English government to the long-sought grant of legislative independence and to the emergence of Grattan's Parliament in 1782. Certain reliefs were later granted to the Catholics, including the right to vote. However, the Irish parliament remained an Ascendancy legislature and Catholics still had no parliamentary representation. Demands for full Catholic emancipation grew.

The French Revolution and its Declaration of the Rights of Man threw light on Ireland's injustices, not only those of the Catholics but of the Presbyterians who were debarred from civil and military office. Theobald Wolfe Tone, influenced by revolutionary ideas elsewhere, preached the cause of republicanism, of Irish national freedom, of civil rights and equality for all classes. Tone's ideals informed the founding of the United Irishmen. By the 1790s the ferment of ideas and political agitation had led to the growth of agrarian strife and sectarian violence, and to increasing Protestant aggression against Catholics in northern counties (the Orange Order was instituted in 1795 in Co. Armagh). The Volunteers were suppressed, political assemblies were banned, other laws were directed at political radicals. The division between Protestants and Catholics grew. There were divisions too within the contending sides. The Catholic hierarchy and most of their clergy were opposed to radical action. When the 2nd Earl Fitzwilliam took up duty as lord lieutenant at the beginning of 1795, he was sympathetic to the Catholics and to parliamentary reform, but his heavy-handed approach to extreme Protestant elements gave rise to vicious reaction. The Bishop of Cloyne wrote to the Earl of Westmorland: ' ... the dinners of the new lord lieutenant are miracles of stupidity, as half of the company tremble for their places, and have been for so many years hostile to the other half; not a word is spoken and Lord Fitzwilliam never speaks himself ...' Fitzwilliam was recalled after fifty days, to the great alarm of the Catholic population. His replacement, the 2nd Earl of Camden, instructed to rally to Protestant interests, arrived in an atmosphere where 'the clangor of trumpets could scarcely drown the hissing of the people' and embarked on a policy of extreme repression. Lady Camden and her children soon returned to the safety of England.[2]

Amidst growing tension, a French invasion fleet with Wolfe Tone aboard, led by General Hoche and intended to secure Irish independence, was destroyed by storm in Bantry Bay in December 1796. Militia and yeomanry forces were put on a war footing for the defence of the government. War was now inevitable. The United Irishmen rose in rebellion in May 1798, first in Dublin and neighbouring counties, then in Wexford, later in Connacht and Ulster. While the rebels enjoyed early victories, and committed atrocities, superior government forces quickly took control, indiscriminately slaughtering rebels and civilians. Dublin Castle itself became a site of death; suspects were tortured and flogged; rebel dead were put on view in its courtyard. By the time a second French force under General Humbert landed at Killala, Co. Mayo, in August, the insurrection was effectively at an end. Humbert's army pushed inland but surrendered to Crown forces at Ballinamuck, Co. Longford, in September.

Government retribution was swift and merciless. Rebel leaders were hanged and their heads exhibited on spikes; Wolfe Tone committed suicide awaiting execution. As the insurrection moved towards its end, Camden was withdrawn and replaced as lord lieutenant by Marquis Cornwallis, also appointed commander-in-chief in Ireland. Cornwallis confronted the undisciplined military repression and brought some degree of clemency into army policy. When the tumult subsided almost 25,000 rebel soldiers and non-combatants had been killed in contrast to 1600 of the Crown forces.[3]

Cornwallis, reflecting the view of the English government, saw an opportunity to abolish the Irish legislature and create a parliamentary union of Britain and Ireland. There followed a period of intense parliamentary activity, managed by Cornwallis and his chief secretary, Viscount Castlereagh, involving negotiation, bartering, intrigue and the dropping of the notion of Catholic emancipation. In order to achieve the Union there was a liberal distribution of peerages, places and pensions. The Irish parliament voted itself out of existence with the Act of Union in August 1800, and the Union was implemented on 1 January 1801. Irish parliamentary representation was transferred to Westminister and restricted to a hundred members. Irish peers elected twenty-eight among them to serve in the London House of Lords, along with four bishops, while the viceroy and his Irish court, now seen by many as an anomaly, remained in existence as a sop to Ascendancy interests.

FIVE

Mushrooming Peers

Nobility had always been the lifeblood of royal courts. The traditional concept of monarchy required a court based on an exclusive circle of families of high birth to maintain and emphasize the power, privilege, status and splendour of monarchy. Edmund Burke defined nobility as 'a graceful ornament to the civil order ... it is the Corinthian capital of polished society.'[1] The Irish viceregal court considered itself on a par with the St James, if not with the courts of other western European countries. It was not unusual for the institution of nobility to be manipulated by governments. Where Ireland was concerned, there were particular political considerations, especially during the latter decades of the eighteenth century, which determined the choice, numbers and background of the Irish nobility. Many could hardly be said to conform to the purity of Burke's image. Often, choice was not influenced by good breeding, or refinement of manners, or even as a reward for military or political services of a high order, but was a consequence of patronage and political blackmail.

An early official ranking of Irish peers in 1585 placed the Earl of Kildare at the head and listed twenty-five other earls, viscounts and lords. When the Irish Parliament sat in May 1689 under James II, the peerage, still headed by Kildare, consisted of 130 to 140 members including fourteen spiritual peers (archbishops and bishops of the established Church) and about twenty peers of doubtful origin. Increased numbers during the seventeenth century arose from the bestowal of Irish peerages on English officeholders and other English seekers of hereditary titles without inflating the English House of Lords. During the eighteenth century a further increase resulted from Irish rather than English demands. At the end of that century there were 22 spiritual peers and 230-odd temporal peers, of whom about 150 were resident in Ireland at the time of the Union. About 70 per cent of the latter were eighteenth-century creations. Over half of the peers attending the Irish House of Lords during the immediate pre-Union period held one or more government positions; some were sinecures, some were appointments with responsibilities.[2]

There were two main influences on the mounting number of Irish peerages between 1700 and 1800. The first derived from the Ascendancy's grandiose notions of the nature of the viceregal court at Dublin Castle. The other was the manipulation of the peerage by successive lords lieutenant as a means of dealing with political problems. Almost all of them used the creation and promotion of peers as an effective device for political ends, appealing to a hunger for advancement and prestige within the Ascendancy. 'Most Irish gentlemen', said Buckingham 'enter my closet with a P in mouths: Place, Pensions, Peerage or Privy Council.' It was a simple act of barter: an honour was awarded, a vote won. Some lords lieutenant were more lavish than others; Townshend, Harcourt, and Buckinghamshire showered awards prodigally.

Honours sought often had little to do with merit. Lady Brandon wrote to Townshend in October 1772:

> ... at the repeated request of your devoted servant, Mr Jo. Mathews, member for Inistioge, or rather of his wife, her heart is set on your makeing her a Lady, if you refuse – answer for her death. The Husband must be a baronet or she dyes – do dear Lord Townshend grant her this speck of honour – it takes from no body and will highly

oblige many very particularly Your Excellency's most humble and obedient Servant.

E. Brandon

Surveying the progress of the Irish peerage during the eighteenth century, Lecky wrote that it 'was systematically degraded; and the majority of Irish titles are historically connected with memories, not of honour, but of shame'.[3]

In the earlier decades of the eighteenth century a large proportion of peers in the Irish House of Lords were absentees. The bishops tended to be a large element of the working majority and this enhanced their importance, although their power diminished later as the number of active lay peers rose. Every bishop was expected to use his influence on behalf of the government and many of the sees were filled by English ecclesiastics because they were more likely to be loyal. The senior clergy assiduously pursued appointments to bishoprics, not just for financial award but for status and the excitements of court life. The fastest way to promotion within the Irish Church lay in securing a post of chaplain to the viceroy. In August 1714, King, the Archbishop of Dublin, complained to the Archbishop of Canterbury about the extent to which Irish clergy pursued preferment, 'attending at court and neglecting their churches'. When Archbishop Boulter became primate, it was said that the choice of bishops gave little or no weight to their religious, moral or theological characters.[4]

None was more perceptive of early intimations of mortality than the senior clergy when the possibility of vacancies arose among ailing members of the peers spiritual. Niceties and sensitivities were ignored, as the papers of various lords lieutenant show. The Bishop of Down, noting at the end of 1746 that the Archbishop of Cashel was 'seventy years old and very corpulent', served notice that he would like to be given the vacancy whenever it arose. In June 1760, Jammett, the Bishop of Cork and Ross, in pursuit of the same archbishopric, wrote to the lord lieutenant, Bedford, that the present incumbent was ill and had but a 'faint prospect' of recovery. James Hawkins, Bishop of Dromore, made representations to North, the prime minister, towards the end of 1776 seeking a better bishopric and suggesting he might be given the more attractive see of Clogher, where John Garnet was in bad health. But Garnet survived until 1782, by which time Hawkins had been translated to the wealthier see of Raphoe. Charles Agar, Bishop of Cloyne, set his sights on the see of Dublin when it became known that the present archbishop, John Cradock, might not have long to live. Agar's determined but unsuccessful pursuit of the Dublin post was a matter of amused public gossip and he felt obliged to write to Buckinghamshire, the lord lieutenant, in December 1778, rejecting the public perception that he 'had limited and confined [his] pursuits to one particular project', offering himself for the 'first suitable preferment which may become vacant'. In the event, the Archbishop of Cashel died shortly afterwards and Agar was promoted. He eventually became Archbishop of Dublin in 1801 and was made Earl of Normanton a few years later. Despite valiant efforts, he subsequently failed to get the post of primate of Ireland when the government refused to relax the rule that no Irishman should hold the post.[5]

ATTITUDE OF ENGLISH PEERAGE

As the number of Irish peers increased there was a strengthening perception among the English that their Irish counterparts were a lesser breed. These attitudes became obvious when the members of the two peerages came together from time to time at the court of St James. When the March 1734 arrangements for the marriage ceremonies of the Prince of Orange and Anne, Princess Royal, were announced, they indicated that all the ranks of Irish peers would be given a lower precedence than the English in the processional walk. Thus, Irish earls and viscounts would have to give way to English lords. The enraged Irish representatives demanded that they be permitted to walk with the English peers of same rank; but the English, adamantly opposed to change, threatened not to walk at all.

The Irish peeresses were infuriated. Not only were their husbands being demeaned but the plan also proposed that they themselves be further humbled by being ranked below the daughters of English peers. According to the Earl of Egmont, who acted as their spokesman and champion, acceptance of these requirements would have enormous implications. During balls their daughters would be at risk of not being asked out to dance according to their rank. And the peeresses themselves would be in a dilemma as to who should defer to whom on entering or going out of doors, or on being seated at card-tables, or in other circumstances where they should be properly acknowledged. Worse still, the queen might end her tradition of kissing Irish countesses on special occasions, a courtesy not extended to their English counterparts.

According to Egmont, Irish countesses had been allowed to walk in the funeral procession of Queen Elizabeth I side by side with their English equivalents. This, and other precedents going back to the fifteenth century, were cited in support of the Irish ladies. But as the day of the royal nuptials grew closer, and in the absence of any change in processional plans, the Irish peeresses informed the queen they would not be attending a special drawing-room arranged to display to her their dresses for the wedding. The drawing-room was called off. The exasperated king, regretting his involvement in the wedding arrangements, tired of the disputing Irish peers and their ladies, and faced with other problems including the lady-in-waiting who was refusing to carve for supper on the wedding night, decided that there would be no changes in the wedding procession. The Irish peers and peeresses withdrew from the celebrations even as spectators.[6]

Three years later, at the funeral of Queen Caroline in December 1737, members of the joint peerages assembled again in London. The Irish representatives were pleased to find that proper precedence had been restored to them and felt that this resulted from their earlier protests. It was not, however, the end of the issue. In August 1761, when ceremonial arrangements for the wedding of Princess Charlotte of Mecklenburgh to George III were being completed, members of the English peerage virulently opposed the giving of equality of precedence to Irish peers. The Irish spokesman, the Earl of Charlemont, was told scathingly 'that they could not expect to walk at any royal procession except a funeral, as they would then be in their proper station as Irishmen, and howl as much as they pleased'. Likening the Irish aristocracy to traditional keeners (or professional mourners) of Irish peasant society was a cruel barb. By now many among the English peerage resented the pretensions of the Irish court and the growing pressures of the patriot faction for more political power. The controversy that followed was spirited and culminated in the king agreeing to the Irish peers walking in certain pre-nuptial ceremonials but not in the coronation ritual itself.[7]

The greater Irish families, who tended to intermarry with the English nobility and to hold both Irish and English titles, were of unchallengeable status, but as the number of peerages of Irish origin increased, the older regime of English aristocracy came to see many as parvenus. Lady Mary Wortley Montague was aghast when Sir John Rawdon was awarded the distinction of Baron Rawdon of Moira in 1750 (he was later promoted Earl of Moira): 'Ever since I knew the world Irish patents have been hung out for sale, like the laced and embroidered coats in Monmouth Street, and brought up by the same sort of people. I mean those who had rather wear shabby finery than no finery at all.' Apart from any other shortcomings, Rawdon was seen as lacking in manly characteristics. When he was punched during a brawl and failed to respond he was reprimanded by Lord Mansel, who told him that no gentleman should take a box in the ear without responding in a spirited manner. Rawdon protested, 'I know that. This was not a box in the ear, it was only a slap in the face.'[8]

Horace Walpole's correspondence directs some of his most astringent observations at newly emerging members of the Irish peerage. He could only find 'brewers and poulterers' among the creations of 1756. Lady Townshend remarked that, every day, she fully expected a bill from her fishmonger signed 'Lord Mount-Shrimp'. Writing to his friend Lord Carlisle, George Selwyn, wit and member of the British House of Commons, expressed concern lest the 'the riff raff' who were being given in titles in Ireland might be confounded with the nobility of England. According to Selwyn, the king had grown 'very averse to promotions of that kind; it is high time to be a little chaste upon that point'. Walpole returned to the attack in 1776, describing the proliferating Irish peers as like 'mushrooms ... half of whom ... will not be gentlemen under a generation or two'. And he compared them to Lord Bateman, whom George I made an Irish peer to avoid him making a Knight of the Bath, 'because', said the king, 'I can make him a lord but I cannot make him a gentleman'. Following his accession in 1760,

George III adopted a policy of refusing peerages to anyone engaged in trade – a rule not applied to Irish creations, thus leaving them open to English supplicants. Some promotions were made on very slight pretexts. Lord North offered an Irish peerage to Sir Richard Philipps, a Welsh baronet, to compensate him for not being allowed to make a carriageway through St James' Park to his front door. He accepted, and was made Lord Milford.[9]

During the 1780s and the 1790s the selection of new Irish entrants for the peerage continued to be influenced by political expediency. The Earl of Charlemont, viewing 'the unthinking and impolitic profusion' of honours, considered that it had one unintended and beneficial effect. It ensured that some illustrious commoners chose to remain in the House of Commons because they were 'perfectly ashamed of going in a vulgar crowd to the upper one'.[10]

THE KNIGHTS OF ST PATRICK

In the latter decades of the eighteenth century, individual Irish peers grew more clamant in their demands for further promotion as the price for loyalty to government policies. There was a huge awareness of rank and seniority. As the numbers of viscounts and earls increased disproportionately, lords lieutenant found it difficult to justify adding to the numbers of an already top-heavy senior peerage. George III became increasingly reluctant to agree to promotions within the Irish peerage. He was enraged in March 1776 to find that Harcourt, without consulting him, had told Lord Drogheda that there would be no difficulty in making him a marquis. The king wrote to one of his circle: 'I desire to hear no more of Irish marquises ... I feel for English earls and do not choose to disgust them.'

When the 2nd Earl Temple (later Marquis of Buckingham) was appointed for his first period of office in 1782, he secured acceptance from the king to create a strictly limited order of chivalry for senior peers acknowledged as the cream of the Irish aristocracy. It was to be known as the Most Illustrious Order of the Knights of St Patrick. The new distinction was intended as a sop to those seeking additional honours whose advancement within the peerage was at a standstill, there being no more room at the top. In England, the Order of the Garter, the highest order of English knighthood dating from the fourteenth century, served a somewhat similar purpose. Temple saw the new order as not only as a way of keeping his senior peers happy and securing their loyalty but as enhancing the Irish court. The original statutes approved by George III in February 1783 established a company of sixteen 'noble and worthy knights', including the reigning monarch. All of them had to be of unchallengeable purity of stock, none would be chosen except he be 'a Gentleman of the Blood' and 'a Knight without Reproach'. He was also required to be 'descended of three descents of Noblesse' on both his father's and his mother's side.[11]

Those chosen were selected by Temple in consultation with Grenville and the king. They consisted of the monarch himself, Prince Edward, the Duke of Leinster, the Earls of Clanrickard, Antrim, Westmeath, Inchiquin, Drogheda, Hillsborough, Shannon, Mornington, Courtown, Charlemont, Ely and Altamont, and the lord lieutenant. Flattering letters of invitation were sent by Temple with assurances that the award was intended as proof of the special esteem in which the king held the recipient. The Duke of Leinster believed it was not an adequate award for his services and made it clear he would have preferred to have been made a Knight of the Garter, but Temple talked him into good humour and he accepted. The Earl of Antrim accepted the honour but on reflection decided that it was beneath him and resigned. He was replaced by the Earl of Arran. In general, though, there was considerable competition for the places and Temple was pleased with the impact that it had made.[12]

The new Order added to the colour, ceremonials and diversity of the social programme of Dublin Castle. Even before its inauguration there was an excited anticipation of the event among the Castle circle. 'Half Dublin is mad about the Order,' wrote Temple to his brother, Grenville. During the six weeks prior to the inauguration, a large number of weavers in the Liberties were required to work day and night to produce the two to three thousand yards of satin required for the ceremonial garb. The vestments, decorations and insignia devised for the Order were hugely elaborate and would have satisfied individuals of the utmost vanity at a period when symbols of rank and status were of great importance. The mantle consisted of sky-blue silk or satin lined with white silk and, on the right shoulder, a hood of the same material was fastened with blue and gold tassels. Silk under-habits were laced with gold. A round hat of black velvet with the Star of the Order was affixed to it, surmounted by ostrich feathers of red, white and blue. The spurs and sword hilt were gilded and the belt and scabbard were of crimson velvet. The boots of white leather had turn-ups of sky blue. The decorations and insignia included a collar of gold with images of harps and roses linked with golden knots. Central to the collar was the image of an imperial jewelled crown surmounting a harp of gold from which hung the gold Badge of the Order bearing specially devised heraldic symbols and the motto of the Order, *Quis Separabit*, which, explained Temple, 'will tend to enforce that ... solid union between the two kingdoms, so necessary to both'. Elaborately jewelled insignia were designed for the Grand Master, to be handed over to succeeding lords lieutenant and designated 'crown jewels'.[13]

The establishment of the Order in March 1783 consisted of elaborate rituals and ceremonials, including an investiture in Dublin Castle followed a week later by an installation ceremony in St Patrick's Cathedral, and the clarification of the order of precedence of participating peers increasingly sensitive about their proper place in court. The Archbishop of Dublin was displeased about his positioning. Temple wrote to Granville, 'the Archbishop [Fowler] is outrageous about the Primate's [Robinson's] prelacy', but an engraving of the inaugural banquet shows, as might be expected, that Robinson was given the higher precedence.[14] The investiture took place in the great ballroom (later named St Patrick's Hall) of the Castle out of sight of public onlookers. The installation in the cathedral followed some days later, on St Patrick's Day.

The lavishness of the installation rituals exceeded in splendour any previous ceremonials of the Irish court. Thousands of regular troops, supported by contingents of the Irish Volunteers, lined the route from the Castle to the cathedral, as the ornately garbed knights and court officials walked in procession. A multitude of ragged onlookers from the grim, overcrowded tenements of the neighbouring Liberties, silenced by the splendour, watched the cavalcade 'not once disturbed by the least unhappy incident'. When Temple, girded in a sword, wearing his cap and plumes, entered the cathedral, the choir and musicians broke into Handel's 'Coronation Anthem' and the long ritual of donning mantles, girding swords, bowing and saluting began. Then, to the triumphant music of a 'Te Deum', the newly proclaimed, sword-begirdled knights set out on their return journey to the Castle where a sumptuous banquet was provided, as cartloads of bread, cheese and beer were distributed to the troops in the streets.

Celebrations continued the following night. The knights were hosts at a supper at the Rotunda Hospital where, according to the *Hibernian Magazine*, 'the grandeur and magnificence exceeded anything of the kind ever given in the kingdom'. The Rotunda was, at that time, regarded as a more elegant setting than the Castle. Some of the pregnant women in the hospital were moved out for the event. As the ragged onlookers watched the bejewelled, richly clothed guests, there was other entertainment to distract their attention — a country vagrant named Molloy being whipped through the streets for pickpocketing. He was to undergo two further days of public whipping, and imprisonment for six months.[15]

IMPACT OF THE UNION ON THE PEERAGE

The Union of 1800 abolished both houses of the Irish parliament. Logically, the union of the kingdoms of Ireland and Great Britain should have brought to an end the creation and the promotion of Irish peers. It did not make sense to go on adding to the peerage of a kingdom that no longer had a separate existence. But it was politically desirable that the Irish Ascendancy should not feel entirely abandoned and that they should retain one of their most valued perquisites, a peerage of their own. Of the 150 resident members of the Irish peerage, about 70 per cent were eighteenth-century creations. It was decided to restrict future creations to one for every three extinctions until the number had declined to 100; thereafter each extinction would be made up by one creation. The Irish peers elected twenty-eight of their colleagues to represent them in the British House of Lords along with four bishops. Vacancies among the representative peers were filled on the vote of the full body of peers. There was intense competition for the twenty-eight places. The Earl of Inchiquin complained to the king about his 'severe mortification' on failing to be selected and sought an English peerage to compensate for his loss of privileges which, in his view, had virtually reduced him to the status of a commoner.[16]

The restricted opportunities for entry to the Irish peerage and for promotion within it quickly became evident. Between 1801 and 1888 there were only twenty promotions. It was always open to the government to appoint Irishmen to the English peerage, as had been done to secure the support for the Union from influential Irish politicians such as Carysfort, Drogheda, Ely and Ormond. But competition was keen and there was a lingering resentment among English contenders about the former ease with which Irish aspirants for ennoblement had moved into and through the ranks of the nobility. Given the limited opportunities for the Irish peerage, the possibility of entry to the Knights of St Patrick became particularly prized. When, in 1810, Richmond, the lord lieutenant, reported to London that Lord Drogheda 'looked as if he would die', a number of senior Irish peers were already in hot pursuit of Drogheda's expected vacancy as a Knight. They included the Marquis of Donegal, the Earl of Rosse, Viscount Mountjoy, the Earl of Courtown and the Earl of Mayo. Faced with the dearth of honours to distribute, the government decided to extend the membership of the Knights of St Patrick beyond the original membership of fifteen. Following the coronation of George IV in 1821 six 'extraordinary' knights were added to the Order on the basis that they would be subsequently absorbed as vacancies arose among the ordinary knights. When William IV was crowned in September 1831, a further four were added to mark the occasion. Eventually, in order to regularize the position, the government decided to extend the membership of ordinary knights to twenty-two and to absorb the then surviving five extraordinary knights in that number.[17]

The election of new Irish peers to the House of Lords ended with the implementation of the Anglo-Irish Treaty at the beginning of 1922. Those elected before then could continue to sit in the House until their death.[18]

The Paddies Appear

Attendance at a post-Union Irish court could be traumatic for the remaining members of the old regime accustomed to the former glories of Dublin Castle. The elderly Lady Clonbrony reported indignantly to her family on her participation in a drawing-room at the Castle where she had accidentally trod on the train of another guest. She was, said Lady Clonbrony, a 'grocer's wife', who had turned angrily on her and said in a strong brogue, 'I'll thank you ma'am for the rest of my tail.' Lady Clonbrony was, in fact, a fictional character in Maria Edgeworth's novel *The Absentee* (1812), but Edgeworth's depiction of Ascendancy society at the beginning of the new century is regarded as accurate.[1]

The changed character of those who now formed Castle society was due not only to the exodus of the Irish aristocracy with their attainments and manners, but to the emergence of the power and the wealth of a commercial and professional middle class as the industrial revolution made its mark. The status of aristocracy and landed wealth, if not under actual attack, was inexorably diminished as bourgeois society grew in political and economic power.

An immediate influence on the quality of post-Union Castle society was the drastically reduced numbers of gentry and aristocracy. On the eve of the Union, 150 or so of the 230 temporal Irish peers lived in Ireland, and many would have habitually attended the social and ceremonial events of the Castle, as would have the 300 gentry who made up the House of Commons. Their womenfolk, wives and daughters provided much of its colour and exuberance. By 1821 there were only thirty-four resident peers and thirteen resident baronets in Ireland, and only five of the former members of the old House of Commons continued to have town houses in Dublin.[2]

Socially, the new order was quickly ousting the old regime. Prospering merchants and bankers, and members of the professions such as engineers, lawyers and doctors whose status had been growing, became the new elite. And if their style of life lacked in elegance and decorum, they were, for all that, acceptable to the Castle administration and loyal to the monarch. One of Maria Edgeworth's characters explained the changing milieu:

> Irish commoners had either retired to London or retired disgusted and in despair to their country houses. Immediately in Dublin commerce rose into the vacated seats of rank: wealth rose into the place of birth. New faces and new equipages appeared; people who had never been heard of before started into notice, pushed themselves forward, not scrupling to elbow themselves even at the Castle; and they were presented to my lord-lieutenant and my lady-lieutenant; for their excellencies, for the time being, might have played their vice-regal parts to empty benches but had they not admitted such persons for the moment to fill their court ...[3]

To the old regime new arrivals were often perceived as Paddies, people of no refinement with peasant origins, historically kept outside the Castle walls, who had pushed themselves into higher society. However, during the immediate post-Union decades the great majority of the arrivistes would have been of lower or middle-class Protestant origins, successful in commerce, in the professions, or in acquiring land. Those with Catholic roots would be slower to emerge, even after Catholic emancipation, and they would always be only a small element of Castle attendances. Even though they were a minority, the aristocracy and gentry who remained from pre-Union days now formed the core of the new court. They provided continuity, smoothed the way for new habitués, and set certain standards of behaviour and respect for the traditional rituals of a viceregal court. From another perspective, opportunity to rub shoulders with an established aristocracy enhanced the prestige and self-importance of the increasing number of merchants and professionals who eagerly sought to be honoured as guests of the Castle.

Politically, the constitutional union of Ireland and the United Kingdom had not been absolute. While the former Irish parliament was integrated with Westminister, the machinery of Dublin Castle remained much the same. The lord lieutenant and his entourage continued with the trappings of a royal court; there was still a colourful military presence on state occasions. The outer manifestations of power and privilege remained to impress the populace. The post of Chief Secretary was now a more powerful one since it was filled by the prime minister; but the balance of power and influence between the lord lieutenant and chief secretary varied according to the strength of personalities and their political influence. Patronage continued to flow from the Castle, and while the creation and promotion of peerages no longer absorbed much of the business of the Castle, there was still a great number of favours to be distributed.[4]

EARLY NINETEENTH-CENTURY VICEROYS

The viceroys who served in Dublin Castle between 1800 and 1830 were of a different calibre to their pre-Union predecessors. All brought with them previous experience in the public service rather than reputations as socialites or courtiers. The office was not a popular assignment because of the political passions and uncertainty about the nature of office under a newly constituted administration and the relative roles of Westminister and the Castle. While the viceroys were all aristocrats, most were not wealthy by eighteenth-century standards, though the pattern of social life continued to be opulent and spirited. It was important for the government to demonstrate to the remaining Ascendancy interests that they were not being abandoned and to show the majority population that they were being treated sympathetically despite the failure to introduce Catholic emancipation. It was difficult to balance the conflicting demands. Most viceroys who served between 1801 and the granting of Catholic emancipation in 1829 had some degree of sympathy towards Catholic grievances, but they were inhibited by the fact that they were serving a Protestant government, administering anti-Catholic laws, and dealing with a minority Protestant population who held most of the offices of power. In the circumstances, viceroys could only reduce tensions and conciliate by being as accessible and hospitable as possible to all parties.

All early-nineteenth-century viceroys complained about the demands on their hospitality and the expense of office. When in 1810 the Duke of Richmond found that his expenses were nearly twice his official allowance and his debts were of the order of £50,000, the chancellor of the exchequer received the reluctant approval of the House of Commons for a £10,000 increase to the allowance fixed since 1783 at £20,000.[5]

HARDWICKE

The appointment of Philip, 3rd Earl of Hardwicke, in 1801 was seen by the government as an appropriate choice at a time of strong emotions following the '98 rebellion and the implementation of the Union. He was easygoing and tolerant, anxious to please and, according to the *Freeman's Journal*, keen to increase 'the happiness of rank and affluence and to better the condition of the manufacturers and the poor'. A contemporary commentator numbered among Hardwicke's distinctions the excellent library he maintained at his London home and his understanding of the fattening of sheep – hardly assets of much value in tackling the many problems facing the new administration. He had little by way of patronage to distribute because of the extent of the commitments already made to secure acceptance of the Union. But, undeterred, the duke and his consort launched a programme of social events along the familiar lines of their predecessors. The usual anniversaries were commemorated, particularly that of William of Orange, despite the resentment of the Catholic population. In November 1801 a large contingent of yeomanry drew up around William's statue in College Green, richly embellished in blue and orange silk, fired a salvo and concluded with 'a general huzza'. It was followed by a levee given by Hardwicke 'numerously attended by personages of rank and distinction', rounded off by a procession of carriages through the streets bearing the lord lieutenant and his suite, the lord mayor and the city regalia, and many members of the nobility and gentry. It was a striking manifestation of Orange triumphalism.[6]

Once again the Castle became the centre of social life for the powerful and privileged. During the disturbed years of the late 1790s the viceroy's apartments had deteriorated, but by the beginning of 1803 the reception areas were refurbished, the long suite of rooms improved and linked with wide connecting arches. They were all newly furnished, and the wall panels were covered with crimson silk to match the furniture. The ball for the queen's birthday in February 1803 was a fitting occasion on which to show off the new embellishments and, in keeping with the policy of broadening the spectrum of society at Castle events and relaxing court protocol, had a larger than usual number of guests. According to *Faulkner's Journal*, 'the vast concourse' had seldom been equalled. There was food and wine 'from every climate'; the magnificent dress worn by the duchess consisted of purple velvet and silver fringes; white ostrich feathers on her head were accompanied by 'a profusion' of diamonds.[7]

But if the guest list for Castle events was less exclusive than before, few Catholics found their way on to it. While Hardwicke showed sympathy towards Catholic grievances, he preferred to keep their dignitaries at arm's length, suspecting some had prior knowledge of Robert Emmet's short-lived rebellion. Lady Hardwicke, writing to a friend in September 1803, described her husband's attitude towards Dr Troy, Catholic Archbishop of Dublin, who had supported the Union: '[Dr Troy] has no footing whatever in the Castle yard. Lord Hardwicke's is the only administration that has never given the heads of the Catholic clergy an invitation to the Castle, he

in no way recognises them further than the law admits them to be priests.'
Despite Hardwicke's assertions, Troy succeeded in developing some con-
tacts with a senior Castle official and secured a preferment for a nephew.
And in a pastoral letter of July 1803, the archbishop praised Hardwicke for
his 'conciliation ... mild administration ... munificent attention of His
Excellency and his amiable consort.'[8]

The Hardwickes maintained the high tempo of social activity until they
were replaced by John Russell, 6th Duke of Bedford, in early 1806. Bedford's period of office was brief, ending with a change of government in
April 1807. He was sympathetic to Catholic grievances and the duchess was
anxious to be popular and to make an impact. The *Dublin Journal* reported
that her first drawing-room was 'more numerously and splendidly attended
than we have witnessed these many years'. The Bedfords revived the practice of celebrating St Patrick's Day at the Castle, a popular initiative with
the Catholics. There was a splendid ball and supper, and in her hair the
duchess wore a specially designed jewel modelled on one worn by an
ancient Irish princess.[9]

THE RICHMONDS

Charles Lennox, 4th Duke of Richmond and Lennox, succeeded Bedford in
April 1807. The two men were married to sisters. The trappings of the
viceregal post appealed to the vanity of the Richmonds, who took easily to
the lifestyle of Dublin Castle while remaining impervious to the poverty of
the surrounding population. The Richmonds inaugurated their reign with a
brilliant ball which established a style they would maintain during their
years in Ireland. They had hoped to be accompanied to Dublin by one of the
most celebrated chefs of the period, to whom they'd promised an extravagant salary; but he decided to remain in England on learning that there was
no Italian opera in Dublin. The duke, in particular, was popular, a hard
drinker, known for his bonhomie, a talented cricketer and adjudged to be
'the finest formed man in England'. John Gamble, visiting Dublin during
Richmond's regime, noted that 'he is what is called a five-bottle man and

after supper drinks grog and smokes tobacco like a West Indies planter'. He was sensitive to the injustices of the penal laws and was pleased when some prominent Catholics were prepared to attend functions at the Castle. The Richmonds caroused regularly and enthusiastically, in private and publicly, surrounding themselves with friends and acquaintances who also lived life to the full. Richmond wrote admiringly of one of Dublin's lords mayor that he had 'a very pretty method of getting drunk. He is so well used to it that he knows his way back in the dark and is always sober when he gets up in the morning'. Satirical journals and cartoonists of the period found plenty of scope for lampooning the lifestyle and foibles of the viceregal circle. Lady Bessborough wrote to Earl Granville in October 1808, 'The Duke of Richmond makes desperate love to [Lady Edward Somerset]; she rides about with him every where and he speaks to no one else. The duchess is, as she always is, very jealous ... and very cross.' When a note from Lady Somerset intended for the philandering duke was opened in error by the duchess, she read: 'What fine fun we shall have! The old Puss will burst with jealousy.' It was an exciting contribution to the gossip of the viceregal circle.[10]

The Richmonds, despite their limited wealth, had a penchant for extravagance and an inclination for flaunting the might and greatness of the empire. The laying of the first stone of the great pillar in Sackville Street (later O'Connell Street) to commemorate Admiral Nelson was used as an occasion for remarkable pageantry. A procession of colourfully caparisoned horses and carriages bore the Richmonds and their suite through the main city streets, accompanied by many gentry, nobility and city officials, and contingents of military and their bands. A large barge on wheels drawn by sailors in white shirts carried a bust of Nelson surrounded by boys from the Marine School. Every window along the route from the Castle to Sackville Street was crowded with 'female beauty and fashion'. At a time of international conflict, with British troops fighting on far-flung battlefields, the viceregal programme included military events with parading soldiery and bands playing exultant tunes like 'Rule Britannia', 'The Conquering Hero Comes' and 'Britons Strike Home'. When the viceroy held a review of the yeomanry at the Phoenix Park, he entertained a great number of guests to breakfast at the Viceregal Lodge where the main table had a gold tea and coffee service 'of exquisite workmanship'. Occasions such as the queen's birthday provided opportunities for celebration in the grand manner, and it was clear, at least during the regency period, that the Crown expected to be honoured in style by its representative in Ireland. Wellesley-Pole, the chief secretary, writing to Richmond from London in July 1812 about arrangements to mark the prince regent's birthday, told him: 'I collected that the more splendidly you did honour to the day the more the proceedings would be approved by the regent.' Some months later Richmond told Earl Bathurst that he was remaining in Dublin only to please the regent; but as long as he was there he would do things 'handsomely but not extravagantly'.[11]

Richmond was anxious to ensure that any patronage available for distribution be entirely within his control. He soon found himself deluged with representations on behalf of clergymen seeking bishoprics or translation to more valuable benefices. In November 1811 he complained to Ryder, the home secretary, 'that almost every clergyman in Ireland is perhaps a little too eager about his own advantage'. He found the character of one candidate for the bench of bishops to be such 'that no person on earth would tempt me to acquiesce his appointment' even though the prince regent was supporting him. The extent of Richmond's intrusion into clerical affairs and his choices for preferment were resented by some churchmen. The Bishop of Limerick complained to the primate, William Stuart, in April 1810, that the lord lieutenant's 'system of clerical barter and extensive line of exchanges sets every jober [sic] at work and draws down a ridicule on the Church by exhibiting a set of clerical jockeys in the Castle yard whenever a government preferment becomes vacant'.[12]

Robert Peel, who served as chief secretary under three lords lieutenant from 1812 to 1818, resisted patronage and did his best to introduce considerations of merit in the making of appointments. But Richmond had been in office for five years before Peel arrived and he found that, by then, Richmond had taken control of the available patronage and 'left me scarcely a voice in the disposal of it'. Peel became one of the most powerful and influential figures in early-nineteenth-century Anglo-Irish relations and overshadowed the lords lieutenant with whom he served. He subsequently served as prime minister for two periods.[13]

By the time Earl Whitworth succeeded him in June 1813, Richmond had acquired notoriety for his hard living. A member of parliament welcoming Whitworth's appointment hoped that the new lord lieutenant 'would show an example of sobriety to the country and that they would not hear of midnight orgies, of songs and toasts tending to influence one part of His Majesty's subjects against each other'. Richmond was remembered more for his conviviality than for his political impact. After leaving Ireland he was appointed ambassador in Brussels. There, in June 1815, the duchess gave the famous ball on the eve of the battle of Waterloo immortalized in Byron's poem, when so many young officers went from the ball to die on the battlefield. Richmond himself died in 1819 from hydrophobia following a bite from a pet fox.[14]

WHITWORTH

Charles, Lord (later Earl) Whitworth, brought to Dublin a number of social distinctions likely to excite the Castle circle. He was a handsome man of considerable polish and had been a minister in Russia during the 1790s, when he was rumoured to be one of the many lovers of Catherine the Great. He subsequently married Arabella, wealthy widow of the Duke of Dorset. Later, when ambassador to France, he had been insulted during a much publicized confrontation with the First Consul, Napoleon, who had addressed him 'only as a monsieur' and had growlingly 'moved his chops like a mastiff' in his direction. Helped by his diplomatic experience at the great courts of Europe, Whitworth fitted easily into the life of the viceregal court. He entertained with style, supported and encouraged by the duchess, who had a reputation for imperiousness, seeking to exclude from Castle functions those not conforming to pre-Union notions of pedigree. Her screening of established lists gave rise to ill-feeling and uncertainty among the professional classes. *The Complete Peerage* commented: 'If her mind was not highly cultivated or refined she could boast of intellectual endowments that fitted her for the active business of life. Under the domination of no passion except the love of money her taste for power and pleasure was also subordinate to her economy.'[15]

Because he was strongly opposed to Catholic claims, Whitworth and his duchess were popular with the Protestant Ascendancy. There was general public sympathy when the son of the duchess, the young duke of Dorset, was killed when hunting in Kilkenny. As far as his political responsibilities were concerned, it suited Whitworth that his chief secretary Peel had similar views and could be safely left to look after the administration of the country. Dublin Corporation, dominated by the Orange faction, had the happiest of social relationships with the Castle. When Whitworth gave a dinner in honour of the lord mayor in April 1815, it was a triumphal occasion. Twenty-six toasts were drunk, including 'The Glorious Memory' accompanied by the words of 'Boyne Water', and 'The Protestant Ascendancy' to the music of 'The Protestant Boys'.[16]

GEORGE IV IN IRELAND

Lord Talbot, who arrived in Ireland in 1817, had an Irish wife, formerly Frances Lambert, whose father was a County Meath gentleman, and they had ten daughters and two sons. He looked like a 'jolly good-humoured farmer' and was nearly nineteen stone in weight. He opposed Catholic emancipation but was perceived by his opponents as honourable and high-minded.[17]

It fell to Talbot to be the host of George IV during his visit to Ireland in 1821. For differing reasons the visit of the king excited the public's imagination. He was the first British monarch to cross the Irish Sea in other than a military role. His visit was a boost to the somewhat flagging social programme of the Dublin Court. It introduced to it a whiff of the contemporary scandals of the London Court, with Queen Caroline rejected by her husband; the king's illegal wife, Mrs Fitzherbert, living in seclusion; and several peripheral mistresses competing for the favours of the self-indulgent monarch. A population exhausted by recurring bouts of famine and typhus looked forward to the spectacle of lavish regal cavalcades, and with it the expectation of the gift of emancipation. William Gregory, under-secretary at the Castle, described the king's advent:

He arrived after a good passage during which much goose pie and whisky had been consumed. Word had just come of the death of Napoleon at St Helena. The story goes – 'Sire, your enemy is dead' were the words he was greeted with. 'When did she die?' was his response. But the Queen was indeed also dead and His Majesty was persuaded to wear a piece of crepe round his arm during the festivities which were in no way curtailed.

Other than the crepe, there were few manifestations of mourning in Ireland. As the king immersed himself in Irish festivities, in London the funeral of the dead queen set out on its journey through rioting crowds to her native Brunswick.[18]

In Dublin the atmosphere was somewhat different. The magnificent processions, ceremonial rituals and social programme at the viceregal court mirrored the golden age of the pre-Union regime. Tens of thousands participated in the colourful cavalcades during the visit. On the occasion of the king's entry, a large contingent of the city's weavers, wearing colourful products of their trade, marched to the music of a band. When the monarch travelled from the Viceregal Lodge to the Castle the route was lined with the gentlemen of the City and County of Dublin dressed in blue coats, buff waistcoats and white trousers, and festooned with a variety of blue, pink and white sashes and scarves. The king himself was resplendent in military uniform, decorated in the regalia of the Order of St Patrick, his hat bearing a huge rosette of shamrocks like a military cockade.[19]

Over succeeding days there was a full programme of celebrations. Nine new Knights of St Patrick were installed with splendour in St Patrick's Cathedral where the king placed the ceremonial collar on each. There were banquets at the Castle and the Mansion House where, the *Freeman's Journal* noted, the king took the soup ladle in 'the most condescending manner' and helped to serve some of the guests in his proximity. The levee held for the king was unprecedented, with between 2000 and 3000 persons participating. Catholics were not often invited to Castle functions prior to George's visit. On this occasion the king, noticeably drunk, met the Catholic bishops in their full episcopal garb in his closet and accepted an address of loyalty from them. They included the Primate of All Ireland, Dr Curtis; Dr Troy, the Archbishop of Dublin; and nine bishops. While the mode of their reception fell short of being received in the throne room, the meeting in the closet was seen as conveying an important mark of distinction to the occasion. Later, during the levee, the king received a presentation from the Catholic laity and Daniel O'Connell was introduced to him. The drawing-room was crammed, colourful and, for the lady guests in particular, hugely exciting. George's stay in Ireland was cheered by the presence of the corpulent Marchioness of Conyngham, his favourite mistress, who had been specially conveyed by royal yacht to Dublin. All in all, the king's visit to Dublin was a social success, an occasion which pleased many and held out expectations of greater justice to others.[20]

WELLESLEY

Talbot, the incumbent lord lieutenant, was now recalled (the immediate cause an Orange toast drunk to 'the pious, glorious and immortal memory' at the lord mayor's dinner); he'd been a weak lord lieutenant and incompatible with his chief secretary, Charles Grant. His dismissal was so sudden that there was no time to arrange the honours usually paid to a departing viceroy. The king's sympathetic gestures towards Catholics and the campaigning fervour of Daniel O'Connell made Catholic emancipation seem inevitable. Richard Colley, Marquess Wellesley, became lord lieutenant in 1821 and was to hold the office until 1828. Brother of the Duke of Wellington and an advocate of the Catholic cause, he arrived in Dublin with an entourage bedecked with shamrocks and a ceremonial carriage drawn by horses similarly festooned. He was greeted enthusiastically. Catholic hopes were strengthened when the new viceroy replaced the serving attorney general, William Saurin, long at the centre of opposition to Catholic claims, with William Conyngham Plunket. O'Connell, believing it marked the beginning of a new era for the Catholic population, moved a public address of welcome to Wellesley before a large assembly of Catholics and attended the first levee held by the new viceroy.[21]

But it was difficult for Wellesley to hold the balance between opposing Catholic and Protestant interests. When the Orange party announced its intention to decorate the statue of King William in College Green to commemorate his birthday, Wellesley forbade it and had the monument surrounded by a military cordon. Some weeks later, in December 1822, he was pelted by an Orange mob with bottles and other missiles as he watched a play at the Theatre Royal. Shortly afterwards O'Connell once again appeared at a Castle levee, wearing the required court dress, with an accompanying group of Catholics and liberal Protestants wishing to show their sympathy with Wellesley.[22]

REMOVAL OF COURT CHAMBERLAIN

Wellesley's term at the viceregal court was marked by the dismissal of Sir Charles Vernon, the long-serving court chamberlain. Vernon had served continuously as chamberlain from the early 1790s until, with two other long-serving courtiers, he was dismissed in 1823. His period of service had linked the pre- and post-Union courts and ensured the continuity of their social and ceremonial programmes. He was an unchallengeable authority on matters of protocol and propriety, and mentor of a succession of viceroys: the professional courtier par excellence.

Vernon was unmarried, with a private apartment at the Castle and a cottage in the Phoenix Park. He was an inoffensive, apolitical popinjay with a talent for mimicry, committed to maintaining the dignity and traditions of the court, an upholder of the importance and artistry of the minuet, and hugely popular with women of the viceregal circle. As well as being in charge of the social life of Dublin Castle, he was close to leading personalities of the period. He gave the Richmonds a lavish farewell party on their departure, and wrote to his sister:

> I gave my grand dinner to their Graces last Monday and without puffing it was as handsome as possible ... fifty-eight to dinner and one hundred and fifteen in the evening ... I had ... all the best I could

from Dublin to meet them ... It was a heavenly night so that dancing on the lawn was pleasant ... we had some fireworks and a band to play between dances.[23]

Vernon was such a pillar of the Irish court that his unexplained dismissal by Wellesley came as a shock. Contemporary periodicals found no difficulty in linking it to a toast given at a dinner organized by the Beefsteak Club, a meeting place for Tories unsympathetic to the Catholic cause. Vernon, a club member, was present when a toast proposed to 'the exports of Ireland' was acclaimed with 'unanimous and protracted applause'. It was greeted with such unprecedented enthusiasm on this occasion as to it were appended the words: 'The Exports of Ireland and may those who would subvert the constitution be first.' It was an obvious insult directed at Wellesley, an exhortation that he should pack his bags and leave. Vernon and two other senior courtiers present on the occasion were dismissed immediately.[24]

The inner world of Castle society was disturbed by the loss of Vernon and there was talk of a petition to the sovereign. The London *Courier* denounced Wellesley for acting with 'Asiatic despotism' towards an innocuous personality. But in general, Dublin periodicals of the period did not take the issue too seriously and poked fun at those who rushed to Vernon's defence. The view of a correspondent in the *Dublin Evening Post* was typical:

> They may apprehend that a less experienced person might not introduce partners so agreeable, so that their trains or their fans might be endangered, if Sir Charles be discontinued. These are weighty matters for a petition to the Sovereign ... one wonders why it has not been thought of to address both houses of parliament. Lackaday! We tremble for His Excellency's government.[25]

When Vernon wrote privately in February 1823 about his removal to his friend Robert Peel, then Home Secretary, he received sympathy but no enlightenment:

You will, I am sure, feel the peculiarity and delicacy of my position as a public man, and will admit the propriety of my abstaining from any act which could be construed as an indirect censure upon those with whom I am acting in office, and whose authority, while I act with them, I am bound not to weaken. Such considerations, however, shall never interfere with the performance of the duties of private friendship. My regard for you, founded on a long acquaintance, on constant intercourse, of the knowledge of the kindness of your heart, and generous and amiable disposition, remains unchanged.[26]

WELLESLEY'S LAVISH STYLE

Vernon's departure did nothing to diminish the busy social programme that the Wellesleys set for themselves. The viceroy's espousal of Catholic claims which generated such resentment among the ensconced Protestant interests encouraged him to display the extent of his popularity. *Saunder's News Letter* reported that the lord lieutenant had ordered a number of Castle events which would 'exhibit a species of magnificence unknown in the annals of the Irish court'. There was a hugely attended levee at the end of February 1823, when a line of carriages extended from the Rotunda to the Castle as they waited to set down the guests. During March, a number of lavish drawing-rooms, dinners and a ball celebrated St Patrick's Day, with dancing led by the Duchess of Leinster and Lord Meath.[27]

Wellesley had lived in splendour in India in the opulent governor-general's residence in Calcutta, which he had had designed by an Italian architect and built by the East India Company at a cost of £180,000. He found the viceregal apartments at the Castle lacking and set about improving them. When the Treasury asked the Commissioners of the Board of Works to reduce expenditure on the improvements, the Board pointed out that 'many expensive works have been done and expensive articles of furniture provided upon superior orders without any communication whatever being made with respect to the same further than an order to defray the expense thereof ...' It cited examples of personal directions to its architect by

Wellesley about the purchase of tabarets and curtains without referral to the Board. Beds and bedding had been acquired for servants 'superior to what is generally allowed by private families to persons of that description'. And costly plants and seeds had been brought from England.[28]

Wellesley had married Hyacinthe Gabrielle Roland, his mistress of nine years' standing, in 1793 when he was growing in public importance and she was anxious to secure her own status. She died in 1816. In 1825 Wellesley married Mary Anne Patterson, a wealthy Catholic widow from Boston with connections through her late husband's family to Napoleon Bonaparte. The marriage ceremony was performed initially by the Protestant primate followed by a Catholic rite imparted by the Catholic Archbishop of Dublin, and attended by a large retinue of courtiers and servants in their colourful court uniforms. The new marchioness was said to be 'distinguished by her beauty, elevation of mind, and dignity of manners'. The marriage added to the viceroy's social presence and underlined his Catholic sympathies, but also provoked some ridicule. The *Dublin Evening Mail* commented, 'At sixty-six, love will make an old man that has more toes than teeth attempt even a more foolish thing than dancing.'[29]

Wellesley held his post until the death of Canning, the prime minister, who had supported his Irish policy. He resigned when his own brother, the Duke of Wellington, followed as prime minister pledged to supporting the Irish Protestant Ascendancy. In September 1833, with Catholic emancipation conceded, he returned to Ireland for a second assignment of little over a year. They were changed times. Daniel Owen Madden, a contemporary historian, summed up his re-appointment: 'His arrival did not produce the slightest excitement ... He appeared on his functions with some degree of languid indifference.' However, the diarist Greville later wrote that while Wellesley appeared to be in the last stages of decrepitude on leaving in 1828, he surprised everyone by his energy during his second period of office.[30]

CHANGING STANDARDS

By Wellesley's time, the quality of the attendance at Castle functions was only a pale reflection of former times. A list of those attending a levee in February 1823 consisted largely of military personnel, Protestant clergy, academics, business and professional persons, with only a small number of the aristocracy. A drawing-room in early March showed a mere thirty titled persons out of an attendance of 500. A subsequent drawing-room listed only ten members of aristocracy among the large number of guests.[31] Vernon's dismissal may have provided an opportunity for the removal of elderly officials who had become incongruous vestiges of a former age. While the new habitués relished the pomp and privilege of the viceregal circle and eagerly sought admission to it, the excessive protocol of the old regime would have made many feel uncomfortable. Guests like the diminutive Lady Morgan, writer of fervid patriotic stories and verses, who scorned the traditional feathers and trains and glided about animatedly in a close-cropped wig, found easier acceptance.[32]

While women of the court circle continued to dress fashionably, standards of clothing for male guests at the Castle were in decline by the 1820s. At a levee in honour of the visit of George IV in August 1821, large sums were offered for the loan of a dress sword. Some of the male guests displayed 'incongruous' swords and there were many 'ludicrous figures' among the attendance.[33] Soon male guests of viceregal functions could rent court dress and other paraphernalia on a commercial basis, a far cry from the individually tailored clothes, specially forged swords and carefully chosen silver buckles and jewellery of the past.

Like other elements of former grandeur, the minuet and gavotte, those artistic expressions of court life, faded into the past during the early years of the century. By 1816, at the ball to celebrate the queen's birthday, the only male dancer available to dance the opening minuets was Vernon. He danced in turn with each of the two Beresford sisters. The spirited quadrille, originating in the old square dancing of France, took over as the ceremonial dance at court. A variation of it, the lancers, became popular as the century progressed. But by far the most popular dancing innovation of the early part of the century was the waltz. Seen as daring, even shocking, the sight of partners clutched in each other's arms as they swirled to the romantic music of brilliant composers of the period was initially regarded as unacceptable. According to one criticism, 'it disordered the stomach and made people look ridiculous'. But by the 1820s the waltz was well established in all circles, surpassing in popularity the country dancing that had long dominated the balls of higher society. Mr Du Val of Mary Street was publishing newspaper advertisements for ladies and gentlemen who wished to acquire 'the present style of dancing', and Mr Dulang of Henry Street offered to teach quadrilles and waltzes with 'ease and elegance'.[34]

ANGLESEY

Wellesley was replaced in 1828 by Henry William Paget, 1st Marquis of Anglesey, one of the most colourful of the nineteenth-century lords lieutenant. He was of striking appearance, tall, hawk-nosed, with one leg, a colourful romantic reputation and a gallant military career behind him. He had an odd variety of relationships with the Duke of Wellington. He'd eloped with the duke's sister-in-law, served with him at the battle of Waterloo where he lost his leg, received from him his initial appointment as lord lieutenant, and was subsequently sacked by him. He had three sons and five daughters by his divorced first wife and three sons and three daughters by his seduced second wife, who already had four children by her first husband. In the course of his marital entanglements he had to fight a duel with one of his brothers-in-law and contest a court case which awarded considerable damages to the aggrieved husband.[35]

Anglesey arrived in Ireland favourably disposed to the Catholic cause but anxious to conciliate rather than to be identified with either party. Expectant Catholics were confident that he was on their side and turned out to welcome him. So, too, did the fashionable set excited by the arrival of such a prestigious social luminary. A contemporary report describes the scene: '... the waving of handkerchiefs, the huzzas drowning the martial music, the dense mass in the streets ...' Another said that every window from the entrance of the city to the Castle was crowded by thousands of elegantly dressed women. When Anglesey had agreed to go to Dublin, he had taken the precaution of seeking advice from Lord Forbes about the pitfalls to be avoided. Forbes, his cousin, who was familiar with Irish realities, urged him to avoid the pomposity of his predecessor, Wellesley, and to adopt a dignified style which would have greater regard for the manners and character of Irish people as a whole. Acting on that advice, Anglesey avoided the usual peacockery of other arriving viceroys and stepped ashore in a blue coat and drab trousers, wearing a single star on his left breast. Forbes had warned that the selection of tradesmen should be impartial as to their religion. And he urged that none of the sixty Castle domestics employed by Wellesley should be retained because of their plundering habits and the likelihood that they would corrupt newcomers. Anglesey acted on the advice he had been given and, anxious to ensure that he was surrounded by familiar, sympathetic faces, had no qualms about the use of nepotism. He appointed Forbes to be comptroller of the viceregal household and his son, Uxbridge, was made its steward. Another son and a nephew were also added to his entourage and he awarded his personal physician a baronetcy.[36]

In keeping with his policy of conciliation, Anglesey launched a lavish social programme directed as much at the loyalist minority as at the Catholic majority, while distancing himself from the more extreme Protestant factions. In general he was perceived as a liberal, tolerant individual anxious to understand the feelings of ordinary people. While he established a rapport with ordinary citizens by going frequently and without ceremony through the streets, he also won the popularity of the Castle set. In a six-week period shortly after taking up duty, he gave fourteen dinner parties and attended three, held three levees, two drawing-rooms and four balls, and went to a number of theatrical events. His first levee was exceptionally big and was attended by a number of Catholic bishops and by Daniel O'Connell. His drawing-rooms and balls attracted the beautiful and the talented. Among the most admired beauties was Letitia Stepney from Durrow, who was related to him. According to *Blackwood's Magazine*, Lady Morgan 'glittered and fluttered, the gayest among the gay in Lady Anglesey's Court' while she derided the prudery and hypocrisy of those who refused to follow her example. According to the *Freeman's Journal*, 'the ethereal lustre' of the grace and elegance of the Countess of Erroll dimmed 'the surrounding constellations'.[37]

He was a generous and entertaining host. Thomas Creevy, a member of parliament who'd dined at the Castle, was charmed, despite being some-what deterred by the 'settled gloom' of Lady Anglesey and the 'forbidding frowns' of his daughters. Another guest, German nobleman Hermann Puckler-Muskau, friend of Goethe, was impressed by his hospitality and by the breeding and intellect of his friends. Anglesey used his single leg as a social asset, making it the butt of fun. It amused him that there were regu-lar visitors to the garden of his former house in Brussels to see where his lost leg had been buried. And he had no hesitation about exhibiting his arti-ficial limb to his guests. A German visitor wrote, 'a more perfect work of art ... I never saw'.[38]

Politically, though, he was moving too fast, increasingly influenced by the arguments for the relief of Catholics. There was concern in England because he was becoming too popular, his views travelling too far ahead of his government's own slow concessions to the Catholic population. Wellington wrote with concern to Lord Bathurst: 'Lord Anglesey is gone mad. He is bit by a mad Papist: or instigated by the love of popularity.'[39] He certainly had become a thorn in the side of his political masters and was recalled to England in January 1829, weeks before the government con-ceded Catholic emancipation.

As Anglesey set out for Kingstown to return to England, crowds lined the route and an accompanying procession of carriages was over three miles long. Thomas Wyse, a contemporary historian, wrote: 'There was no unseemly riot; no turbulence; no invective; the blessings were not loud but deep ... Banners ... enwreathed in crepe were borne by the different trades before him ... there were few guards; an insignificant escort; no troops; he went escorted by the affections of the people.' And Lady Cloncurry, who observed the scene at Kingstown, said 'the Duchess of Leinster and all the great Ladies as well as the lower orders cried most dreadfully'.[40]

CATHOLIC EMANCIPATION

Hugh Percy, 3rd Duke of Northumberland, who succeeded Anglesey in January 1829, was regarded as a nonentity of little talent, but his personal qualities, in the view of prime minister Wellington, were appropriate to the prevailing atmosphere in Ireland. His appointment ended with a change of government in 1830. Northumberland was unsympathetic to Catholic emancipation, but by now the government privately decided to concede it while making an insincere gesture to the extreme Protestant point of view. He was amiable and charitable, hugely wealthy, an eternal talker who, according to Greville, was 'a prodigious bore'. Daniel Madden, a contemporary historian, observed that Northumberland believed that the best way to rule the Irish was 'to exhibit fine clothes, fine coaches and fine horses and to subscribe liberally to public institutions'. His wife, who had been governess to the young Princess Victoria (later queen), was sensible and good humoured, 'ruling her husband in all things' and particularly generous in benefactions to Catholic charities. Their official entertainments at the Castle maintained the generous standards of the Anglesey administration. They were regal in attitude with an attachment to old standards of etiquette and to the stiffer court regimen of the past.[41]

Northumberland's period of office marked an ending of the long period of penalization of the Catholic population. The Catholic Emancipation Act came into operation during 1829. Catholics were enabled to enter parliament and, with few major exceptions, to hold offices of state. The removal of the political, civil and religious disabilities that had for so long been imposed on them provided, in theory at least, the basis for social and economic advance. But for most Catholics the possibility of such progress was still very distant; there was an expanding population, growing unemployment and poverty, aggravated by intermittent famine and epidemic disease. The more immediate beneficiary of the new freedoms was the developing Catholic middle class, economically and educationally positioned to take advantage of fresh opportunities. And the fact that they had now been acknowledged as full citizens of the state was a boost to their self-confidence and social status. Those who aspired to be members of the viceregal circle would now find it easier to secure acceptance. While there were certain criteria to be met in regard to office or loyalty to the Crown, 'Castle Catholics' were no longer there merely on sufferance.

SEVEN

The Court in Victorian Times

Victoria became queen in 1837 and would remain on the throne for sixty-three years. Her reign had little impact on the course of Irish history but it did influence the narrow world of the viceregal court at Dublin Castle. The pre-Union Irish court had relative freedom in developing its own character and had not been expected to mirror the practices of St James'. There was little change in that position during the early post-Union years, but Victoria had clear views about court conduct and expected the same criteria to be applied to her subordinate court in Dublin.

Victoria's court was far more formal, less spirited and relaxed than those of her immediate predecessors. From the beginning of her reign she'd set about establishing more clearly defined procedures at St James with emphasis on restrained and dignified ceremonials. Etiquette tightened up, rakishness became taboo, the morals and manners of earlier court society were no longer acceptable. There was a sharper awareness of class distinction. To the end of her reign, Victoria's levees and drawing-rooms were virtually closed to those who were not members of the aristocracy and the old gentry or of the higher echelons of the Church, the army and the professions. Those who were involved in literature, or on the stage or in trade, were viewed with reserve. In Irish court society, meanwhile, a policy developed of assimilating, as far as possible, the main standards and practices of St James'.

THE CASTLE IN FAMINE TIMES

In 1836 a government commission enquiring into the condition of the Irish poor found that for at least thirty weeks of the year in 'normal times', well over two million people were destitute.[1] The period was marked by the implementation of a demeaning Poor Law and the establishment of a national system of workhouses. Disease and hunger swept away a million people during the years of the Great Famine, 1845-9, and about one and a half million others emigrated in circumstances of gross hardship. Politically, the main issue was O'Connell's intensifying campaign for the repeal of the Union.

The routine of social life in Dublin Castle was unaffected by prevailing social conditions. There was no reason why it should have been otherwise. By its very nature, the viceregal court and most of its participants were cocooned from hardship. If there was death and disease on a huge scale in rural areas, especially in the west and the south, it was out of sight of those attending the levees, drawing-rooms and balls at the Castle, although a few lords lieutenant reduced their social spending. Some events showed insensitivity to prevailing conditions, for example the shows of one the most favoured societies of the court, the Royal Horticultural Society of Ireland, of which the Duke of Leinster was president. The seasonal shows were fashionable occasions for lavish displays of flowers, fruit and vegetables, the produce of gardens of the gentry and nobility. They were usually attended by the lord lieutenant and an entourage of friends and courtiers. Shortly after the exhibition hall opened to the public for the autumn show of 1849, there was a sudden rush for the exhibits; all the produce was carried away by the spectators or consumed on the spot. Policemen on duty participated in the plunder. An uncomprehending *Irish Farmer's Gazette*, a voice of the landed gentry, later wrote of the 'vulgarity, ferocity ... total disregard to ... decency'.[2]

Following Wellesley's departure there had been no particularly flamboyant displays of viceregal hospitality until the end of the 1840s. Anglesey held office for a second period from the end of December 1830 to September 1833. While he'd been a popular champion of Catholic emancipation, he found himself in a hostile environment in his second period of office when he opposed demands for the repeal of the Union and had to quell the disturbances arising from the collection of tithes. In an effort to reduce the cost of his administration, and in response to the pervasive poverty of the times, he toned down the social and ceremonial aspects of his court. Sinecures, pensions and salaries were reduced, as were his own emoluments, which were reduced to £20,000 a year, the level operating in 1784. The appointment of battleaxe guards ceased and the number of aides-de-camp was reduced. One of the most colourful features of the court came to an end with the extinction of the state musicians, a tradition dating from 1662. They'd varied in number over the years but by Anglesey's time had amounted to almost thirty, including a master and composer, and a variety of string, wind and percussion instrumentalists. But gestures such as these carried little weight with the general population. With the tide of popular opinion running against him and in failing health, Anglesey resigned from office in September 1833.[3]

A succession of viceroys held office briefly and did not have the resources or inclination for demonstrations of wealth out of the ordinary. The Earl of Haddington held office for four months at the beginning of 1835; the Earl of Mulgrave (later Marquis of Normanby) was in office from May 1835 to March 1839; Viscount Ebrington (later Earl Fortescue) from April 1839 to September 1841; Earl de Grey from September 1841 to July 1844; Baron Heytesbury from July 1844 to July 1846; and the Earl of Bessborough was viceroy from July 1846 to May 1847.

Mulgrave was the most popular of this group. He was friendly with Daniel O'Connell and with the Catholic population. Because he was not a man of wealth — in any event, many of the Castle elite spurned his hospitality due to his Catholic leanings — social functions at the Castle were not conducted on a grand scale. But he was dashing, charming and theatrical in manner and dress, and his public appearances caught the imagination of the public. A contemporary commentator describes his style:

> And what added to the charm of his appearance and deportment in Irish eyes, was that he really looked and bore himself like a brilliant and accomplished Irishman. He was not a bluff, red-faced Englishman, or a phlegmatic British peer, stiff and stubborn as one of his ancestral oak trees ... He possessed the art of returning public salutations to perfection; the wave of his hand was quite inimitable; his bow was worthy of Mr Charles Kemble ...

But Mulgrave's policies were resented by the powerful Protestant minority, particularly his leniency towards political crime. When he visited Cork, members of the Royal Cork Yacht Club refused to dress their yachts for the occasion and few of the local gentry went sailing on that day. Eventually the prime minister decided to relieve the situation by creating him Marquis of Normanby and, retiring to London, he was appointed secretary for the colonies.[4]

Mulgrave's successor restored to the entrenched minority a more acceptable Castle, attitude although Dublin society did not like the looks of Ebrington. It was said that he looked 'just like a farmer'. They would have wished for a viceroy of more polished and patrician appearance, someone unlikely to invite to the Castle's drawing-rooms persons like the ridiculous, archetypal O'Looneys of Ascendancy jokes, the type favoured by Mulgrave. Ebrington had strong views about who would be *persona grata* at the Castle. He discouraged professional, middle-class support for O'Connell's repeal movement by making it clear that support for repeal of the Union was synonymous with the destruction of empire. Ebrington was a widower; but with the assistance of Lady C. Fellowes, he maintained the customary programme of social events. On the eve of his return to England he married for the second time, at the Viceregal Lodge, Elizabeth, widow of Sir Marcus Somerville.[5]

Ebrington's successor, Thomas Philip, 2nd Earl de Grey, married a woman of considerable charm, daughter of the Earl of Enniskillen. They spent generously and entertained well, encouraging native dressmakers, and the earl's retirement in 1844 was much regretted by Dublin society. However, he made little impact on the general population. Few people, for instance, turned up to witness the changing of the guard at the Castle on St Patrick's Day 1842, when the lord lieutenant traditionally made an appearance swathed in shamrocks and expected the populace to acclaim him. The *Freeman's Journal* reported that his presence was not recognized by 'by a single cheer'. It may have been influenced by the counter-attraction: a parade of thousands of 'the temperate sons of Ireland's metropolis' with bands playing and gaily decorated carriages supporting the total abstinence campaign of Father Mathew. De Grey had a long-term interest in architecture. He became first president of the Royal Institute of British Architects when it was founded in 1834 and remained in office until he died in 1859.[6]

Heytesbury, who had long service in diplomatic posts, was described by Peel who had appointed him as 'a very calm and dispassionate man'. He was, perhaps, too dispassionate about prevailing conditions in Ireland and the gathering omens of famine. When he was confronted in November 1845 by a deputation of prominent citizens that included Daniel O'Connell and the Duke of Leinster, he reacted 'very coldly' to their fears about the accelerating hunger. The *Freeman's Journal* commented angrily: 'They may starve! Such in spirit, if not in words, was the reply given yesterday to the English viceroy.' It was an unfair comment; Heytesbury was to be reasonably energetic in seeking funds for famine relief. However, the normal social routine continued at the Castle; the levees and the drawing-rooms were crowded. But the programme was dimmed by the death of Heytesbury's wife at the Viceregal Lodge within a few months of his taking office. His daughter, Miss A'Court, subsequently acted as hostess. When Peel's government was replaced by Russell's Whig administration, Heytesbury had to resign.[7]

Bessborough came into office on the eve of the total failure of the potato crop. He was a resident Irish landlord, high-minded, with easy manners and good sense, but in poor health and clearly unfitted for the demands of the post. He complained to the prime minister that it was 'the balls and the

A viceregal ball in the time of Lord Clarendon, mid-nineteenth century (*Courtesy Gorry Gallery and Brian P. Burns Collection; photo: Irish Architectural Archive*)

Visit of the Prince and Princess of Wales to Ireland, 1865

Investiture of the Prince of Wales as a Knight of St Patrick, at St Patrick's Cathedral, 1868

John Poyntz Spencer, 5th Earl Spencer, from *Zozimus*, 1871. His long red beard tickled the faces of the debutantes.

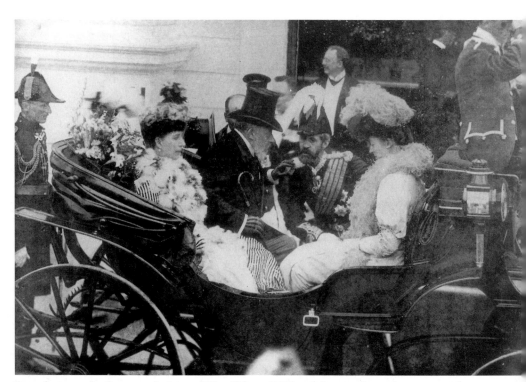

Two photographs from royal visits of King Edward VII and Queen Alexandra: at a garden party in 1903 (*top*), and in their coach with the Aberdeens after attending an art exhibition in 1907 (*National Library of Ireland*)

Sir Arthur Vicars, Ulster king-at-arms, in his ceremonial tabard. Vicars was removed from office following the theft of the Irish crown jewels in 1907, and subsequently murdered in Kerry in 1921. (*National Library of Ireland*)

Debutantes being received by the Aberdeens (*National Library of Ireland*)

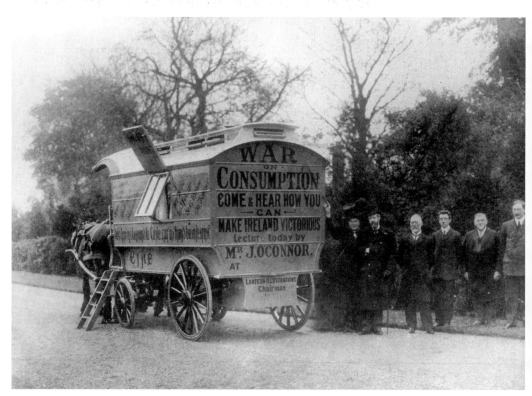

The 'Health Caravan', part of Lady Aberdeen's 'War on Consumption', c. 1910 (*National Library of Ireland*)

Dublin Castle gate, 1920 (*Courtesy George Morrison*)

Kevin O'Higgins and Michael Collins arriving at Dublin Castle for the handover of power to the Provisional Government of Ireland, 16 January 1922 (*Hulton Getty*)

Lord and Lady Fitzalan at Stormont, Belfast, for the opening of the Parliament of Northern Ireland, 1921 (*Courtesy George Morrison*)

drawing-rooms' rather than his other duties that he found most wearying. When he eventually became ill and had to cancel his social programme, Dublin society found it a tiresome interruption, and hopes were expressed that death or resignation would allow early resumption of the gaieties. He died during the 'season' of 1847 when death and epidemic were at their height. The Earl of Clarendon agreed reluctantly to fill his vacancy and to accept 'the terrible task imposed on me' by Russell, the prime minister. It was, indeed, a frightening responsibility: five years of office amidst famine, the Young Ireland movement, Orange disturbances and economic disarray.[8]

A YOUNG WOMAN'S DIARY

The social round at the Castle continued unabated throughout the mid-century. Clarendon, liberal and learned, believed that no matter what the conditions of the times, traditional hospitality had to be maintained. He maintained it in style although he had difficulty in meeting expenses. Writing to his brother-in-law, George Cornewall Lewis, he lamented: 'I have no prospect but the Watford workhouse before me when I leave this, particularly, as I now have to undergo another season at about £3000 a month.'

On viceregal occasions he adopted a regal manner. The young Ellen Palmer, daughter of Sir Roger Palmer of Kenure Park in Rush, recorded in her unpublished diary a dinner with the Clarendons at the Viceregal Lodge in August 1847. Ellen was the great-granddaughter of Eleanor Ambrose, the great beauty and 'dangerous papist' who had fascinated the earlier Irish viceregal court of Chesterfield.[9] She wrote of the Clarendons:

> We found ourselves in the dreaded presence of the representatives of majesty and indeed regal etiquette was indeed kept up ... [it was] in the last degree formal and solemn, so much so that I felt on entering the room as if I had been plunged into ice all at once. Lord and Lady Clarendon received us with a condescending bow and then we sat down to twiddle our thumbs till dinner time. When the doors were opened all my pleasing visions of agreeable neighbours and pleasing

conversation during dinner were to be awfully deceived for horror on
horror I perceived a hobbling white-haired man was to be the partner to lead me in … This gay Lothario had lost the palate of his
mouth and all his teeth so at not one word of what he said was intel-
ligible … It was the dullest of all dull parties I have ever been at.
Wore my pink silk dress, hair in ringlets, no flowers.[10]

But there were other occasions when Ellen's company was more ani-
mated and to her liking. For the young and privileged, the Castle continued
to be a place of excitement and romance. She was part of a charmed circle
who managed to keep the harsher world at bay. Her diary reflects some of
the atmosphere of a viceregal ball at the beginning of 1850, the flirtations,
inconsequential chatter, preoccupations and pursuit of a beautiful heiress,
for which the Castle was a popular hunting ground:

Everyone was as surprised to see me as if I had stepped from the
clouds and Lord Mountcharles told me that one of my acquaintances
had offered him a bet that it was not me at all whereas he declared
that it was. However, everyone declared they were charmed to see
me in Dublin once more and Lord Catto, Captain Lindsay and Lieutenant Ponsonby took the trouble of rushing across to tell me so. I
danced with Mr Bickerstaff, Lord Mountcharles, Mr Vacher (twice),
Mr Vernon, Mr Doherty, Captain Saunderson etc. etc. I was asked by
Capt. Saunders [and] Mr Foster (introduced by Mr Bruten) but was
engaged and could not dance with them … Several of the ADC's
whom I had cut for their conceit in London returned the compliment
to me here. In Dublin they are great Dons and can play off the grand
airs which they are forced to suspend during the London season.
Everyone enquired with the greatest interest if I was not going out
again in Dublin and Mrs Doherty (who was as full of compliments as
ever) said in a sentimental way that it was 'too cruel just to show my
face and then leave them all to pine over my absence'. Mr Vacher was
very inclined for a strong flirtation and kept reminding me of all my
sayings and doings of two years ago (even to the way I wore my hair).

He also enquired particularly whether Kenure were too far for a visit and wanted to know what train I was going back tomorrow with the evident intention of accompanying me if he were encouraged to do so. Lord Mountcharles was particularly polite. He asked me to dance a third time but I happened to be engaged. He would enquire the name of every partner he had seen me dancing with and wanted sadly to induce me to stay in town for the Garrison theatricals, likewise offering to procure me a horse for 'a quiet ride in the Park tomorrow'. Then he asked me with the greatest interest if I were not coming to the Drawing Room and begging me repeatedly to do so [and] just as I was going to my chaperon he said again 'and do you mean to say, Miss Palmer, that we shall not, that I shall not, have the pleasure of seeing you at Court'. These would be suspicious symptoms with anyone else but Lord Mountcharles is such a well known flirt that I must beware of falling in love with him. The beauty [Captain Saunders] wouldn't know how to flirt but he kept pertinaciously in my way until I bowed to him and then gave me a most friendly greeting and asked me twice to dance (which I couldn't do) and then watched an opportunity to come and sit out a quadrille with me ... We did not get to bed until 4 o'clock ... Wore my cerise dress and white [?] wreath, hair waved and rolled behind à la Jenny Lind.[11]

VISIT OF QUEEN VICTORIA, 1849

With parts of the country still in the grip of famine, the summer of 1849 seemed an inappropriate time for Queen Victoria to visit Ireland. But Russell, the prime minister, and Clarendon, the lord lieutenant, believed that a young queen, just thirty and still pretty, would boost the people's spirits as well as provide a tonic for trade. The official announcement of the visit emphasized that it was not a State Visit because 'of the general distress' and her desire to avoid 'ill-timed expenditure and inconvenience to her subjects'. Catholic and loyalist opinions were divided. The *Freeman's Journal* echoed the views of many: 'sumptuous festivities would be, not the token of an exuberant loyalty, but an insult to the sufferings of the living and the sepulchres of the dead'. The queen first landed at Cobh from the royal yacht, visited Cork city, then sailed up the coast to Kingstown where she stepped ashore in a large shawl of red plaid and a plain straw bonnet, accompanied by her husband and four children. The procession from Kingstown to the city was 'cold, formal and scant' and the welcoming crowds not especially enthusiastic, but over the next four days her crowded official programme brought greater crowds onto the streets who responded to her with unexpected warmth.[12]

The queen and her consort stayed with the Clarendons at the Viceregal Lodge. Clarendon was anxious that the costs of the visit be kept as low as possible, but carpets and chintzes had to be replaced because they were 'in such a disgusting state for dirt and old age that they were quite unfit for decent people'. However, only three rooms were re-papered. The extra costs of Victoria's visit, including those of the levee and drawing-room, were estimated by Clarendon to be £4340. The Lord Chamberlain came from London to supervise the arrangements at the Castle and to ensure that protocol was in accordance with that at Buckingham Palace and St James'. There were unprecedented numbers at Castle functions; about 4000 persons attended the levee and 900 ladies were presented at the drawing-room where the queen wore a dress of emerald green poplin embroidered with golden shamrocks. As she passed through the Dublin streets on the way to the Castle the queen caught glimpses of Dublin's poverty. Writing later from the Lodge to the King of the Belgians she remarked, 'You see more ragged and wretched people than I ever saw anywhere else.'[13]

By the end of her visit the *Freeman's Journal* had tempered its views. It acknowledged 'the deep sympathy [that] the womanly bearing of the Sovereign awoke in the heart of all who had an opportunity of watching proceedings'.[14] But the people had nothing to thank her for, and since she had no political power, nothing to expect from her. Nor was there any perceptible change in Irish conditions following her visit. If acute famine was coming to an end, grinding poverty and large-scale emigration would remain during the following decades. But it had been a pleasant interlude; a passing cavalcade in a grim world. Increasingly the Irish people saw the way ahead in terms of separation from Britain; the manifestations of monarchy grew less relevant to their lives. Victoria returned to Ireland in 1853, 1861 and 1900, with diminishing public enthusiasm. Towards the end of the century she had become ensconced in folk memory as 'the famine queen'. The disrespect was mutual. She came to view the Irish representatives at Westminister, clamouring for Home Rule and showing such disregard for the traditional trappings of monarchy, as 'mostly low, disreputable men, who were elected by order of Parnell, and did not genuinely represent the whole country'.[15] In that respect, she was mistaken.

THE ULSTER KING-AT-ARMS

The office of Ulster King-at-Arms had been in existence since 1552, when it was created by Edward VI. The main role of the king-at-arms was to act as chief herald, granting arms, registering pedigrees, keeping the official list of Irish peers, ruling on disputes about title and establishing precedence. His heraldic office was independent of the viceregal court but, in a secondary role, he also regulated the proceedings of the court with its rights, privileges and ceremonies. That role had been confirmed by an ordinance of the Duke of Bolton in August 1717, when he assigned the king-at-arms the highest-ranking place among the officials of the court. While this heraldic role was remunerated by fees, duties at the court were purely honorary.[16]

During the eighteenth century the detailed regulation of the privileges and ceremonies of the court were left largely to the chamberlain. William Hawkins, who held office as king-at-arms from 1765 to 1785, appears to have taken little part in the direction of court affairs; nor did the short-serving Gerald Fortescue, who died in 1788. His successor, Sir Chichester Fortescue, held the post from 1788 until 1820. He spent much of his time at either his County Louth home or in London, making irregular appearances in Dublin at ceremonial events such as when leading the procession of carriages when a new lord lieutenant arrived to take up office. On such occasions he was bedecked in his tabard, an ornate jacket of medieval origin.[17]

However, following Vernon's departure in 1823, the office of court chamberlain ceased to be the chief regulator of court etiquette and rituals. None of the chamberlains subsequently appointed to the office held it long enough to acquire the prestige and experience of chamberlains of the past. The latter-day holders of the office were given the limited role of preparing the lists of invitations for the drawing-rooms and the balls, presenting by name the ladies who attended and ensuring that the ritual of Going into Supper left no lady unaccompanied or embarrassed. And, as the century progressed, the chamberlain was also expected to dance the opening country dance with the wife of the lord lieutenant at the St Patrick's Day ball, the remaining vestige of the old tradition of the chamberlain dancing the first minuet at all state balls.[18]

After Vernon's departure, the Ulster king-at-arms increasingly became the main regulator of the business of the court. Sir William Bentham served from 1820 to 1853, his impact on the court being relatively low-key, involving himself more in the regulation of major ceremonials such as the reception and swearing-in of the lords lieutenant rather than in details of its social events. But Bentham's successor, Sir J. Bernard Burke, who held office from 1853 to 1892, had a much greater involvement and became the major influence on the organization and operation of the Victorian Irish viceregal court during his long period of service. He had practised earlier as a lawyer and acquired experience in genealogical and peerage issues. His main claim to fame was as the compiler of *Burke's Peerage*, the monumental work, first compiled by his father, that he revised annually throughout his lifetime. When he took public office and became close adviser on the management of their court to the succession of viceroys with whom he served, he was quick to profit personally from the environment of patronage of which he was a part. He managed to create official appointments under his office for his three sons, devised new heraldic and genealogical services, and established generous fees for himself and his staff. When a new office was created within the nobility, Burke received a fee which varied according to the status of the office. Thus a new knight paid a fee of £3-3s-4d, an archbishop £10-13s-4d, an earl £19-13s-10d and, at the top, a Knight of St Patrick paid £50. But there were few honours being created during the late Victorian period. Burke found it to his advantage to hand over to the Treasury all the fees received by him and to receive in return a fixed annual salary for his heraldic duties with certain allowances for his assistants. He pursued his fees assiduously. When Charles Cameron, medical officer for Dublin City, had an knighthood conferred on him in an informal manner by Earl Spencer at the Viceregal Lodge, Burke, within days, requested a fee of £16.[19]

Burke was as energetic and as persistent in supervision of the business of the court as he was in pursuit of genealogical and heraldic activities, issuing constant directives about all aspects of the conduct of the business of the court. To ensure similarity of practice he routinely received copies of instructions and regulations issued at St James' and also sought occasional advice from its officials, including the queen's private secretary. Whenever a question of any consequence was raised about a court issue at Dublin Castle, there was, as Burke saw it, little or no scope for departure from the London approach. Rules and procedures once settled became sacrosanct. A contemporary described him as a self-important 'cock-sparrow figure' who regarded lords lieutenant and their ceremonials 'as something supernatural'. He laid great emphasis on pomp and precision in the performance of rituals, no matter how ridiculous they may have appeared to the onlooker. The *Daily News* described the inauguration of two new Knights of St Patrick in August 1871. The ceremony began with the Grand Master intoning, 'Ulster, summon the Knights':

> Whereupon Sir Bernard Burke first bowed deeply and then floated down the room, a vision of splendour ... The effect was on the whole most striking and impressive though some of the incidents provoked a few titters ... the whole ceremonial resembled a theatrical performance of an usually brilliant description.

To many Burke was a figure of fun, to others an embarrassment and irritation. When he once ran foul of Archbishop Whately following a muddle about a court ritual, the enraged archbishop snapped, 'Why, sir, you don't even understand the foolish rules of your own business.' This was probably apocryphal; a similar remark was ascribed on an earlier occasion to Lord Chesterfield during an encounter with an official at the court of St James. But Whately was undoubtedly unhappy about the content of some of the court ceremonials, particularly the oath-taking during the induction of new Knights of St Patrick. He believed oaths should be used only 'in a cause of faith and charity', and he conveyed this view to the queen.[20]

In January 1878, Rudolph, the crown prince of Austria, arrived incognito in Dublin in an unofficial capacity. A member of his entourage, the Count of Bombelles, contacted the Castle to say that the prince was in town and the latter was immediately invited by the lord lieutenant, Marlborough, to dine with him at the Castle. In response, Bombelles enquired whether it was the intention that the prince should 'go out first' and thus lead the procession of guests into dinner. He explained that the prince expected reciprocity, viz., that the Emperor of Austria was accustomed to giving such an honour to foreign crown princes visiting his court and that the crown prince should be similarly treated on his visit to Dublin. Marlborough, advised by Burke, rejoined that, as he was acting as representative of the queen, he was not prepared to yield place to the prince. The prince declined the invitation.

When Burke subsequently informed Henry Ponsonby, the queen's private secretary, about the incident, Ponsonby supported the advice given by Burke and observed that if the precedence sought by the crown prince had been conceded, 'I imagine that the Prince of Wales would have complained if it was refused to him'. But the queen took a different view when informed about the incident. Her imperious annoyance about the handling of the event was evident in the letter sent on her behalf to Burke:

> Her Majesty thinks that on such occasions it would be more customary ... that a royal guest should take in the lord lieutenant's wife first and that the viceroy should follow ... The queen commands me to ask you whether you do not think it should be desirable to enable the lord lieutenant to act on these matters with the same freedoms as the Sovereign, so that he could offer this courtesy to the members of royal and imperial families.[21]

SOCIAL STATUS AND DUBLIN CASTLE

While Burke succeeded in maintaining a viceregal court at Dublin Castle based firmly on upper-class and bourgeois society, he had, as a result of economic and political developments, to contend with a rising tide of persons of lesser social provenance holding public positions entitling them to recognition. It must have been some relief to him, of course, that many of those being lifted by that tide found the activities of the viceregal court ridiculous and irrelevant to their lives, and were increasingly hostile to its very existence.

But for others who took seriously the issues of status and precedence at the Castle, Burke's frequent directives carried all the force of a ukase. For example, only a small, clearly designated elite, predominantly aristocratic, were accorded the privilege of being present in the throne room when presentations were being made to the lord lieutenant. They had to be peers, peeresses or their unmarried daughters; mothers of peers not peeresses whose husbands had they survived would have been peers; archbishops, their wives and their unmarried daughters; dukes' daughters; peeresses' eldest sons; and the senior officers of state such as the lord chancellor. In keeping with the practice at St James, divorced women could not be presented at the Castle prior to 1888. Then, in January of that year, Burke was informed by the lord chamberlain's office that the queen had relaxed the rule 'so that those who have divorced their husbands, being themselves blameless, on account of breach of matrimonial vows, are now permitted to be presented to Her Majesty ... Every case is, however, submitted to Her Majesty's decision.'[22]

At the top of the viceregal social pyramid was the small aristocratic element; next, and in far greater numbers, were the landed gentry. The land legislation of the latter nineteenth century had regulated the relationships of the gentry with their tenants, reduced their incomes, and induced some to leave the country.[23] But they remained an influential, economically valuable element in Irish provincial society, and their wives and daughters, in particular, saw in an invitation to the Castle a recognition and confirmation of their social status. Another social grouping of growing significance were senior public officials. From the mid-century onwards, the composition of guests at levees and drawing-rooms reflected the growth of government services as the *laisser-faire* policies of the past faded. New government departments and services emerged and expanded. The number of officials of status grew in number, all anxious their importance be recognized by the viceregal court. Inclusion in the attendance lists of Castle levees was the ultimate accolade in the public service. Burke received a constant stream of requests for recognition. The growing attendances thronging the Castle on state occasions, particularly for levees, included representatives of the Board of Works, the Poor Law Commissioners, the Education Commissioners, the Local Government Board, the various revenue authorities, the prisons, the Inspectors of Lunacy and many others.

The numbers of members of the professions invited to the Castle increased due to their growing wealth and roles in the expanding public services. Some of the old order perceived the new professionals as jumped-up tradesmen. William Thackeray, in his satirical *Irish Sketch Book* of 1842, rejected the notion that they were on a par with the aristocracy:

> Brass-plates are their titles of honour, and they live by their boluses and their briefs. What call have these worthy people to be dangling and grinning at lords lieutenant's levees and playing sham aristocracy before a sham sovereign? Oh that old humbug of a Castle![24]

However, distinguished members of the medical profession had been welcome at the Castle from the early days of the post-Union court. Visiting Dublin in the early past-Union period, John Gamble noted that 'a physician here is almost at the pinnacle of greatness'. Until well on in the century almost all doctors holding senior appointments in the medical schools and hospitals were Protestants of Ascendancy origin and, therefore, perceived as of good breeding and loyal to the Crown. This reflected the absence of opportunity for Catholics to be educated as doctors until the emergence of university education for them in the latter part of the century.

Despite the acceptability of the medical profession, Burke became somewhat alarmed about the disproportionate number of doctors attending viceregal functions who held formal appointments at the court and were thus entitled to the privilege of walking in procession with the viceroy on state occasions as members of the viceregal household. It was a privilege that they obviously valued even though they ranked lowest in the procession of courtiers. The surgeon-dentist, in turn, ranked lowest among the medical group so that on the occasions of levees, drawing-rooms and important banquets the procession entered the reception chamber headed somewhat incongruously by the viceroy's dentist, followed in ascending order of status by the other medical personages, then other officials of the court, building up in importance to the chief secretary bearing the sword of state, and then the viceroy himself, followed by the ladies of his household. When the large medical involvement in the processions gave rise to increasing comment, Burke decided to limit it to two doctors, the physician-in-ordinary and the surgeon-in-ordinary, thus ending the ceremonial roles of the other doctors involved, including the oculist and the dentist to the household.[25]

While the medical profession had long been acceptable, the court authorities did not have the same unquestioning attitude towards the other professions. While Burke himself was a lawyer, he appeared to have some doubts about the social standing of lawyers in general and their suitability for inclusion in court events. This was possibly because many of the more troublesome political agitators of the period were lawyers. When he consulted Frederick Willis, a long-serving gentleman-usher, on the subject, he was advised that while that there had been once a rule excluding lawyers, they had by then become acceptable.[26]

CATHOLIC ATTITUDES

Despite the impact of emancipation on the majority Catholic population, Castle attendances remained solidly Protestant and royalist in character. The gulf that had for so long separated the subjected and penalized Catholics from their Ascendancy masters could not be easily bridged. It took time for

Catholics to acquire the education to move into the professions and posts of status. But an important consideration was that the Catholic population as a whole had become closely identified with the repeal movement. The majority of their clergy, including many of the bishops, became deeply involved in the campaign, despite strictures from the Vatican. Grievances about the education system further inflamed attitudes against government policies. For these reasons, the social activities and public ceremonials of the Castle remained forbidden territory for the political and religious leaders of the majority population and their followers. The epithets 'Castle bishops' and, later, 'Castle Catholics' were used offensively to describe the relatively small number of Catholics who, for whatever reason, became identified with the viceregal court. Archbishop Murray of Dublin occasionally participated in viceregal functions during the 1840s, but when his successor, Archbishop (later Cardinal) Cullen, was in office (1852-78), bishops ceased attending Castle functions altogether. Cullen feared that attendance at the court might give the impression that he was a Castle hack, suspect in regard to his atti- tude to government policies, and likely to lose his influence with the people. The other bishops followed his example. But Cullen had reluctantly gone to see Spencer when he was lord lieutenant in 1867 to intercede for the life of a Fenian, and he had a further contact with him to discuss legislation on Church lands. Following Cullen's death, his successors, Cardinal McCabe and Archbishop Walsh, occasionally participated in the annual banquet for the queen's birthday. But at the banquet to celebrate the sixtieth year of Vic- toria's reign in 1897 the only representative of the Catholic clergy appears to have been Monsignor Molloy, rector of the Catholic University, who was also present on other important viceregal occasions.[27]

LATE-NINETEENTH-CENTURY VICEROYS

If some of the old aristocracy and the gentry were less than enthusiastic about attendance at viceregal events, nevertheless these events were still seen as the peak to be reached by all those with pretensions to status within Irish society. While most invited would have been sensitive enough to prevailing political currents, an invitation to the Castle was beguiling regardless of the political context. The invitees included the bulk of the minor aristocracy, gentleman farmers, business and professional classes, and officials and military who had little choice in the matter. Towards the end of the century the 'Castle Catholics' were increasing in number; but no self-respecting nationalist, in the unlikely event of getting an invitation, would wish to be seen entering the portals of Dublin Castle. In the five weeks of the 1891 season, 16,310 persons were entertained at the viceregal functions.[28] Servicing the social life of the Castle had become an important economic activity. Hundreds were required for catering, food supplies and dressmaking, and the services of many other tradesmen and merchants were needed by the court and its guests.

Generous hospitality was expected and given. As in the past, the degree of lavishness varied with the extent to which a lord lieutenant was able to supplement his official allowance. The 13th Earl of Eglinton, who served for two periods between 1852 and 1859, made an impact more because of the regal style of his court than his political abilities. When he opened an industrial exhibition in Cork in 1852, it was carried out with elaborate ceremonial, including military bands and troops, a mass choir singing the 'Hallelujah Chorus' and the knighting of the mayor of the city. Edward Granville Eliot, 3rd Earl of St Germans, who had previously served as chief secretary for Ireland, organized a splendid round of celebrations for the second visit of Queen Victoria in 1853 when she opened the Grand Exhibition in Dublin. The 7th Earl of Carlisle, who served from 1855 to 1858 and again from 1859 to 1864, was also a generous host. Unmarried, cultivated and articulate, anxious to improve agricultural and industrial output in Ireland, his style of administration made him very popular. An indignant guest complained to the *Dublin Evening Post* in January 1861 about the great crush at one of Carlisle's levees where he was 'shot into His Excellency's presence like a pea from a pop-gun'.

When Carlisle retired due to ill health, the *Irish Times* expressed disappointment that his successor should be Baron Wodehouse (1864-6), not only because of his lack of political standing and low rank, but because he had insufficient resources to maintain the level of hospitality of his predecessor. Wodehouse got a cool reception on arrival in Dublin. He arrived by train at Westland Row and, mounted on horseback, joined a procession to the Castle. The *Irish Times* reported, 'We have, we are sorry to confess, witnessed processions of lords lieutenant but never before did we witness before one so cold, formal, and heartless.' The most enlivening feature of the occasion occurred when a rocket from the Castle intended to greet his arrival misfired and fell on a cab in Dame Street. The injured passenger received a gift of five pounds from the new viceroy. Wodehouse's leavetaking in July 1866 was no warmer. By then he had to deal with the Fenian rising, had sharpened nationalist antagonisms, and was being mocked as 'Wodelouse'. His embarkation at Kingstown elicited 'no manifestation of public feeling one way or the other'.[29]

His successor James Hamilton, 2nd Marquis of Abercorn (later Duke), served two periods of office, July 1866 until December 1868 when Disraeli's Tory government was replaced by that of Gladstone, and March 1874 until November 1876 after Gladstone's defeat, eventually resigning office because of his wife's ill-health.[30] Abercorn, haughty in demeanour, was concerned about maintaining the proper trappings for his court. When employing professional waiters, he went to the expense of dressing them up in tights, black silk facings and shoe buckles to ensure that they kept to the traditions of the court. A visit by the Prince of Wales in 1868 led to a lavish spectacle at St Patrick's Cathedral when the prince was installed as a Knight of St Patrick. Encouraged by Burke, the king-at-arms, with his propensity for elaborate ceremonial, Abercorn arranged for the closure of the cathedral for a month to improve the seating and decoration. The event was a *coup de theatre*. Abercorn had hoped that the festivities would help to distract attention from the high level of agrarian violence, but it had no obvious impact and a Westmeath landlord, Mr H. Fetherston-Haugh, on his way home from the viceregal celebrations, was shot through the heart after arriving at Killucan station. The installation of the prince was the last such event in St Patrick's. The following year the Irish Church Act disendowed the Church of Ireland and the cathedral was thereafter closed to official ceremonials.[31]

Percy Fitzgerald, who wrote an entertaining account of the end-of-century viceroys, *Recollections of Dublin Castle and of Dublin Society*, tells a story of the contrasting demeanour of Carlisle and Abercorn, as perceived by two natives:

> Ah sure I'm for Abercorn any day. Now Carlisle, you see, would receive you in the most cordial way, and talk and be delighted to see you; ask how you were and all that. But give me Abercorn. Shure there he stood, without a word, looking down with the utmost contempt on you, just as if you were the very dirt of his shoe.

Abercorn and his family established marriage bonds with some of the highest-ranking nobility of the day. He himself married a daughter of the Duke of Bedford. He had six sons and seven daughters; all the daughters married peers: four earls, a marquess and two dukes.[32]

The Spencers (1868-74 and 1882-85) were a particularly engaging couple. The tall, red-bearded John Poyntz Spencer, 5th Earl, a commanding figure with attractive manners, and his wife, Charlotte, a woman of rare beauty, were welcomed as an exciting acquisition to Irish society. Extremely wealthy, they were already noted in England for the magnificence of their hospitality. Spencer served for two periods under separate Gladstone governments. As far as entrenched upper-class Irish society was concerned, he started with the disadvantage that he had been chosen by Gladstone, disestablisher of the Church of Ireland and of its special status, and begetter of protective legislation for tenants to the disquiet of the landlords. They were times of agrarian disturbance. Nonetheless the Spencers, and particularly the beguiling charms of the vicereine, overcame any overt political antagonisms. Their first drawing-room, in February 1869, was a hugely fashionable, crowded affair, at which the countess, resplendent in an ensemble of white and silver, established herself incontestably as head of Irish society. Over a century later one of her kinswomen, Diana Spencer, Princess of Wales, would illuminate a broader world than that of Dublin Castle. But if Earl Spencer was popular with viceregal society, the ordinary citizen was no more enthusiastic about him than other lords lieutenant. In May 1882, during his second period of office his chief secretary and under-secretary were assassinated in the Phoenix Park, and his repressive policies in dealing with agrarian violence made him deeply disliked. Lord Charles Dilke strolled with Spencer through the streets of Dublin in 1885; he later wrote that while Spencer was universally recognized, only one man raised his hat to him. And some persons met him with shouts of 'murderer'.[33]

John Winston Spencer Churchill, 7th Duke of Marlborough (1876-80), father of Randolph Churchill, grandfather of Winston, was also wealthy and entertained on a large scale, travelling widely throughout the country and espousing popular causes such as religious toleration in the north and land purchase for small farmers. His duchess, too, sought personal popularity, developed influential contacts among Catholic bishops, and valued the support of the press, enquiring anxiously at functions, 'Have the press been fed?' She sponsored a fund, with her son Randolph assisting as secretary, from which contributions came from abroad to relieve Irish distress. But she could be out of touch; when one of her ladies' committees sent clothes for the children of the poor of western counties, they were nearly all Little Lord Fauntleroy suits.

The Marlboroughs left office with the demise of the Tory government in May 1880. The Cowpers followed. Francis Thomas de Grey, 7th Earl of Cowper, courteous, intelligent, 'one of the old school', and his attractive wife, were most acceptable to the traditional viceregal circle. They took up office at the height of Parnell's power when the campaign of the Land League against landlordism was destabilizing rural Ireland. Parnell was arrested and when Cowper was told that Gladstone was prepared to discuss peace terms in order to allay current tensions, he resigned.[34]

By the 1880s the viceregal court at Dublin retained, on the surface, only a small vestige of the aristocratic element that had for so long sustained it. The attendance at the first levee of the 1881 season held by Earl Cowper numbered about 800, consisting of about 200 army officers of all ranks, several hundred persons drawn from commercial, academic and public service life, fifty members of the medical profession (including army doctors) and about twenty-five Protestant clergymen. There were only seventeen artistocrats listed among the attendance.[35] Many of the aristocracy and old county families were increasingly uncomfortable with the social provenance of many of their fellow guests; and others would indicate by their absence their disdain for government policies favouring the notion of Home Rule. No matter what the prevailing political atmosphere may have been – the changing perceptions of Parnell and the Irish Party, the contentious issues of land reform and Home Rule, the growing force of nationalism – the private circle of most lords lieutenant remained solidly aristocratic and royalist, undiluted by nationalistic or democratic elements. The guest lists of private functions at the Castle and Viceregal Lodge throughout the Victorian decades reflected that position. And when loyalty to the Crown needed to be demonstrated, the peerage was not wanting. On Queen Victoria's golden jubilee in 1897, sixty-two noblemen participated in the banquet in her honour at the Castle; there were about 200 others present but, according to the *Express*, a great many invited persons 'were prevented by a variety of unavoidable causes from being present'.[36]

HOME-RULE POLITICS

During the 1870s and the 1880s the Irish Party developed under the leadership of Charles Stewart Parnell into a powerful, disciplined force within the House of Commons. For much of this period the party held the balance of power between the Conservatives (Tories) and the Liberals (Whigs), which increased its clout in advancing its demand for Home Rule for Ireland. Up to the end of the century and during the dying years of British rule in Ireland, government swung back and forth between the Tories and the Whigs, and the lords lieutenant who held office in Ireland were adjudged either pro- or anti-Home Rule.

The emergence of the 4th Earl of Carnavon as lord lieutenant was the product of a brief flirtation between the Conservatives and the Parnellites from 1885-6. Henry Robinson said of him that he was an excellent viceroy whose speeches, while received with enthusiasm, when analyzed 'meant absolutely nothing at all'. His seven-month term of office ended with a change of government.

When the general election of 1885 led to the return of eighty-six Irish nationalists and the loss of many Liberal seats, their leader Gladstone combined with the Parnellites to secure power. The arrangement secured the support of the Liberal government for Home Rule. Lord Aberdeen, friend of Gladstone and ardent home ruler, was appointed lord lieutenant and came to Dublin accompanied by his wife Ishbel, a woman of great determination and many causes. Lady Aberdeen arrived with her four children, aged from sixteen months to seven years, dressed in suits of green velvet, but was persuaded at the last minute, in deference to unionist sensitivities, to have their suits dyed blue before the family travelled in procession in an open coach through the streets. The Aberdeens were a well-meaning couple who quickly became popular with the nationalists but were anathema to unionist opinion. However, the general election that followed the defeat of Gladstone's first Home Rule Bill was disastrous for the Liberals and led to a change of government. The Aberdeens had to return to England after only six months in office; but they would later have an opportunity for a more prolonged stay in Dublin.[37]

The Aberdeens were followed by Charles Stewart Vane-Tempest, 6th Marquis of Londonderry (April 1886 to July 1889), and Lawrence Dundas, 3rd Earl of Zetland (July 1889 to August 1892). The social programme of the Castle had by now a momentum of its own, little influenced by whomever was viceroy, but both maintained high standards of hospitality that pleased the traditional Castle circle. Prince Albert and Prince George visited in 1887 and Londonderry gave a brilliant state banquet for them at the Castle. Neville Wilkinson, who later became Ulster king-at-arms, described being present at a viceregal dinner in Zetland's time where 'a long table gradually filled with Switzer's most expensive frocks, and black coats coruscating with stars and orders'.[38]

When the Salisbury ministry ended and Gladstone returned to power, there was once again a Home Ruler in Dublin Castle. Lord Houghton (1892-5), young, good-looking, rich and a widower, brought added excitement to the drawing-rooms and balls even if his strong Home-Rule sympathies were repugnant to older loyalists. Many unionists refused his hospitality and according to Henry Robinson, vice-president of the Local Government Board, 'the lower strata of society which flocked to the Castle were people who had nothing in common with him'. Houghton himself, writing to the queen's private secretary in February 1893, confirmed that he was being shunned by unionist supporters. He reported that his first levee of the season had consisted mainly of official and military personnel and that the landed gentry were, with few exceptions, absent. The Lord Chief Justice, Sir Peter O'Brien, 'did his best to induce others to stay away', while many young debutantes boycotted the drawing-rooms.[39]

DRESS CODES, DEBUTANTES, DANCING AND KISSING

Throughout the nineteenth century there was insistence on formality of dress at state functions, but during the latter part of the century it became less elaborate. Among male guests, much of the colour came from the varying dress uniforms of officers of the different military detachments. Judges were required to wear their gowns of office and senior churchmen wore the appropriate purple and red of their rank. Until the latter part of the century, male civilians attending the Castle were expected to follow the practice of St James: full court dress of cloth or velvet, lined with white silk; embroidered white silk waistcoat; breeches of the same colour and material as the coat; white silk hose; shoes with buckles; sword, cocked hat, lace frill and ruffles. By now there were many among those at court who were uncomfortable about the garb they were required to wear. During 1865 the London *Times* said that levees at Dublin Castle were being 'rendered almost ridiculous' by the archaic dress and that many gentlemen were refusing to attend levees because of 'their unconquerable repugnance to appearing in court dress'. So the rules eased and by 1866 Castle occasions required only 'ordinary dress [evening] coat and waistcoat with black knee breeches and black stockings', according to a note of Burke, the king-at-arms. White knee breeches were no longer appropriate. Wodehouse, when lord lieutenant, decided that it was unnecessary to have shamrocks embroidered on the ceremonial jackets of viceroys as in the past, but the accoutrements of sword, buckles and a cocked hat continued even after court dress was formalized by an official directive of 1898. The growing number of officials from government departments entitled to viceregal invitations were required to wear 'the civil service uniform', for which it has not been possible to find a specific prescription, but it appears to have been only another name for the dress required for all civilian guests.[40]

Much of the colour, imagination and excitement came from the ladies' dresses. As with pre-Union society, there was a constant quest for the up-to-date ideas of London and Paris, and Dublin Castle was the stage on which they were displayed. By the 1830s women of fashion wore several layers of petticoats with widely protruding skirts. The quest for even fuller skirts led to the use of small pads, consisting mainly of horsehair, or crin, from which the word 'crinoline' was eventually derived. The crinoline was a construction of hoops, which avoided the need for swathes of petticoats and horsehair. In the pursuit of the ultimate fashionable impact the skirts grew wider and wider, reducing the number of persons who could be accommodated with comfort in the Castle and wherever women of fashion congregated. In Dublin, the original Shelbourne Hotel was founded in 1824 largely as a base for the country gentry attending viceregal and other social events of importance. By the 1860s, as the spatial demands of the crinoline grew, there was difficulty in negotiating doorways and staircases when large crowds of ladies prepared for Castle events. To overcome the problem, the hotel owners found it necessary to redesign the premises to provide wider doorways, corridors and stairways, allowing greater freedom of movement.[41]

By the end of the 1860s the crinoline era was over, with a movement away from encumbering fashion, and ladies of the court were permitted greater freedom in what they wore; but certain features remained imperative, such as a long train, ostrich feathers in the hair and white veils and lappets. There was a clear directive for guests at the London and the Dublin courts: 'feathers should be worn so that they can be clearly seen in approaching The Presence ... coloured feathers are inadmissible'.[42] Personal milliners and tailors began to be displaced by the products of the so-called 'monster' shops. At the beginning of 1860 Brown Thomas and Co. of Grafton Street and McBirney Collis and Co. were advertising a wide variety of fabrics for the approaching Castle season. While the quality of ladies' fashions at the court remained on a high level, there was some roughening of general impact. A representative of the *Freeman's Journal* noted in January 1874:

... here and there the eye was caught by a style of dressing which the slang phrase 'loud' most accurately characterises. The decolleté fashions of the Second Empire are out of fashion at an Irish court and no one can watch without horror the revival of the days of our great grandmothers when the rouge pat and the puff powder were parts of the regular paraphernalia of the dressing table.

Male attire at court was also on a downhill slope. Samuel M'Comas and Sons were offering society gentlemen a large assortment, for sale or hire, of hats, lace, ruffles, swords and buckles for levees and drawing-rooms. The cost of purchasing a full court suit was about £45 but its hire for use at both occasions was usually two guineas. The clothes were often 'dreadfully venerable garments already worn by scores of people'. And some of the wearers themselves were not always of acceptable quality. Following Lord Wodehouse's first levee at the beginning of 1865 the *Mail* suggested that it would have been better 'if a more careful selection had been made of those who were admitted'. Later, as lords lieutenant emerged strongly supportive of Home Rule, such as Houghton and Aberdeen, some of their guests tended to ignore former niceties. A court official noted with distaste the appearance at court functions of 'blue reefer coats and brown boots'.[43]

Even if the majority of the populace were at best indifferent to the social life of the viceregal court, Victorian Dublin could never have been left unaware of the occasion of a levee, drawing-room or ball at the Castle. On a levee day a great procession of carriages moved slowly up Dame Street to drop the many colourfully attired males deemed acceptable in Irish society. The *Freeman's Journal* describes such a day in January 1871 in the anteroom of the Castle:

Here are the fathers of the city in robes of fur and scarlet, brave as the alcades of Murillo, as the burgomasters of Teniers. Here are the officers of every branch of the Service. Here are the rich scarlet of the Line; here the dark coats of the Rifles; here blaze the splendid uniforms of the Lancers. The red coat of the deputy lieutenants relieved by the sombre gown and monstrous wig of the Queen's Counsel and,

for the rest, the gentlemen who have no right to wear a special costume are disguised in the laced ruffles and fronts, the swords, cocked
hats and peach-coloured suits of Georgian Macaronis ... [44]

The most colourful and most eagerly attended events of all, however,
were the drawing-rooms and balls. Whatever their other attractions, these
occasions during the Victorian years became an important marriage mart
for daughters of the middle and upper classes. George Moore's 1887 novel
A Drama in Muslin recounts realistically the social progress of Olive Barton, daughter of a Connacht landlord, who comes to Dublin for the season
accompanied by her mother. There were many daughters in real life who
embarked on similar quests, some with considerable success, for instance
Daisy Burke from Galway, who 'did' various Castle seasons and ended up as
the wife of the Earl of Fingall, for a time steward of the viceregal household.[45] Moore's novel gives an accurate account of the excitements and turmoil associated with a presentation at the Castle, describing the crush as
excited daughters and accompanying mothers surged towards the lord lieutenant while an orchestra played waltzes in the background:

> The air was agleam with diamonds, pearls, skin and tulle veils. Pow-
> dered and purple-coated footmen stood, splendid in the splendour
> of pink calves and salmon-coloured breeches on every landing ...
>
> An hour passed wearily and in this beautiful drawing-room
> humanity suffered in all its natural impudence. Momentarily the air
> grew hotter and more silicious; the brain ached with the dusty odour
> of *poudre de ris* and the many acidities of evaporating perfume; the
> sugary sweetness of the blondes, the salt flavours of the brunettes,
> and this allegro movement of odours was interrupted by the garlicky
> andante ... that the perspiring arms of a fat chaperone slowly exhaled.

Then, at last, it is the turn of the debutante. The chamberlain calls out
her name, her mother presents her, the lord lieutenant kisses her on both
cheeks, she curtsies and passes on, her train caught up and handed to her
by two aides-de-camp. Then into St Patrick's Hall:

In a top gallery, behind a curtain of evergreen plants, Liddell's orchestra continued to pour an uninterrupted flood of waltz melody upon the sea of satin, silk, poplin and velvet that surged around the buffet, angrily demanding cream ices, champagne and claret cup. Every moment the crowd grew denser and the red coats of the Guards and the black corded jackets of the Rifles stained like spats of ink and blood the lugubrious pallor of the background.[46]

A journalist viewing one such occasion in the Hall, with its thousand lamps lighting up its rich gilding, elaborate paintings and splendid ceiling, wrote, '... here is one of the brightest and richest scenes to be witnessed in the world'.[47]

For those who had already been presented, the subsequent balls were even more exciting and colourful. By now, the quadrille had taken over as the ceremonial dance at the court, the initial one usually danced by the lady of the lord lieutenant and the court chamberlain. Waltzes, the universal favourite, with their echoes of the romantic milieu of great European courts, and a popular version of the quadrille, the lancers, were joined at the close of the century by new American dances, the two-step and barn dance (or military schottische), facilitated by the less encumbering dresses of the period. The military bands were gradually replaced at Castle dances by private bands which adapted more quickly to the changing modes and preferences of popular dancing. During the 1850s and 1860s Kelly's String Band and Hanlon's Band usually provided the music for Castle balls. They were popular for many years until supplanted by Liddell's Band. Liddell was a talented and flamboyant musician who developed his initial group into a large orchestra that played at viceregal functions throughout the 1880s; the band was in huge demand at society events and was eventually invited to play at Buckingham Palace. Military bands often gave public performances in the Upper Castle Yard. The 7th Earl of Carlisle, when lord lieutenant, always appeared on the balcony and selected the music himself.[48]

In 1879 the king-at-arms, Burke, became concerned about the extent of formal kissing during official presentations at the Castle, compared with the court of St James. It had become the practice for lords lieutenant to kiss the cheek of all ladies presented to them at drawing-rooms, a practice that Marlborough, the ageing, incumbent viceroy, was finding exhausting. When Burke consulted the early precedents for the Irish court dating from the mid-eighteenth century, there were no references to kissing in the ceremonial procedures then devised. It appeared that the Georgian kings subsequently set a pattern of their own for public kissing which became accepted practice at both the Dublin and London courts. When George IV visited Dublin in 1821 there was a palpable frisson of excitement at the drawing-room in his honour and, according to a contemporary account, 'many Ladies who were never at Court before attended ... the ambition of getting a Royal Smack induced all to come'. The king kissed over 1000 ladies on that occasion.[49]

Queen Victoria introduced a degree of reserve into her court which was a deterrent to warmer forms of greetings. Ladies presented to her were kissed only if of appropriate rank: peeresses; daughters of dukes, marquises and earls; wives of eldest sons of dukes, marquises and earls; and the wives of younger sons of dukes and marquises. Burke proposed a procedure to relieve the overburdened Duke of Marlborough whereby all ladies would continue to be kissed on being received at the drawing-rooms, but the duchess would stand alongside her husband and share the task. When the queen was informed of this proposal she rejected it on the grounds that the duchess had not a representational role. So, kissing the lord lieutenant himself remained one of the excitements of being presented. The young Daisy Burke from Galway describes in her later memoirs as Countess of Fingall being tickled by the long red beard of the Earl of Spencer when she was presented to him.[50]

PROPOSALS TO ABOLISH THE POST OF LORD LIEUTENANT

From the implementation of the Union there had always been a view among some British politicians that the post of lord lieutenant was an unnecessary and expensive incumbrance to the machinery of governing

Ireland. The question surfaced sharply from time to time during parliamentary discussions or in legislative proposals that were later dropped or rejected. Proposals for the abolition of the office came before the Commons in 1823, 1830, 1844 and 1850. At various times the proposal had the support of Whigs, Conservatives and Radicals and a number of major political figures of the period. Usually, the view prevailed that while the existence of a viceregency did not confer any great benefits, neither did it do any great harm, and there was always the possibility that any move to abolish it would stir up trouble. It was better to let sleeping dogs lie. When Lord John Russell got approval in 1850 for the second reading of a bill in to abolish the posts of lord lieutenant and chief secretary and replace them by a minister for state, the opposition came mainly from Irish members who feared that the abolition of the offices would end the last vestige of a separate administration for Ireland. But the proposal was dropped because of other parliamentary priorities.[51]

The arguments for and against abolition of the office were social and commercial rather than political. It was argued that ending of the Dublin court would deprive the most steadfast and loyal citizens of the kingdom of a prestigious ceremonial provision where their loyalty could be publicly acknowledged, and that the merchants, hoteliers and milliners would lose out. A large public meeting in March 1850, claiming to be representative of all trades and professions, protested that the abolition of the lord lieutenancy would 'inevitably bring desolation upon this City and its Trade'. When Carlisle was lord lieutenant in 1857 he wrote to Palmerston, the prime minister, suggesting that it was not worth the bother changing things and urging the acceptance of the view that there would be a heavy loss to tradesmen if country gentry stopped coming to Dublin for the season. But the tax-paying British public took a contrary view. *The Times* declaimed that 'in conceding a mock court to Ireland ... Englishmen only do as they would give glass beads to savages'. During 1858 Roebuck, the member for Sheffield, proposing the abolition of the office, argued that it was wrong to base its existence mainly on the income it provided for the shopkeepers of Ireland. He suggested that 'a lord lieutenant who exhilarates the people of Ireland by his dancing propensities and may give music and good parties ...

is merely a pageant'. Roebuck got considerable support but the resolution was rejected.

When Spencer was lord lieutenant he held the private view that the post should not be continued and sounded out Larcom, the under-secretary, in 1871 about the merits of having, as an alternative, a royal prince living in Dublin carrying out non-political duties. While Larcom thought that the idea was worthy of serious consideration he warned against a 'false step'. However, Gladstone, who consulted both Spencer and Larcom, got the somewhat reluctant agreement of the queen to the notion that the Prince of Wales or another royal personage might take up residence in Ireland as a just step towards abolition of the post. Victoria clearly had doubts about her son because of his character and susceptibility to flattery, while Spencer felt it would be difficult for a member of the royal family to retain a position of neutrality. Once again the issue fizzled out. Nationalist members of parliament continued to target the ridiculousness and extravagance of the court when there was any House of Commons discussion on the subject. Mac Neill, a Donegal member, objected to four aides-de-camp being paid £200 each for 'standing about in more or less picturesque attitudes'. He also thought it ridiculous that the state steward should be paid £505.19.4 for the 'important and delicate duty' of introducing ladies to gentlemen at dances.[52]

Over the next few decades the post of lord lieutenant continued to be seen as a relatively unimportant element in the broader structure of government, its limited political influence waning further as Westminster and Irish parliamentarians determined the path of Irish politics. By 1900 the government viewed the lord lieutenant as a constitutional monarch with no real political role. Viceroys gave an increasing portion of their time to social functions and charitable events, accepting a duty to encourage reconciliation, discourage unrest and to keep the flag of empire flying in Dublin. While the levees, drawing-rooms and balls continued to be popular among the Castle set, some of the traditional ceremonials were dropped or muted as nationalism gained ground amidst increasing indifference or hostility to public displays of viceregal pomp.

The ceremonial changing of the guard in the Upper Castle Yard on St Patrick's Day, when the lord lieutenant would appear on the balcony, was one index of public feeling. Up to the 1860s the event usually attracted a large crowd of onlookers, many of them poor and idle, seeking entertainment. Carlisle, thirsty for popularity, liked to encourage the crowd to react to the traditional music of the band while whetting their behaviour by mimicking the ebullient Paddy. On one occasion he threw down cakes and bread to the scrambling mob. Sometimes coins were thrown. They were humiliating scenes; the *Freeman's Journal* wrote of drunken ragamuffins 'cheering and dancing ... vying with each other in the thoroughness of their degradation'. When the Spencers appeared on the balcony on St Patrick's Day 1869 for the first time, they attracted a large and orderly crowd. However, by the time they returned for their second period of office during the 1880s the general public were no longer allowed into the Castle yard because of continuing disturbances. A small crowd 'of disemployed labourers and artisans', closely watched by police and military, peered through the gate as the nobility and gentry arrived for the first levee of the 1883 season. On St Patrick's Day 1885 a military band played in the Upper Yard mainly, according to the *Freeman's Journal*, 'for the delectation of a strong body of detectives and of some idlers who looked and listened through the gateway'. The Marquis of Londonderry did not observe the trooping of the colours on St Patrick's Day 1887, but nationalist bands paraded through the city streets to commemorate the occasion. Zetland was determined to revive the ceremony and in 1890, when the colours were trooped as he stood on the balcony, the *Irish Times* reported that the attendance was small and that the police had carefully screened those seeking admittance to prevent demonstrations.[53]

The cheering crowds, the flag-waving, the long train of carriages associated with arriving and departing lords lieutenant, had long ceased. As the arrival procession of Cadogan, the last to hold office during the nineteenth century, moved up Dame Street towards the Castle in August 1895, bystanders watched its progress 'with apparent indifference', according to the *Evening Telegraph*: 'A slight effort at a cheer was made by some people ... but it was followed by considerable groaning and hooting. His Excellency, evidently determined to make the most of the display irrespective of its merits, bowed with a diplomatic smile ...'[54]

The state apartments at the Castle were largely neglected during late Victorian times despite the huge traffic of social activities. Ignoring political realities, however, the Board of Works had elaborate ideas in 1870 for their refurbishment. A member of its staff was sent to view the personal accommodation of the queen and the late prince consort at Buckingham Palace and Windsor Castle as a guide to what might be appropriate. He secured admission to the queen's personal bedroom at the palace, where he was surprised to find that it was 'very plain' and had not been renovated since she had moved in. On the other hand, the prince consort's apartments were highly decorative. Subsequently, when the Board of Works put forward elaborate plans for the Castle based on the standards of the royal palaces, they were quickly rejected by Larcom, the under-secretary.[55] As Irish political preoccupations moved away from land and landlords, and as nationalist consciousness developed, attention was focused on the whole nature of the British overlordship, and the demands for Home Rule grew stronger.[56]

EIGHT

The Last Years of British Rule

Cadogan's term of office straddled the turn of the century, marking the end of the Victorian era. Dudley followed. Their ten combined years of office represented a last, defiant refulgence of gaiety in the history of what was now a moribund court.

The arrival of George Henry, 6th Earl of Cadogan, and his wife, revived the flagging social life of the Castle even if they were greeted with indifference by the populace at large.[1] As far as the traditional Castle circle was concerned, the Cadogans had all the desirable qualifications for the viceregal role. They had been sent to Ireland by a Tory administration and, therefore, were likely to be favourably disposed towards the unionist minority. Unlike the majority of Irish lords lieutenant, Cadogan had a seat in the cabinet and was in a position to influence government policy. The Cadogans spent generously, were charming in manner, liked to entertain, and were intimate with the Prince and Princess of Wales, who visited in 1897. But the social highlight of the viceregency was the visit of Queen Victoria, who, close to the end of her reign, arrived in April 1900. She stayed with the Cadogans at the Viceregal Lodge but her visit was a private one and there were none of the ceremonial rituals of a state visit. Nevertheless, Cadogan used the occasion to encourage enthusiastic displays of loyalty to the monarch. There was a colourful review of the Dublin garrison held in the Phoenix Park, and a huge assembly of school children from the Dublin schools, estimated to number 52,000, was organized, also in the park, through which the queen drove in an open carriage.[2] However, prominent nationalists such as Maud Gonne agitated against the visit, and half of the members of Dublin Corporation stayed away.

DUDLEY

Cadogan retired from public life in July 1902 with the departure of Salisbury as prime minister, and was succeeded by William Humble Ward, 3rd Earl of Dudley. Cadogan and Dudley had similar styles, socially and politically. Dudley was rich and extravagant, spending in his first year in Ireland £60,000 above his official annual allowance of £20,000. He would telegraph his usual London barber to come to Dublin when he needed a haircut, once sending him home peremptorily when he arrived late. Educated at Eton, a landowner of about 30,000 acres with a large ironworks, he spent three years touring the world in the 1880s and liked to live in the grand manner.[3]

The Dudleys were determined to revive some of the former glory of the viceregal court. The countess organized a *bal poudre* at the Castle early in March 1903, where the guests were expected to dress in costumes representing historic events or famous paintings. There was a great gathering in St Patrick's Hall and the *Irish Times* reported that it was 'a memorable occasion ... We take off our hat to the Countess of Dudley'. Later in the month at a hugely attended St Patrick's Day ball, court dress and full uniforms were obligatory. The countess, resplendent with a large spray of shamrock and a diamond tiara in her hair, danced the opening country dance with the chamberlain, Sir Gerald Dease. For the first time St Patrick's Day was declared to be a public holiday, with the Dudleys marking the occasion by attending the Trooping of the Colour in the Castle courtyard.

There was 'a goodly assemblage' of the public, whose admission had been subjected to the 'judicious discretion' of the police.[4]

The Dudleys did their best to be popular. The earl travelled throughout the country by motor car to familiarize himself with social realities. The countess took a special interest in promoting a better nursing service for the more deprived areas. They made a determined effort to secure a widely representative attendance at the levee held in honour of the visit of Edward VII in July 1903. Dr Walsh, the Catholic Archbishop of Dublin, wearing his ecclesiastical gown, came to a Castle function for the first time and was given precedence over his Protestant counterpart when presented to the king, an event, reported the *Daily Chronicle*, 'fraught with the utmost significance'.[5]

By the time Cadogan and Dudley completed their periods of office, the loyalist opponents of Home Rule had come to be disillusioned with their performances. The glitter of their courts, their more discriminating choice of guests, the deference shown to old county families and the nobility, while making some gestures of sympathy to the old regime, were not really strengthening of the bonds of empire. It would have been impossible for any lord lieutenant to ignore the sharpening nationalism of the majority population, and it was essential that nothing should be done to incite further disloyalty. As in the past, the dilemma confronting lords lieutenant was how to keep both sides reasonably happy or, at best, unprovoked. The *Irish Protestant* found that Cadogan lost no opportunity of promoting the power and influence of the 'Italian Hierarchy and the priests at the expense of the loyal inhabitants'. Dudley was seen as having developed nationalist sympathies which were a 'disgraceful betrayal of the loyalists' and had their 'parallel in the infamies of James the Second'.[6]

In reality, the lord lieutenant was now no more than a symbol, powerless to influence political trends of the times. The battle for Ireland was being fought in Westminister, not in Dublin Castle. Despite the best efforts of Cadogan and Dudley, the vestiges of the old order were fast vanishing. If the majority of a traditional loyalist population were indifferent to the rituals associated with the viceregal court, there were, on the other hand, others anxious to make up any shortfall in attendances at Castle functions as an increasing number of middle class Catholics sought to distance themselves from the peasant origins from which most had sprung. Some in the professions had benefitted from the expanding university education; some had been small farmers, or small-town shopkeepers who had prospered. The strongly nationalist journal *The Leader* constantly railed against the snobbish, un-Irish attitudes engendered by fashionable Catholic boarding-schools for boys, like Castleknock and Clongowes Wood, or by elitist convents for girls, where the Irish language and other areas of Irish culture were given little attention and nationalist influences were diverted. *The Leader* termed the products of these schools *seoiníní*, or West Britons, who had allied themselves politically and culturally to British values. Mary Butler, a nationalist writer, lamented in the *New Ireland Review* in 1901 that 'the depth of anglicization in which the Irish gentlewoman is sunk is truly deplorable'.[7]

Augustine Birrell, who became chief secretary under the Liberal admin-istration in 1907 and was in office until he resigned following the Rising of 1916, quickly recognized that the viceregal administration had ceased to have any relevance to political or social life in Ireland. His speech in the House of Commons in May 1907 was a *cri de coeur*:

> I do not think that any chief secretary with the slightest tincture of popular feeling in his bones can enter the gloomy portals of Dublin Castle without a sinking of the heart almost amounting to an aban-donment of hope. It is not that Dublin Castle is a sink or seat of job-bery or corruption. It may have been once. It is certainly so no longer. But it is, to use a familiar expression, 'switched off' from the current of national life and feeling ... No pulse of real life runs through the place.[8]

The seven individuals, four Liberals and three Tories, who held vicere-gal office from 1892 to 1921 accepted that their main role was placatory. Only two, Cadogan and French, had seats in the cabinet; the others were completely subservient to their chief secretary. By the time Aberdeen arrived to take up office in December 1905, the best that he could hope for was that he should be kept informed about what was going on.[9]

THE ABERDEEN PERIOD

If there had been any lingering hopes among traditional loyalists that the viceregal court would have continued to acknowledge old values and provide occasion for civilized social intercourse among the established ruling classes, the return to office of Aberdeen was the *coup de grace*. His earlier brief sojourn in the Castle during 1886 had left no doubts about the strength of his commitment to Home Rule. His reappointment at the end of 1905 was to give him ten continuous years in office, longer than that of any previous holder of the post, during a period when successive proposals about the nature of Irish Home Rule dominated the business of Westminster. Aberdeen's persistent espousal of the nationalist views effectively ended the days of the viceregal court as a focus of the social life of that minority.

One Dublin architect, P.L. Dickinson, a member of the traditional Castle circle, wrote with indignation of Aberdeen's impact:

> The Liberal business was alright in England but in Ireland it was ill understood and Liberalism was translated as licence and licence it was. Social amenities were flung to the winds and the rag-tag and bobtail of Dublin went to court. After a few years of Aberdeen's term of office many people of breeding gave up all idea of going to the Castle and social life in Dublin underwent an amazingly rapid decline. Man after man of my own generation who formerly would, as a matter of course, have gone to the court functions, avoided them and laughed when the Castle was mentioned. Without being a snob, it was no pleasure, and rather embarrassing, to meet the lady at dinner who had measured you for your shirts the week before. As a result of this upsetting of values, social life in Dublin from the point of view of good breeding rapidly declined ...[10]

Gordon John Campbell, 7th Earl of Aberdeen (later 1st Marquess of Aberdeen and Temair), had always been an ardent liberal who from the early days campaigned zealously for the welfare of various groups, notably railway workers and small farmers in Scotland. His deeply felt religious and humanitarian concerns were shared by his wife, formerly Ishbel Maria Marjoribanks. They were a physically contrasting pair. He was small and bearded and usually wore kilts, sometimes handing out sprigs of heather on social occasions. She was large, domineering and outspoken. Once they had been assigned to Ireland they set out single-mindedly in pursuit of its interests, even though the viceregal post had become devoid of any power or influence. They were entirely sincere and tireless, anxious to advance the health and general welfare of the Irish, enthusiastic about encouraging Irish culture and promoting employment, always available to participate in a wide range of charitable events. *The Leader* commented that by the time he left Dublin, Aberdeen had opened everything in the city except the House of Parliament in College Green and the safe containing the crown jewels.[11]

Ishbel, as she was often popularly referred to, was indefatigable in the advancement of good health. Particularly conscious of the high toll of death in Ireland from tuberculosis, she founded the Women's National Health Association, which developed Peamount Sanatorium, sought better provisions for maternity and children, arranged a travelling exhibition on health education, campaigned against the habit of spitting, and encouraged householders to open their windows to let in fresh air. As an appendage to her travelling exhibition she brought into the more inaccessible parts of the country a horse caravan called Eire equipped with a magic lantern, a gramophone and an accompanying doctor. Her Irish crusade against tuberculosis became so well known in Britain that it was said that Irish domestic servants had difficulty in getting employment there because it was feared that they might spread infection.[12]

The legendary tight-fistedness of Aberdonians was often unfairly ascribed to the earl, and he and his wife took pains to demonstrate their generosity. In their memoirs they claimed to have entertained more people during their nine Castle seasons than any of their immediate successors. Innovations were introduced: afternoon receptions were held for members of the non-dancing community who 'liked to drop in, meet their friends and have a cup of tea'. This tea-and-buns hospitality was far removed from the grandeur of the Dudleys. During 1907 an Irish Lace Ball was held where all guests, male and female, were expected to wear something of lace; a later ball was organized to represent tableaux of different Irish industries. But attendance at the Castle was widely disdained by the nobility and the gentry and became ineffably middle-class. The list of 2000 participants at the St Patrick's Ball in 1907 shows that only about fifty or sixty titled persons were present, a reflection of the extent to which Aberdeen's espousal of Home Rule had made him anathema to loyalists. At the other extreme, those of strong nationalistic inclinations found it impossible to stomach the spectacle of the diminutive, kilted representative of the king dancing jigs and reels on the national feast day in the bastion of British power in Ireland. There were some exceptions. Constance Markievicz, prominent in Sinn Féin and other independence groups, and a later participant in the 1916 Rising, moved in the viceregal circle and danced at the Castle. But in general, according to Dickinson, an invitation to the Castle appealed only to those 'who liked to feel they were dressing up in feathers and trains and strutting in rarely worn evening suits and swimming in a dashing social life entirely foreign to their upbringing but congenial to their worldly ambitions'.[13] The personality of the lord lieutenant and his policies was a matter of indifference to them.

The Aberdeens found some of the ceremonial rituals to be irksome. On their first Sunday at the Castle, when they decided to walk the few hundred yards to a service in Christ Church Cathedral, they were required to become part of an accompanying procession: two policemen, two detectives in plain clothes, two aides-de-camp, two detectives, two policemen.[14] Anachronistic practices of this sort were dropped or ignored, but the traditional ceremonials and behavioural rules for levees, drawing-rooms and banquets continued to be observed, if not always treated with the same degree of reverence as in the past. Long-serving officials were often offended by Aberdeen's disregard for established niceties. When he decided to allow the filming of ceremonial processions in St Patrick's Hall and the installation of powerful arc lights for the purpose, it was seen as an intrusion into the traditional solemnity of the occasions. This led to a peremptory direction from London and a dropping of the proposal.[15]

The Aberdeens loved Ireland and disliked leaving it. To many they were figures of fun, even if at heart there was an underlying liking and respect for their sincerity and good intentions. They were the subject of satirical cartoons, ballads and amusing anecdotes of doubtful origin. As they left the Viceregal Lodge for the last time the massed band of the Royal Irish Constabulary broke into a popular music-hall tune, 'Hold your Hand out, Naughty Boy', said to have been intended as a rebuke to the marchioness for earlier declaring that the Artane Boys' Industrial School band was her favoured one. And as the farewell procession of the viceregal pair passed through the indifferent streets on their way to embark for England, an old apple-woman was heard to shout, 'There they go! There they go with their microbes and the crown jewels!'[16]

THEFT OF THE IRISH CROWN JEWELS

The great sensation of the Aberdeen administration was the theft of the Irish crown jewels.

On his death in 1893, Sir Bernard Burke had been succeeded as Ulster king-at-arms by his assistant Arthur Vicars, who was subsequently knighted. Vicars' father had died when he was young and his mother, a native of County Wicklow, remarried Pierce Mahony, who claimed descent from a high king of Munster. Vicars became very attached to his step-brothers George and Pierce. Pierce eventually inherited the old Irish title The O'Mahony and became a nationalist member of parliament, uncomfortable that his step-brother should hold office at the viceregal court.[17]

While his heraldic post was secure and independent, it would appear that by the end of 1903 Vicars' role in the ordering of the rituals of the viceregal court had become open to question. The official papers of the court show that his name had been dropped from the list of members of the household of lord lieutenant proposed for the 1904 edition of *Thom's Directory*. The decision to delete his name had been taken by Lord Plunket, private secretary to Dudley, the lord lieutenant, without consulting Vicars. Vicars became aware of his exclusion before the directory went for printing and as a result of vehement representations to Dudley had his name restored. Vicars claimed that he was the only official with responsibility for ensuring the continuation of the court's traditions; but the omission of his name in the first instance appears to have implied doubts about his role.

However, by 1905 standing orders governing the viceregal household and its staff clearly show that the king-at-arms had the main responsibility for overseeing and guiding ceremonial and social activities of the court. His heraldic status had also been strengthened following a revision of the constitution of the Order of Saint Patrick when posts of various heralds and pursuivants previously allowed to lapse were revived. In keeping with a long-standing tradition of nepotism, Vicars was able to give the post of Cork Herald to his nephew Pierce Gun Mahony, the post of Dublin Herald to his close friend Francis Shackleton, younger brother to the explorer, and that of Athlone Pursuivant to Francis Bennett-Goldney, an English friend with whom he had developed a mutual interest in silver, antiques and heraldic objects. None of these posts had salaries attaching to them but they carried a certain cachet and entrée to the viceregal circle.[18]

Among Vicars' responsibilities were the custody and care of the regalia of the Order of St Patrick, which came to be known as the Irish crown jewels. They included a great diamond star and diamond badge of the Grand Master, and five jewel-encrusted golden collars worn on ceremonial occasions by the knights companions. A statutory order of July 1905 provided that the jewels were to be deposited in a steel safe in the strong room of the Order alongside Vicars' office in Dublin Castle. On 6 July 1907, on the eve of a state visit by Edward VII during which the jewels were to be used in a ceremonial investiture, the safe was found open and all the badges and collars gone. They were never seen again. The theft of the jewels, then valued at about £50,000, was a sensation. A police investigation failed to unearth any clues. It was obvious that the strongroom and safe had been opened by their own keys and there was no indication of a forced entry. Various allegations and theories were aired publicly, culminating in the establishment of a commission to enquire into the loss of the regalia and into whether Vicars had 'exercised due vigilance and proper care as the custodian thereof'. Vicars himself refused to appear before the commission but he had already made statements to the police.[19]

The evidence showed obvious laxity in the control of keys in use in Vicars' office. There were at least seven keys giving admission to his office which were freely available to cleaners and messengers as well as to Vicars himself and Mahony, the Cork Herald. Four other keys gave access to the strongroom. There were only two keys to the actual safe which Vicars claimed were always in his custody: one carried on his person and the other in his home. But various persons had access to his home, including Francis Shackleton, with whom Vicars shared his house in Clonskeagh. The commission had no hesitation in concluding that Vicars had failed in his duty to care properly for the jewels and he was dismissed from his post. When he refused to hand over the keys of the strongroom to his successor as Ulster king-at-arms, Sir Neville Wilkinson, arrangements had to be made for the Board of Works to break into the room to recover the sword of state and other remaining regalia. Lord Aberdeen also asked for the resignations of Shackleton, Bennet-Goldney and Mahony. The first two resigned in 1907 but Mahony was allowed to continue in office, probably as a result of public agitation by his father against the findings of the commission.[20]

Vicars subsequently denied vehemently any suggestion that he was involved in the theft. However, evidence to the commission and subsequent information and public gossip revealed some extraordinary facts about the personalities and lifestyle of Vicars' office in Dublin Castle. Parties were held there frequently. Vicars himself was relatively abstemious but at times became intoxicated after a few glasses of sherry. The authors Bamford and Bankes describe an occasion when Vicars collapsed drunk and some of his staff removed the keys from his pocket and took the crown jewels to give him a fright.[21]

Vicars' colleagues were an odd group. Shackleton, who had been invalided out of the army, had an arrangement to pay half of the costs of the house that he shared with Vicars. According to evidence given to the commission, Vicars had difficulty in meeting his own share and had to borrow money from Shackleton, who in turn borrowed money to meet Vicars' needs from professional money-lenders and 'furniture men' in London. Bennet-Goldney, the Athlone Pursuivant, helped out by giving guarantees to the money-lenders.[22]

Shackleton, described by a friend as 'extremely depraved' and by the *Gaelic American* as an associate of men 'suspected of unspeakable and disgusting offences',[23] had an unsavoury reputation. Bennet-Goldney was a shadowy figure with no obvious reason to be attached to Irish affairs. A private report circulated by the under-secretary at Dublin Castle, Sir Augustine MacDonnell, indicated that Augustine Birrell, the chief secretary, believed that the theft of the jewels could have been brought about by Vicars' financial troubles and his entanglements with Shackleton and with a group of London homosexuals. The concentration of impecuniosity, fecklessness, ineptitude and moral turpitude within the coterie of the Ulster king-at-arms and his attendant heralds and pursuivants provided fertile territory for conspiracy and crime.

The mystery of the disappearance of the jewels was never solved, although over the years many theories were advanced, some bizarre. An eccentric barrister sought on a number of occasions to have Lord Aberdeen himself indicted for the theft. In November 1912 a story in a scurrilous weekly paper, the *London Mail*, suggested an alternative sexual orientation to the background to the stealing of the jewels. It alleged that Vicars had slept at the Castle with a mistress, Molly Robinson, on the night of the theft. She departed in the morning with the jewels. She was said to have been aggrieved with Vicars because he was simultaneously conducting an affair with Lady Haddo, daughter-in-law of Aberdeen. The paper refused to withdraw the allegations but, following a libel action taken by Vicars, a London court awarded him £5000 and costs after a short deliberation. It was a huge amount for the times. Lady Haddo, who gave evidence, said that she had met Vicars only once, in a casual way.[24]

Mahony, the Cork Herald, eventually resigned, practised for a while as a lawyer, and in July 1914 was found shot dead near his Kerry home with a shotgun by his side. Bennett-Goldney later became an independent unionist member of parliament for Canterbury and died in 1918. Shackleton was tried for fraud in England during 1913 and was imprisoned for fifteen months. He died in Chichester, England, in June 1941. In April 1921 Arthur Vicars was taken from his home, Kilmorna House near Listowel, County Kerry, by an armed group. He was murdered and a placard was attached to his body which read, 'Spy. Informers beware. IRA never forgets.' His home was burnt to the ground. The IRA later denied responsibility.[25]

ROYAL VISITS

The period from the turn of the century to the beginning of the world war in 1914 was remarkable for the number of visits by British monarchs to Ireland. Victoria arrived in 1900; Edward VII and Queen Alexandra in 1903, informally in 1904, and again in 1907; and George V and Queen Mary came in 1911. The frequency of the visits was influenced by threats to British-Irish links arising from the demands for Home Rule and the more distant rumbles about national independence. Royal visits were seen as affirmations of support for the union and were viewed by the government and particularly by the unionist minority as a means of encouraging loyalty to personalities who clearly projected no political or physical threat, while conveying a sense of continuity, solidarity and even benevolence. When Edward's proposed visit was announced in 1903, English newspapers sympathetic to the unionist viewpoint hoped for a warm Irish welcome. The *Daily Mail* reported that the royal couple were received 'quietly but cordially' apart from minor gestures of dissent, such as the refusal of Dublin Corporation to present an address of welcome. This, according to the *Daily Express*, was orchestrated 'by Mrs Maud Gonne MacBride and the 'bhoys in the gallery'. Mrs MacBride also tried to deter 'patriotic children' from attending a gathering in the Phoenix Park of children from the slums to honour the king. About 1800 children went to the park; only about 100 children attended Mrs MacBride's rival mustering.[26]

If the majority population was at best indifferent to its royal visitors, cavalcades, circuses and marching bands were certain to draw crowds into the streets. It was not always necessary to know who or what was being feted. When Edward VII visited Killary harbour during a tour of Connemara in 1903 a local dignitary called for three cheers for 'King Henry VI', a call taken up with enthusiasm by the onlookers. There were large crowds in the streets when Edward again visited Dublin in 1904 to lay the foundation of the new College of Science. Dublin Corporation for a second time refused to give him an address of welcome. When Edward returned to Ireland in 1907, the *Irish Independent*, encouraging a trouble-free visit, went to pains to point out that the king was 'a strictly constitutional monarch who is no way responsible for the misgovernment of Ireland'.[27]

When the newly crowned George V and Queen Mary arrived for a four-day visit in July 1911 there was an elaborate programme of festivities and large numbers in the streets. Once again Dublin Corporation refused to recognize the visit. A stand erected at Baggot Street bridge to allow dignitaries to watch the traditional presentation of the city's keys to the king on his arrival was found to have been daubed with green paint on the morning of the ceremony and could not be used. And Walter Carpenter, secretary of the Socialist Party of Ireland, addressing a crowd in Beresford Place, protested about being asked to honour 'the offspring of one of the vilest scoundrels that ever entered the country'. He was charged with disturbing the peace and sent to jail for a month in default of a fine. But the protests were muted. Huge numbers attended the levee and the drawing-room at the Castle as well as the military review in the Phoenix Park and the garden party at the Viceregal Lodge.[28] If the loyalist community had turned its back on Aberdeen and had been shunning the Castle, it was prepared to return in great strength to it, albeit temporarily, for royal visits.

WIMBORNE

Ivor Churchill, 1st Viscount Wimborne, a cousin of Winston Churchill, was attached to the staff of the British forces in the Curragh when appointed lord lieutenant in February 1915. He was enormously rich, a connoisseur of the arts, and a sportsman with a reputation as a polo player. He and his wife, a smart and sophisticated duo, fitted easily into the leading parts of what had become the charade of the Irish viceregal court. In deference to war conditions, the court's social programme was largely confined to the Viceregal Lodge rather than the Castle.

Even in its reduced scale there was some questioning of the flamboyant hospitality of the Wimbornes at a time of increasingly calamitous casualty lists from the Western front. They dined off gold plate with a retinue of powdered, colourfully liveried footmen, who, according to one guest, looked like 'a strange assembly of clowns'. Lady Cynthia Asquith, daughter-in-law of the prime minister, visited the Wimbornes during 1915 and early 1916 and later commented frankly and amusingly on what she saw. The lord lieutenant and his lady assumed all the attitudes and affectations of a regal couple. At dinner parties there was much fawning and deferring and standing about while 'Their Majesties' moved around bestowing a few words on each guest. The curtseying when one left the room was 'terrifying'. She described Lady Wimborne played her queenly role to perfection with 'a heaven-born manner', while Wimborne was 'just a fairly frank bounder' who swilled brandy and had 'a terrible way of flapping his furry eyelids at one'. Lady Cynthia was relieved not to be invited into his private sitting-room, a practice extended to other ladies from time to time.[29]

THE GREAT WAR AND EASTER 1916

The viceregal lifestyle was now at an utter remove from the grim realities of the conflict and upheaval around it. At the Western front thousands of young men were dying without knowledge or understanding of the reason why. Among them were many sons and brothers and other members of Irish Ascendancy families for whom the Castle had been a familiar haunt. They had gone to war unquestioningly as a duty to be fulfilled, an inseparable part of their loyalty to England. At the same time, many other Irishmen, mainly of humble origin, for whom the life of Dublin Castle had been remote, even forbidden, were also dying in Flanders, on the Marne, the Somme and on the other fronts in Belgium and northern France. They died together, gentry and peasant, united in valour, mingling blood in the mud of battlefields.

Others chose to die in a different war, in Ireland for Ireland. At Easter 1916 the Irish Volunteers and Citizen Army struck for national freedom and occupied the General Post Office and other central Dublin buildings. After almost a week of intense fighting, hundreds of insurgents died before the survivors surrendered to British forces. Within days of the surrender fifteen rebel leaders were executed by the English, planting the seeds of a freedom that was now inevitable.

Wimborne was recalled to London after the Easter Rising but later exonerated from blame for failing to anticipate it. He returned to Dublin and remained in office until May 1918 when he was replaced by Lord French.[30] French had resigned as commander-in-chief of British forces in France because of his military shortcomings in the conduct of war. In Ireland he found himself in another, smaller theatre of conflict, as the war of independence developed and intensified from 1918 to 1921. The general election of 1918 was a triumph for Sinn Féin, which won 73 of the 105 Irish seats. Sinn Féin members of parliament met separately and constituted themselves an independent parliament, Dáil Éireann, and provisionally established a republic.

By 1920 the machinery of British administration of Ireland at Dublin Castle had been put out of action. The traditional role and rituals of the viceregal court at the Castle were at an end, but for those prepared to brave the hazards of the Phoenix Park, French managed to provide a social programme of dances and dinners at the Viceregal Lodge while presiding over a policy of military aggression and reprisal against the population at large. He resigned in April 1921 during the last few months of a dying administration to make way for the legislative changes then contemplated, and was replaced by Edmund Bernard Talbot, Lord FitzAlan.[31]

A SUNSET TOUCH

The Castle itself reverted from 1918 onwards to its historic role as a fortress in the midst of a hostile territory. There was a drawing in of forces, an encircling of wagons. The gate of the upper yard remained closed; the main gate in the lower yard had a permanent guard of police and military who challenged all comers. French applied a spartan economy to the viceregal staff of the court, retaining only the minimum entourage necessary for essential official routines. Others were added to the population of the Castle: senior police personnel, army officers, intelligence officers, English civil servants working in Irish departments and moved into living quarters for their own protection, typists brought surreptitiously from England to support the beleaguered regime as Irish typists were suspect. A well-guarded hostel was established outside the lower gate for wives and typists who could not be accompanied within.

Social life of a kind went on within the walls. During the afternoons some loyalist members of Dublin society would take part in *thés dansants* to the accompaniment of popular tunes of the period. At nighttime others would brave the hazards of a curfew to join the engarrisoned personnel and their womenfolk for dances in St Patrick's Hall to the music of a military or police band. From pre-war years it had become customary to have the odd party at the Castle for children of senior officials; a highlight was the annual Christmas fancy-dress dance hosted by the lord lieutenant. Enid Starkie, whose father was a commissioner of education, wrote in her memoirs that it was unheard of for a family to refuse an invitation to that party, such was the status it carried. The children themselves were not always impressed by the event since it was usually overcrowded, the band small and inaudible, and the refreshments, provided by a firm of school caterers, 'undistinguished and uninteresting'. One such children's party at the beginning of January 1922 marked the last social function held in Dublin Castle before the British administration handed over to the Provisional Government of Ireland.[32]

The last ceremonial event of the Irish viceregal court took place some days later, on 16 January 1922, when members of the Provisional Government led by Michael Collins arrived by taxi at the Castle where by arrangement they met the lord lieutenant, Viscount FitzAlan, and heads of the outgoing departments in Ireland. A red carpet was laid down but this appeared to be in deference to the lord lieutenant rather than in recognition of the Irish leaders. There was no prescribed court dress. Collins and his colleagues arrived somewhat dishevelled. An observer described their tweed caps and unpolished boots, their hair, collars and ties in disarray, their unshaven faces.[33] FitzAlan received from Collins the formal ratification of the Treaty with Britain and in turn handed over Dublin Castle and the entire administration of government to the Irish representatives, introducing them to the heads of departments. It was a ceremony without ceremonial. There were no rituals, no trumpets, no liveried courtiers, no drinks on the sideboard. The following day the *Irish Times* summed up the event:

> After its fluctuating history of seven centuries Dublin Castle is no longer the fortress of British power in Ireland. Having withstood the attacks of successive generations of rebels, it was quietly handed over yesterday to eight gentlemen in three taxicabs.

The Lords Lieutenant of Ireland 1700–1922

	Date of Appointment
Laurence Hyde, Earl of Rochester	December 1700
James Butler, 2nd Duke of Ormond	February 1703
	Returned November 1704
Thomas Herbert, Earl of Pembroke and Montgomery	April 1707
Thomas Wharton, 1st Earl of Wharton	December 1708
	Returned May 1710
James Butler, 2nd Duke of Ormond	October 1710
Charles Talbot, Duke of Shrewsbury	September 1713
Charles Spencer, Earl of Sunderland	September 1714
Charles, Viscount Townshend	February 1717
Charles Plowett, 2nd Duke of Bolten	April 1717
Charles Fitzroy, 2nd Duke of Grafton	June 1720
	Returned August 1723
John Carteret, 2nd Baron Carteret	May 1724
Baron Carteret	October 1727
Lionel Cranfield Sackville, 1st Duke of Dorset	June 1730
	Returned September 1733
	Returned September 1735

William Cavendish, 3rd Duke of Devonshire	April 1737
	Returned March 1740
	Returned September 1741
	Returned 1743
Philip Dormer Stanhope, 4th Earl of Chesterfield	January 1745
William Stanhope, 1st Earl of Harrington	November 1746
	Returned September 1749
Duke of Dorset	December 1750
	Returned September 1753
William Cavendish, Marquis of Harrington, 4th Duke of Devonshire	April 1755
John Russell, 4th Duke of Bedford	January 1757
	Returned October 1759
George Montague-Dunk, Earl of Halifax	April 1761
Hugh Percy, 2nd Duke of Northumberland	April 1763
Thomas Thynne, 3rd Viscount Weymouth	June 1765
Francis Seymour-Conway, Earl of Hertford	August 1765
George William Hervey, 2nd Earl of Bristol	October 1766
George Townshend, 4th Viscount Townshend	August 1767
Simon Harcourt, 1st Earl Harcourt	October 1772
John Hobart, 2nd Earl of Buckinghamshire	December 1776
Frederick Howard, 5th Earl of Carlisle	November 1780
William Henry Cavendish Bentinck, 3rd Duke of Portland	April 1782
George Nugent-Temple-Grenville, 3rd Earl Temple	August 1782
Robert Henley, 2nd Earl of Northington	May 1783
Charles Manners, 4th Duke of Rutland	February 1784
George Nugent-Temple-Grenville, Marquis of Buckingham	November 1787
John Fane, 10th Earl of Westmorland	October 1789
William Wentford Fitzwilliam, 2nd Earl Fitzwilliam	December 1794
John Jeffreys Pratt, 2nd Earl Camden	March 1795
Charles Cornwallis, 1st Marquis Cornwallis	June 1798
Philip Yorke, 3rd Earl of Hardwicke	March 1801
Edward Clive, 1st Earl of Powis	November 1805
John Russell, 6th Duke of Bedford	February 1806
Charles Lennox, 4th Duke of Richmond	April 1807
Charles Whitworth, 1st Baron Whitworth	June 1813
Charles Chetwynd Talbot, 2nd Earl Talbot	September 1817
Richard Wellesley, 1st Marquis Wellesley	December 1821
Henry William Paget, 1st Marquis of Anglesey	February 1828
Hugh Percy, 3rd Duke of Northumberland	February 1829
Marquis of Anglesey	November 1830
Marquis Wellesley	September 1833
Thomas Hamilton, 9th Earl of Haddington	December 1834
Constantine Henry Phipps, 6th Earl of Mulgrave	April 1835
Hugh Fortescue, Viscount Ebrington	March 1839

Thomas Philip de Grey, 2nd Earl Grey	September 1841
William A'Court, 1st Baron Heytesbury	July 1844
John William Ponsonby, 4th Earl of Bessborough	July 1846
George William Frederick Villiers, 4th Earl of Clarendon	May 1847
Archibald William Montgomerie, 13th Earl of Eglington	February 1852
Edward Granville Eliot, 3rd Earl of St Germans	January 1853
George William Frederick Howard, 7th Earl of Carlisle	February 1855
Earl of Eglinton	February 1858
Earl of Carlisle	June 1859
John Wodehouse, 3rd Baron Wodehouse	November 1864
James Hamilton, 2nd Marquis of Abercorn	July 1866
John Poyntz Spencer, 5th Earl Spencer	December 1868
Duke of Abercorn	March 1874
John Winston Spencer Churchill, 7th Duke of Marlborough	November 1876
Francis Thomas de Grey Cowper, 7th Earl Cowper	May 1880
Earl Spencer	May 1882
Henry Howard Molyneux Herbert, 4ht Earl of Carnarvon	June 1885
John Campbell Hamilton Gordon, 7th Earl of Aberdeen	February 1886
Charles Stewart Vance-Tempest-Stewart, 6th Marquis of Londonderry	August 1886
Lawrence Dundas, 3rd Earl of Zetland	July 1889
Robert Offley Ashburton Milnes, 2nd Baron Houghton	August 1892
George Hanry Cadogan, 6th Earl Cadogan	June 1895
William Humble Ward, 3rd Earl of Dudley	August 1902
Earl of Aberdeen	December 1905
Ivor Churchill Guest, 2nd Baron Wimborne	February 1915
John Denton Pinkstone French, 1st Viscount French of Ypres and High Lake	May 1918
Lord Edmund Bernard Talbot	April 1921

Source: *A New History of Ireland*, vol. 9, pp. 491-500

Notes

CHAPTER ONE

1 Maguire, J.B. *Dublin Castle – Historical Background and Guide* (Dublin 1992), pp. 8-13. Bayley, William J., *Historical Sketch and Description of Dublin Castle*, pp. 15-20. O'Dwyer, Frederick, 'Dublin Castle and the State Apartments 1997' in *The Court Historian* (February 1997).
2 Cal. MSS Marquis of Ormond, pp. 133-4, 497-9, HMC 7 1912: Rep. MSS Marquis of Ormond 2, p. 256 (London 1899). *Dict. Nat. Biog.* 19, pp. 331-3.
3 Beattie, John M., *The English Court in the Reign of George I* (Cambridge 1967), p. 11. Stanhope, Earl, *History of England comprising the Reign of Queen Anne 1701-1713* (London 1870), p. 566. Molloy, J. Fitzgerald, *Court Life Below Stairs*, 4 vols (London 1883), 2, p. 121.
4 Stanhope, op. cit., p. 82.
5 MSS of Earl of Onslow, HMC Rep. 14, app., pt. 9 (London 1895), p. 508.
6 *Dict. Nat. Biog.* 19, p. 1038. O'Mahony, Charles, *The Viceroys of Ireland* (London 1895), pp. 137-8.

CHAPTER TWO

1 McCracken, J.L., 'The Political Structure 1714-60' in T.W. Moody and W.E. Vaughan (eds), *A New History of Ireland*, vol. 4, p. 58. Johnston, Edith M.,

Great Britain and Ireland 1760-1800 (London 1963), p. 19.

2   Calendar of MSS of Marquis of Ormonde, New series vol. 8 (London 1920), pp. xxxviii-liii. Report MSS Mrs Frankland-Russell-Astley (London 1900), p. 194. *Lives of the Stuart Age 1603-1714* (London 1976), pp. 46-7. *Dict. Nat. Biog.* 3, pp. 512-17. Smith, Robert, *Court Cookery or the Compleat English Cook* (Dublin 1724).

3   O'Mahony, op. cit., p. 129.

4   O'Mahony, op. cit., pp. 129-32. Jonathan Swift (ed. Herbert Davis), *Miscellaneous and Autobiographical Pieces etc.* (Oxford 1982), p. 258. 'A Short Character of His Excellency Thomas Earl of Wharton, Lord Lieutenant of Ireland' in *Prose Works of Jonathan Swift* (ed. Temple Scott) 5, pp. 1-28. Carswell, John, *The Old Cause* (London 1954), pp. 109-10. Swift, *Prose Works* 2, p. 34

5   O'Mahony, op. cit., pp. 134-5. *Dict. Nat. Biog.*, pp. 301-7. *The Wentworth Papers 1705-1739* (London 1887), pp. 213-14, 263, 424, 439. *Whalley's Newsletter*, 30 Aug.–2 June 1716. *The Complete Peerage* 11, pp. 720-4.

6   Maxwell, Constantia, *Dublin Under the Georges 1714-1830* (London 1936), p. 100.

7   Froude, James A., *The English in Ireland in the Eighteenth Century*, 2 vols (London 1872), 1, p. 533. Walpole, Horace, *Memoirs of the Last Ten Years of George the Second*, 2 vols (London 1822), 1, p. 157-9. Burns, Robert E., *Irish Parliamentary Politics in the Eighteenth Century*, 2 vols (Washington 1989), 1, p. 113. Swift, *Miscellaneous and Autobiographical Pieces etc.*, p. 258. *Irish Happiness Compleated or a new Poem on His Grace the Duke of Grafton* (Dublin 1723). O'Mahony, op. cit., p. 138. Waldegrave, James Earl, *Memoirs from 1754–1758* (London 1821), p. 114. *The Complete Peerage* 6, pp. 45-6.

8   Walpole, Horace, *Memoirs of the Last Ten Years of the Reign of George the Second*, 1, p. 146. *Dict. Nat. Biog.* 3, pp. 1119-24. O'Mahony, op. cit., pp. 139-44. Granville, Mary, Mrs Delany, *Autobiography and Correspondence*, First Series (London 1861), 1, p. 290. Pemberton, W. Baring. *Carteret: The Brilliant Failure of the Eighteenth Century* (London 1936), pp. 108-10. Ballantyne, Archibald, *Lord Carteret: A Political Biography 1690-1763* (London 1887), pp. 133-8.

9   Pemberton, op. cit., p. 110.

10 *A Contest between Marsyas and Apollo to be presented at the birthday of George, King of Great Britain etc, Dublin, May 1723*; *A Serenade to be presented ... at Dublin Castle, May 1725*; this collection of pamphlets in Trinity College, Dublin, also includes celebratory verses for 1726 and 1727. Burns, op. cit., 1, p. 191.

11 Fitzmaurice, Edmond, Life of William, Earl of Shelburne (London 1875), 1, p. 341. Walpole, op. cit., 1, p. 84. Hammond, Joseph W., *The Hell-fire Club* (Dublin n.d.), pp. 4-5.

12 *Pue's Occurrences*, 13 Oct., 3 Nov., 6 Nov. 1733; 22 Jan., 2 March 1734. *Faulkner's Dublin Journal*, 24 Feb.–2 March 1734.

13 Granville, op. cit., 1, pp. 289, 290, 294, 301, 308, 337. Murray, Margie, 'Enter-

tainment in Eighteenth-Century Dublin' in *Dub. Hist. Rec.* 22 (4), p. 293. *The Correspondence of Jonathan Swift*, 5 vols (Oxford 1905), 4, p. 423. Henrietta, Countess of Suffolk, *Letters*, 2 vols (London 1824), 2, p. 34.

14 *Dict. Nat. Biog.* 17, pp. 582-3. Walpole, op. cit., 1, p. 244. *Faulkner's Dublin Journal*, 7-11 January 1755. *The Orrery Papers*, 2 vols (London 1903) 2, pp. 118-25. Molloy, J. Fitzgerald, *The Life and Adventures of Peg Woffington*, 2 vols (London 1884) 1, p. 267; 2, pp 2-10. Report on the MSS of Mrs Stopford-Sackville, vol. 1 (London 1904), p. 183.

15 Burns, op. cit., 2, p. 36. O'Mahony, op. cit., p. 146.

16 Gilbert, Sir J.T. and Lady (eds), *Calendar of Ancient Records of Dublin*, 19 vols 4, pp. 460, 461; 6, pp. 90, 178. O'Carroll, Joseph, 'Towards the Homeless Poor 1725-1775' in *The Gorgeous Mask* (ed. D. Dickson) (Dublin 1987).

17 *Faulkner's Dublin Journal*, 23-26 April 1737. Robins, Joseph, *The Lost Children* (Dublin 1980), p. 17.

18 O'Mahony, op. cit., pp. 146-51. Stanhope, Philip Dormer, Earl of Chesterfield, *Miscellaneous Works*, 3 vols (Dublin 1777), 2, p. 272; 3, pp. 400-4. Burns, op. cit., 2, pp. 72-83. *Annual Register* (London 1774), pp. 22-3. *Lives of the Georgian Age* (London 1978), pp. 403-5. Craig, op. cit., pp. 162-3. Buckinghamshire, Earl of, Manuscripts HMC, Fourteenth Report, app., part 9 (London 1895), p. 131. *The Orrery Papers*, 2 vols (London 1903), 2, pp. 40-1. Ernst-Browning, William, *Memoirs ... Fourth Earl of Chesterfield* (London 1906), pp. 252-7. *The Letters of Lord Chesterfield*, 6 vols (London 1932), 1, pp. 121, 130. Shellabarger, Samuel, *Lord Chesterfield* (London 1935), pp. 225-36.

19 Orrery Papers 1, p. 320.

20 Orrery Papers 2, Orrery to Mead, 21 Nov. 1749. O'Mahony, op. cit., pp. 152-6. Foster, op. cit., pp. 238-9. Burns 2, p. 117. Montgomery, K.L., 'Successful Beauties of the Last of the Century' in *New Ireland Review* (Dublin 1896), 5, pp. 227-9. *Dict. Nat. Biog.* 18, pp. 927-31.

21 O'Mahony, op. cit., p. 161. *Faulkner's Journal*, 19-22 April, 3-6, 6-10, 10-13, 13-17, 24-27 May 1755.

22 *Faulkner's Journal*, 30 May–3 June 1755, 8-11 Nov. 1755. *Dict. Nat. Biog.* 3 pp. 1284-5. MSS Leinster Papers, correspondence of James Edward Fitzgerald 1752-62; to his wife, 13 May 1755. Hardy, Francis, *Memoirs of James Caulfeild, Earl of Charlemont*, 2 vols (London 1812), 1, p. 91

23 Walpole 2, pp. 254-9. O'Mahony, op. cit., pp. 162-3. *Faulkner's Journal*, 22-5 Oct.; 29 Oct.–1 Nov.; 8-12 Nov. 1757; 3-7 Jan.; 24-8 Jan. 1758. *Correspondence of John, Fourth Duke of Bedford*, 3 vols (London 1842), 2, pp. xx-xxii, 335. Correspondence of Emily, Duchess of Leinster, 2, p. 85. Manuscripts of Theodore J. Hare, HMC Rep. 14, app., pt. 9 (London 1895), letter R. Marsham to F. Naylor, 13 Nov. 1761. Charlemont, *Memoirs*, 1, p. 107. Craig, Maurice, *Dublin 1660-1860*, pp. 104, 107, 173.

24 Foster, op. cit., pp. 222-3. O'Mahony, op. cit., p. 163.

25 O'Mahony, op. cit., pp. 164-7. *The Complete Peerage* 6, p. 247. *Dict. Nat.*

Biog. 6, pp. 199-201. *Gentleman's Magazine* 32 (1762), pp. 133-4.

26 O'Mahony, op. cit., pp. 167-9. *The Complete Peerage* 9, p. 743. Greig, James, *The Diaries of a Duchess* (London 1926), pp. xiv-xvi; 57-8. *Dict. Nat. Biog.* 15, pp. 803-05. *Freeman's Journal*, 20-24 Sept. 1763. *Journals of the Irish House of Commons 1761-1764*, 7, p. 360.

27 Walpole, Horace, *Correspondence with the Countess of Upper Ossory*, 3 vols (Yale 1965), 1, pp. 14-15. Bedford Correspondence, 3, p. 322. *The Complete Peerage* 6, pp. 509-10. *Dict Nat. Biog.* 4, p. 496. *Gentleman's Magazine* 64, pt. 1, p. 581. Delany, op. cit., p. 129.

CHAPTER THREE

1   Vernon-Barton Papers: The court chamberlain's records of the households of the lords lieutenant of Ireland, rules of precedence etc., 1713-71 (NAI).

2   Hatton, Ragnhild, *George I: Elector and King* (London 1978), pp. 141-3.

3   Buckingham Papers MSS 13035 (12).

4   Harrowby Papers PRONI MSS T3228/1/10, Bishop of Down to Sir Dudley Ryder, 25 Oct. 1743. Willes, Baron, PRONI MSS T 2855/1, Miscellaneous Observations on Ireland 1759-60.

5   Burke, Bernard, *The Rise of Great Families* (London 1873), pp. 234-8.

6   Berry, H.F., 'Notes from the Diary of a Dublin Lady' in *JRSAI*, 8, fifth series, 1898, p. 147.

7   VB Papers: papers of establishment of Duke of Devonshire: attendances to be observed by the lord lieutenant's household. Hatton, pp. 141-3. Beattie, John M., *The English Court in the Reign of George I*, pp. 5-31.

8   *Faulkner's Dublin Journal*, 11-15 March 1755.

9   Johnson, Edith M., *Great Britain and Ireland 1760-1800* (London 1963), p. 21.

10 *Freeman's Journal*, 5-7 Nov. 1782; 10-13 March 1787.

11 Harcourt Papers (ed. W.E. Harcourt), 14 vols, 1880 etc., 3, p. 131.

12 VB Papers: diary of Lord Carlisle's household and successive lord-lieutenants' 1781-1784; duties of the gentleman usher to the ladies c. 1780. *Dict. Nat. Biog.* 17, pp. 66-88. Barrington, Jonah, *Personal Sketches of His Own Times*, 3 vols (London 1832), 1, pp. 115-18.

13 Carlisle Diary: 8 March, 15 Nov., 25 Dec. 1781; May 1783.

14 Sharpe, J. Cecil, *The Dance: an Historical Survey of Dancing in Europe* (London 1924), pp. 24-8. Sachs, Curt, *World History of the Dance* (London 1938), pp. 391-8.

15 O'Dwyer, Frederick, 'The Ballroom of Dublin Castle' in *Decantations*, ed. Agnes Bernelle (Dublin 1992). Report on MSS of Reginald Rawdon Hastings, 3, p. 152 in HMC (London 1934), Willes MSS, Miscellaneous Observations, p. 37.

16 Swift, Jonathan, *Correspondence* (ed. Harold Williams), 5 vols (Oxford 1905),

4, p. 467 fn.

17 Leinster Papers: Louise Connolly correspondence, 29 Nov. 1775. *Freeman's Journal*, 8-11 Feb. 1772.

18 *Freeman's Journal*, 25-27 Sept 1770: *Dict. Nat. Biog.* 9, p. 377. O'Keeffe, John, *Recollections of the Life of John O'Keeffe* (Dublin 1826), 2, p. 256.

19 Cassidy, James p. , *Treatise on the Theory and Practice of Dancing* (Dublin 1810).

20 VB Papers: The forms of the state ceremonies attending the lord lieutenant of Ireland c. 1798.

21 VB Papers: Diary of the Carlisle household etc., 19 Feb 1782. Harcourt Papers, 11, p. 760.

22 VB Papers: Diary of the Carlisle household etc., 1781-84. The forms of the state ceremonies attending the lord lieutenant of Ireland (undated but water-marked 1798). Carswell, John, *From Revolution to Revolution: England 1688-1776* (London 1973), pp. 91-2. MacCaffrey, James, *History of the Catholic Church in the Nineteenth Century* (1789-1908), 2 vols (Dublin 1909), 2, pp. 104, 115.

23 MSS of Duke of Rutland in HMC Fourteenth Report, app., pt. 1 (London 1896), p. 78

24 Dunlevy, Mairead, *Dress in Ireland* (London 1989), p. 92. Laver, James, *Taste and Fashion from the French Revolution until Today* (London 1937), pp. 25-8. *Hibernian Magazine*, April 1787, p. 174. *Gentlemen's Magazine*, 1788, pt. 1, p. 355.

25 *Pue's Occurrences*, 15 Jun. 1731. Dunlevy, pp. 93-4. *Freeman's Journal*, 19-23 Feb. 1765; 26-8 Feb., 20-23 April 1782; 27-9 May, 5-8 June 1784. Leinster Papers: Charlotte Fitzgerald correspondence, 3 June 1778.

CHAPTER FOUR

1 Townshend Papers (NAI) M730 (53), Thomas Allan to Townshend, 26 Dec. 1770.

2 Froude, James A., *The English in Ireland in the Eighteenth Century*, 2 vols (London 1872), p. 116.

3 Townshend Papers: M734 NAI. Hunt, William (ed.), *The Irish Parliament 1775* (London 1907), p. xix.

4 Walpole, Horace, *Memoirs of the Reign of George the Third*, 4 vols (London 1845), 3, pp. 109-12; 4, pp. 348. Tenth Report HMC, The MSS of Charles Fleetwood Weston (London 1885), p. 417.

5 *The Hibernian Magazine*, 1771, pp. 452-3.

6 Bartlett, Thomas, *Macartney in Ireland 1768-1772* (Belfast 1982), p. 268.

7 O'Mahony, op. cit., pp. 173-8. Montgomery, K.L., 'Successful Beauties of the Last Century' in *New Ireland Review* 5 (Dublin 1896), pp. 227-44.

8 Bartlett, op. cit., p. 163. *Faulkner's Journal*, 12-15 Sept. 1772.

9 *Walker's Hibernian Magazine*, October 1776, p. 664. *Dict. Nat. Biog.* 8, pp. 1209-10. Charlemont, *Memoirs*, 1, p. 317.

10 Froude, op. cit., 2, p. 158.

11 Howard, Hugh, Parliamentary History of Ireland, HMC Rep. 3, 1872-4, p. 433. Harcourt Papers 10, pp. 143, 157. Darnely Papers MSS T251/2 Lady Clanwilliam to John, third Earl of Darnely, 1776.

12 Cornforth, John, 'Dublin Castle' in *Country Life*, July-Aug. 1970, pp. 342-3. O'Mahony, op. cit., pp. 179-80. Harcourt Papers (ed. W.E. Harcourt), 1880 etc., 14 vols, 3, Harcourt to Lady Nuneham, 25 Dec. 1772; Lord Nuneham to Whitehead, 22 June 1777. *The Complete Peerage* 6, p. 300.

13 Fitzgerald, *Correspondence of Emily Duchess of Leinster*, 3, p. 168. Howard, p. 433.

14 *Dict. Nat. Biog.* 8, pp. 1209-10.

15 Buckingham Papers: MSS 13034 (4), 13035 (3). Leinster Papers: MSS 617. Dickson, David, *New Foundations: Ireland 1660-1800* (Dublin 1987), pp. 130-1. Dunlevy, p. 95.

16 MSS 13035 (3). Buckinghamshire Papers in Report on MSS of Marquis of Lothian, HMC (London 1905), p. 337.

17 Foster, op. cit., pp. 172 fn., 240: *Dict. Nat. Biog.* 9, pp. 926-7. Leinster Papers: correspondence of Charlotte Fitzgerald, to her mother, 28 July 1778. *The Complete Peerage* 6, p. 401-2.

18 *Dict. Nat. Biog.* 10, p. 15. O'Mahony, op. cit., pp. 181-6. MSS of Earl of Carlisle in Fifteenth Report HMC (London 1897), app., pt. 6, p. 532.

19 Carlisle MSS, pp. 544-5.

20 Falkiner, op. cit., pp. 483-4. O'Dwyer, 'State Apartments', p. 4.

21 Diary of Carlisle's household (NAI), 10 April 1782. *Freeman's Journal*, 20-23 April 1782.

22 Foster, op. cit., pp. 247-55.

23 O'Mahony, pp. 186-7. Lecky, op. cit., 2, p. 461. MSS diary of Carlisle's household, 21 April, 12 Aug. 1782; 8 Jan., May 1783. *Freeman's Journal*, 5-7 Nov. 1782, 11-14 Jan. 1783. Fortescue MSS in Thirteenth Report HMC (London 1892), app., pt. 3, p. 180. Walpole, *Memoirs ... George the Third*, 2, p. 622. Charlemont, *Memoirs*, 1, p. 88, 2, p. 65. O'Connell, op. cit., pp. 359-61.

24 *The Complete Peerage* 9, p. 700. O'Connell, p. 361. Diary of Carlisle household Nov. 1783–Feb. 1784. Charlemont, *Memoirs*, 2, p. 81. Foster, op. cit., p. 228.

25 Foster, op. cit., p. 252.

26 Lecky, op. cit. 2, p. 461: Grattan, Henry, *Memoirs of the Life and Times of the Rt. Hon. Henry Grattan*, 5 vols (London 1839), 3, pp. 278-9. *Freeman's Journal*, 15-18, 27-9 May 1784: Wraxall, N.W., *Posthumous Memoirs of his Own Times*, 3 vols (London 1836), 2, p. 354. Hardy, Francis, *Memoirs of James Caulfeild, Earl of Charlemont*, 2nd ed., 2 vols (London 1812), p. 143. Gordon, James, *A History of Ireland*, 2 vols (Dublin 1805), 2, p. 298. 'Sixty Years Ago' in *DUM* 21, p. 733.

27 VB Papers. Diary of Lord Carlisle's Household etc.: 17 March 1784. *Hibernian Magazine*, March 1784, p. 164.
28 Lyons, Mary, ed., *The Memoirs of Mrs. Leeson, Madam, 1727-1797* (Dublin 1995), pp. 143-4.
29 MSS of Duke of Rutland, vol. 3 in HMC Fourteenth Report, app., pt. 1 (London 1894), pp. 253, 266, 274, 276, 291, 331, 335, 345, 363. *Hibernian Magazine*, 1785, p. 1613. Wraxall 2, p. 350. Buckinghamshire Papers in Report on MSS, Marquis of Lothian, HMC (London 1905), p. 29. Barrington, Jonah, *Historic Memoirs of Ireland*, 2 vols (London 1835), 2, p. 188.
30 Trench, Mrs Richard, *The Remains of the Late Mrs Richard Trench* (ed. Dean of Westminister), 2nd ed. (London 1862), pp. 8-16. MSS of the Earl of Donoughmore in Twelfth Report, HMC (London 1891), app., pt. 9, pp. 313-15.
31 Gamble, J., *Sketches of the History, Politics, and Manners taken in Dublin ... Autumn of 1810* (Dublin 1811), p. 53. Wilkinson, Neville R., *To All and Singular* (London 1925), pp. 42-3. Wraxall, 2, p. 351. MSS of Duke of Rutland, vol. 3 in Fourteenth Report, HMC, app., pt. 1, pp. 142-3, 159.
32 *Dict. Nat. Biog.* 12, pp. 931-3. *Freeman's Journal*, 17-20, 20-22 Nov. 1787. *Gentlemen's Magazine* 17, pt. 2, pp. 1016, 1021. Gilbert, J.T., *A History of the City of Dublin*, 3 vols (Dublin 1978), 3, p. 133. *Freeman's Journal*, 30 Oct.–1 Nov., 27-30 Oct. 1787. Charlemont, *Memoirs*, 2, p. 161.
33 *Freeman's Journal*, 24-27 Nov., 18-22 Dec. 1787; *Gentlemen's Magazine*, 17, p. 1116; 18, pp. 828-9, 842. MSS and correspondence of James, first Earl of Charlemont, vol. 1, 1745-1783 in HMC Twelfth Report, (London 1891), app., pt. x, p. 157. Cloncurry, Lord Valentine, *Personal Recollections of his Life and Times* (Dublin 1849), p. 256 fn.
34 *The Life and Letters of Lady Sarah Lennox* (eds Ilchester and Stavordale), 2 vols (London 1901), 2, p. 73. MSS of J.B. Fortescue in HMC, Thirteenth Report (London 1892), app., pt. 3, p. 466. *Freeman's Journal*, 7, 10 June 1788, 23-5 Sept. 1788. O'Dwyer, 'State Apartments', p. 4.
35 *Dict. Nat. Biog.* 6, p. 1040. O'Mahony, pp. 193-8. Brialmont, M., *History of the Life of Arthur, Duke of Wellington*, 4 vols (London 1858), 1, pp. 10-12. Barrington, Jonah, *Rise and Fall of the Irish Nation* (Dublin 1843), p. 415.
36 McDowell, p. 675. Grattan, Henry, *Memoirs of the Life and Times of Henry Grattan*, 5 vols (London 1839), 1, p. 151. Harcourt Papers 3, p. 116. Carlisle MSS, p. 507.

INTERLUDE

1 Hewitt, Esther (ed.), *Lord Shannon's Letters to his Son* (Belfast 1982), p. 174.
2 Charlemont, *Memoirs* 2, p. 350. Westmorland Papers, 3/718/4 (126), Bishop of Cloyne to Westmorland, 12 Jan. 1795. *Dict. Nat. Biog.* 16, pp. 290-2.
3 Bartlett, Thomas, et al., *Rebellion: A Television History of 1798* (Dublin 1998), p. 144.

CHAPTER FIVE

1   Burke, Edmund, *Reflections on the Revolution in France* (Dublin 1790), p. 205.
2   *The Complete Peerage* 1, app. A, pp. 457-9: 3 app. D, pp. 631-4. McDowell, R.B., 'Ireland in 1800' in T.W. Moody and W.E. Vaughan (eds), *A New History of Ireland*, vol. 4, pp. 680-1. James, Francis G., *Lords of the Ascendancy* (Dublin 1995), p. 126.
3   McCracken, *The Irish Parliament in the Eighteenth Century*, p. 7. Lecky, W.E.H., *A History of Ireland in the Eighteenth Century* 1, pp. 178-9. Townshend Papers M, 732 (65).
4   Mant, Richard, *History of the Church of Ireland* (London 1840), pp. 274, 424. McCracken, J.L., 'The Political Structure 1714-1760' in T.W. Moody and W.E. Vaughan (eds), *A New History of Ireland*, vol. 4, p. 71. McNally, *Patrick, Parties, Patriots and Undertakers* (Dublin 1997), p. 164.
5   Harrowby Papers MS T3228/1/33. Bishop of Down to Sir Dudley Ryder, 31 Jan. 1746/7. Bedford Papers MS T 2915/5/50, Strangford to Bedford, 29 Sept. 1758; MS T2915/9/58 Bishop of Corke and Ross to Bedford, 10 June 1760. Lecky, 1, p. 196. Buckinghamshire Papers: MS 13034 (3) Memo from North Dec. 1776; MS 13044 Ager to Buckinghamshire 6 Dec. 1778, 30 May and 6 June 1779. MacDonagh, Michael, *The Viceroy's Postbag* (London 1904), p. 94.
6   *Gentlemen's Magazine* 4 (1734), p. 163. Hervey, Lord, *Memoirs of the Reign of George the Second*, 2 vols (London 1848), 1, pp. 306-7. Egmont, second Earl of, Manuscripts HMC (London 1923), 1, pp. v, 405-65; 2, 46, 53-4, 60-1. Egmont, *The Question of the Precedency of the Peers of Ireland etc.* (Dublin 1739).
7   Egmont, 2, 452-6. Charlemont, *Memoirs*, 1, pp. 120-5.
8   Foster, op. cit., p. 172. Wortley Montague, Lady Mary, *Letters and Works* (ed. Lord Wharncliffe), 3 vols (London 1837), 3, p. 185.
9   Cannon, John, *Aristocratic Century: the Peerage of the Eighteenth Century* (Cambridge 1984), p. 16. Carlisle MSS, pp. 245-6. Walpole, Horace, *Letters* (ed. Paget Toynbee) (Oxford 1904), 9, p. 390. Wraxall, *Posthumous Memoirs*, 1, p. 77.
10 Charlemont, *Memoirs*, 2, p. 244.
11 Harcourt Papers 3, fn. p. 130. Hartnell, Crawford, 'The Most Illustrious Order of St Patrick' in *The Lady of the House*, 20 (224), 1908.
12 *Freeman's Journal*, 18-21 Jan., 15-18 April 1783. Fortescue, J.B., Manuscripts in HMC, Thirteenth Report, app., pt. 3 (London 1892), p. 183. Temple to Grenville, 15 Jan., 2, 5, 9, 16 Feb. 1783. Charlemont, *Memoirs*, 2, pp. 67, 71.
13 Fortescue Temple to Grenville, 5 Feb 1783. *Hibernian Magazine*, March 1783, p. 166. Hartnell, p. 3.
14 Fortescue Temple to Grenville, 7 March 1783.

15 Hartnell, p. 4. *Hibernian Magazine*, March 1783, pp. 166-7. Ross, Ian Campbell, *Public Virtue: Public Love* (Dublin 1986), p. 77. *Freeman's Journal*, 18-20 March 1783.

16 Jupp, Peter, *Lord Grenville 1759-1834* (Oxford 1985), pp. 268-9. McDowell, p. 681. *Faulkner's Journal,* 25 Sept. 1804. *The Later Correspondence of George III* (ed. A. Aspinall), 5 vols (Cambridge 1967), Inchiquin to king, 18 Oct. 1800.

17 Richmond Papers MSS 62 (501). Corkayne, G.E., *State of the Peerage of Ireland at and since the Time of the Union* (London 1889), pp. 1-2, 42-5. Cannon, op. cit., p. 28.

18 *Burke's Peerage and Baronetage* (106th edn, London 1999), pp. xli-xlii.

CHAPTER SIX

1 Edgeworth, Maria, *Castle Rackrent and The Absentee* (London 1910), p. 179.

2 McDowell, R.B., 'Ireland in 1800' in T.W. Moody and W.E. Vaughan (eds), *A New History of Ireland*, vol. 4, pp. 680-1. Maxwell, Constantia, *Dublin under the Georges 1714-1850* (London 1936), p. 113. Hill, Jacqueline, *From Patriots to Unionists: Dublin Civic Politics and Irish Protestant Patriotism 1660-1840* (Oxford 1997), p. 292.

3 *The Absentee*, p. 180.

4 Foster, op. cit., p. 289.

5 Brynn, Edward, *Crown and Castle: British Rule in Ireland 1800-1830* (Dublin 1978), pp. 26-9, 104-5. Hansard first ser., 17, pars. 527-30.

6 O'Mahony, p. 210. *Freeman's Journal*, 25 July, 25 Aug., 5 Nov. 1801. Cobbett quoted in *The Complete Peerage* 6, p. 307. Connolly, S.J., 'Aftermath and Adjustment' in T.W. Moody and W.E. Vaughan (eds), *A New History of Ireland*, vol. 5 , pp. 1-2.

7 *Faulkner's Journal*, 22 Feb. 1803. *Freeman's Journal*, 18 Jan, 1803. O'Mahony, p. 210.

8 Abbot, Charles, Lord Colchester, *Diary and Correspondence*, 3 vols (London 1861) 1, p. 443. *Archivium Hibernicum* xi (Maynooth 1944), pp. 13, 21, 27-30.

9 *Faulkner's Journal*, 14, 19 March 1807. Brynn, p. 30.

10 O'Mahony, pp 213-15. Melville, Edward, *Sketches of Society in France and Ireland 1805-1807*, 2 vols (Dublin 1811), 2, p. 112. *The Dublin Satirist*, Feb.–Mar 1810. Sir Robert Peel from his Private Papers, 3 vols (London 1899), 1, p. 106. Richmond Papers 63 (555). Gower, Lord Granville Leveson Gower, *Private Correspondence 1781-1821*, 2 vols (London 1916), 2, pp. 332-3. Hayward, Abraham, *The Art of Dining* (London 1899), p. 86 fn.

11 *Walker's Hibernian Magazine* 7, p. 573: 1808 pp. 124-5. Richmond Papers 60 (298). Bathurst Papers HMC vol. 129 (1923), pp. 220-1.

12 Richmond Papers 60 (258, 304), 63 (562, 601).

13 Peel Papers 3, p. 41.

14 *The Complete Peerage* 10, 842-4. Peel Papers 1, p. 101. Brynn, p. 31.
15 *The Complete Peerage* 12, pt.2, pp. 169, 618-20. Gash, Norman, *Mr Secretary Peel: the Life of Sir Robert Peel to 1830*, p. 131.
16 *Faulkner's Journal*, 14 Feb., 1 April 1815.
17 *Dict. Nat. Biog.* 19, pp. 308-9. Gregory, Lady (ed.), *Mr Gregory's Letter Box 1813-1830* (London 1898), pp. 108-9.
18 Fraser, Flora, *The Unruly Queen* (London 1996), p. 446. Gregory, p. 152.
19 Anon., *The King's Visit to Ireland* (Dublin 1821), pp. 22-7.
20 *The Freeman's Journal*, 21, 23, 24, 25, 30 Aug. 1821. Foster, op. cit., p. 296. Molloy, *Court Life Below Stairs*, 4, p. 345. *The King's Visit*, p. 74.
21 MacDonagh, Oliver, *O'Connell: The Life of Daniel O'Connell* (London 1991), p. 178. Gregory, pp. 166, 184. Cloncurry, *Personal Recollections*, p. 278.
22 MacDonagh, pp. 180-1. Wellesley, Richard Marquess of, *Memoirs and Correspondence*, 3 vols (London 1846) 3, pp. 369-79.
23 VB Papers, Letter to Helen Vernon, 21 Aug. 1813.
24 *Saunder's News Letter*, 5, 20 Feb. 1823.
25 *Dublin Evening Post*, 13 Feb 1823. Quoted by *Saunder's News Letter*, 20 Feb. 1823.
26 VB Papers, Robert Peel to Vernon, 24 Feb. 1823.
27 *Saunder's News Letter*, 24, 25, 28 Feb.; 6, 8, 14, 19 March 1823.
28 MSS Minute books Comms. of BOW, 31 Aug. 1826. Farrington, Joseph, *The Farrington Diary* (ed. James Grieg), 8 vols (London 1922-1928), 8, p. 263.
29 *The Wellesley Papers*, 2, pp. 150-1. *Dublin Evening Mail*, 19 Oct. 1825. O'Mahony, op. cit., pp. 222-5. Wellesley, *Memoirs*, 3, pp. 387-90.
30 *Dict. Nat. Biog.*, 20, pp. 1122-34. Madden, Daniel Owen, *The Castle and the Country*, 3 vols (Dublin 1850), 2, p. 45. *The Wellesley Papers*, 2, pp. 236-7.
31 *Saunder's News Letter*, 28 Feb., 8, 14 March 1823.
32 Fitzpatrick, William J., *Lady Morgan: Her Career, Literary and Personal*, p. 245.
33 Croker, John Wilson, *Correspondence and Diaries* (ed. Louis J. Jennings), 3 vols (London 1884), 1, p. 204.
34 Sharp, Cecil J., *The Dance: An Historical Survey of Dancing in Europe* (London 1924), pp. 28-30. Young, G.M. (ed.), *Early Victorian England*, 2 vols (London 1934) 1, p. 120. *Faulkner's Journal*, 3 March 1816. *Freeman's Journal*, 21 Nov. 1821. *Saunder's News Letter*, 12 March 1823.
35 Hinde, Wendy, *Catholic Emancipation: A Shake to Men's Minds* (Oxford 1992), pp 49-52. O'Mahony, op. cit., p. 229. *The Complete Peerage* 1, pp. 138-9. *Dict. Nat. Biog.* 15, pp. 54-8.
36 Anglesey, Marquis of, *One Leg: The Life and Letters of Henry William Paget, first Marquis of Anglesey 1768-1854* (London 1961), pp. 184-5. Tighe, Gregory, *A Brief Sketch of the Marquis of Anglesey's Administration* (Dublin 1829), p. 6. *Freeman's Journal*, 3 March 1828. Hinde, p. 52.
37 Fitzpatrick, *Lady Morgan*, p. 256. Daunt, W.J. O'Neill, *A Life Spent for Ireland* (London 1896), p. 295. Anglesey, op. cit., p. 192. Hinde, op. cit., p. 53.

Freeman's Journal, 11 March, 24 April 1828.

38 Maxwell, Herbert, *The Creevey Papers*, 2 vols (London 1904), 2, pp. 162, 188-9. Puckler-Muskau, Hermann, *Tour in England, Ireland and France in 1828 and 1829*, 2 vols (Bermingham 1832), 2, pp. 83-4.

39 Anglesey, op. cit., pp. 210-11.

40 Wyse, Thomas, *Historical Sketch of the Late Catholic Association of Ireland*, 2 vols (London 1829), 2, p. 37. Anglesey, op. cit., p. 217.

41 *Dict. Nat. Biog.* 15, pp. 867-9. Madden, Daniel, *Ireland and its Rulers since 1828*, 3 vols (London 1844), p. 55. Greville, *Memoirs*, 1, pp. 162-4; 3, p. 408. O'Mahony, op. cit., pp. 232-4. VB Papers, Notes and Letters, Francis Vernon to Sir Charles Vernon, 19 May 1829.

CHAPTER SEVEN

1 Third Rep. Cond. Poor Ire., pp. 1-34, HC 1836 (43) 30.

2 Robins, Joseph, 'History of Royal Horticultural Society of Ireland' in *Irish Gardening and Horticulture* (Dublin 1979), pp. 71-91.

3 Anglesey, *One Leg*, pp. 268, 276, 380-1 fn. Report from Sel. Comm. on Civil Government Charges, Oct. 1831, p. 13, HC 1831 (337) 4.

4 Madden, Daniel Owen, *The Castle and the Country*, 3 vols (Dublin 1850), 2, pp. 278-80. O'Mahony, p. 240.

5 MacDonagh, *O'Connell*, p. 471. Madden, *The Castle*, 1, p. 113.

6 *Dict. Nat. Biog.* 8, p. 651. O'Mahony, pp. 243-4. *Freeman's Journal*, 18 March 1842.

7 *Dict. Nat. Biog.* 9, p. 779. *The Complete Peerage* 6, p. 518. Woodham-Smith, Cecil, *The Great Hunger: Ireland 1845-1849* (London 1962), pp. 48-9. *Freeman's Journal*, 31 Jan., 7 March 1845.

8 Woodham-Smith, pp. 104, 299, 301. *Dict. Nat. Biog.* 16, p. 87; 20, pp. 347-50.

9 Burke, Bernard, *The Romance of the Aristocracy*, 3 vols (London 1855), 2, pp. 5-9. Maxwell, Herbert, *The Life and Letters of George William Frederick, Fourth Earl of Clarendon*, 2 vols (London 1913), 1, p. 323.

10 MS Diary of Ellen Palmer, 26 Aug. 1847.

11 MS Diary of Ellen Palmer, 14 Feb. 1850.

12 Woodham-Smith, pp. 384-406. *Freeman's Journal*, 6 Aug. 1845.

13 Maxwell, 1, p. 302. Victoria, Queen, *Letters* (eds Benson and Esher), 2, p. 225. Woodham-Smith, p. 400. *Freeman's Journal*, 7, 9, 10, 13 Aug. 1845.

14 *Freeman's Journal*, 10 Aug. 1845.

15 Victorian Journals 3rd ser. 1, p. 36, 1 Feb. 1886.

16 Hood, Susan, *Ulster's Office: The Irish Office of Arms*, pp. v-vii. Gen. Off. MSS. 337, vol. 1, p. 14; 339, 3, p. 79.

17 Hood, pp. 4-21.

18 MS 337, 1, p. 18.

19 Forms of ceremonial to be observed at the reception and swearing of Marquis

of Anglesey, Dec. 1830. MS PCO XB7 (NAI) Hood, pp. 47-51. Cameron, Charles, *Reminiscences* (Dublin 1913), pp. 142-3.

20 Fitzgerald, Percy (A Native), *Recollections of Dublin Castle and of Dublin Society* (London 1902), pp. 30-1. *The Daily News*, 3 Aug. 1871. *Quarterly Review* 49, p. 337. Whately, E. Jane, *Life and Correspondence of Richard Whately*, 2 vols (London 1866), 1, p. 405.

21 MSS 337 (123).

22 MSS 321 (12); MSS 338 Viceregal court, vol. 2, p. 34.

23 Gribbon, H.D., 'Economic and Social History 1850-1921' in T.W. Moody and W.E. Vaughan (eds), *A New History of Ireland*, vol. 6, pp. 331-2.

24 Thackeray, William Makepeace, *Works*, 13 vols (London 1908), 5, p. 578.

25 Meenan, F.O.C., 'The Medical Consultants of Dublin: a Social and Political Portrait' in *Essays in Honour of J.D.H. Widdess* (Dublin 1978), pp. 57-67. Gen. Off. MS 321 (pp. 13 and 157); 339 (p. 3); 337 (p. 53). Gamble, John, *Sketches of the History, Politics and Manners taken in Dublin and the North of Ireland Ireland 1810* (London 1811), p. 26.

26 Gen Off. MSS. 321 (157).

27 MacDonagh, Oliver, 'The Politicization of the Irish Catholic Bishops 1800-1850' in *The Historical Journal* 18 (London 1975), pp. 38-49. Kerr, Donal A., *Peel, Priests and Politics* (Oxford 1982). Norman, E.R., *The Catholic Church and Ireland in the Age of Rebellion 1859-1873* (London 1965), p. 359. Gen. Off. MSS 337 (pp. 89, 90); 338 (p. 13); 339 (pp. 26, 57). *Freeman's Journal*, 7 March 1845.

28 Ross, F.E., *Historical Reminiscences: Dublin Castle* (Dublin 1896), p. 70.

29 *The Illustrated London News*, vol. 20, sec. supp. , 19 June 1852. O'Mahony, op. cit., pp. 257, 261. *Dublin Evening Post*, 31 Jan. 1861. *Irish Times*, 4 Oct. 1864. *The Express*, 9 Nov. 1864. *Saunder's Newsletter*, 18 July 1866. *Dict. Nat. Biog.* 13, pp 750-1.

30 O'Mahony, op. cit., pp. 262-72.

31 Hood, op. cit., p. 55. *Dublin Evening Mail*, 16 April 1868.

32 Fitzgerald, *Recollections*, pp. 46-7, 52-3. *The Complete Peerage* 1, p. 9.

33 *Dict. Nat. Biog.*, pp. 362-72. *Freeman's Journal*, 4 Feb. 1869. Gwynn, Stephen and Gertrude Tuckwell, *The Life of Sir Charles W. Dilke*, 2 vols (London 1917), 2, p. 138. Foster, op. cit., p. 395.

34 Wynne, Maud, *An Irishman and his Family: Lord Morris and Killanin* (London 1937), pp. 97-8, 159, 208. Foster, R.F., 'To the Northern Station: Lord Randolph Churchill and the Prelude to the Orange Card' in *Ireland and the Union*, eds Lyons and Hawkins (Oxford 1980), pp. 237-40. Robinson, Henry, *Memories: Wise and Otherwise* (London 1923), p. 72. Fitzgerald, *Recollections*, p. 58. O'Mahony, pp. 274-5. *The Complete Peerage* 3, pp. 486-8. Foster, op. cit., p. 405.

35 Gen. Off. MS 337, Viceregal Court, 2, p. 53.

36 MSS. 339 Viceregal court, vol.3, p. 19. Cameron, p. 122. *The Express*, 15 March 1897.

37 O'Mahony, op. cit., p. 295. Pentland, Marjorie, *A Bonnie Fechter* (London 1952), pp. 56-7. Robinson, op. cit., p. 76.

38 T.W. Moody and W.E. Vaughan (eds), *A New History of Ireland*, vol. 9, pp. 499. *Irish Times*, 18 March 1887; 18 March 1890. O'Mahony, op. cit., p. 30. Wilkinson, Neville R., *To All and Singular* (London 1925), p. 38.

39 Wynne, op. cit., p. 159. Robinson, op. cit., p. 106. *Letters of Queen Victoria*, Third series, Selection of correspondence 1886-1901 (ed. G.E. Buckle), 3 vols, 2, Houghton to Ponsonby, 9 Feb. 1893.

40 MSS 321 (76, 145, 147, 253). *The Times* quoted in *The Mail*, 12 Feb. 1865. Dunlevy, op. cit., p. 145.

41 Laver, op. cit., p. 59; Bowen, Elizabeth, *The Shelbourne* (London 1951), p. 98.

42 Dunlevy, op. cit., 145-6. Gen. Off. MS 339, Viceregal Court, vol. 3, p. 77.

43 *Irish Times*, 2, 10 Jan. 1860. *The Mail*, 1 Feb. 1865. Fitzgerald, *Recollections*, p. 36. *Freeman's Journal*, 29 Jan. 1874. Wilkinson, Neville R., *To All and Singular* (London 1925), p. 195. Hone, Joseph, *The Life of George Moore* (London 1936), pp. 100-1.

44 *Freeman's Journal*, 28 Jan. 1871.

45 Hinkson, Pamela, *Seventy Years Young: Memories of Elizabeth, Countess of Fingall* (Dublin 1991), p. 64.

46 Moore, George, *A Drama in Muslin* (Dublin 1886), pp. 172-5.

47 *Freeman's Journal*, 29 Jan. 1874.

48 Fitzgerald, *Recollections*, pp. 40-5. *Freeman's Journal*, 19 March 1850. *Irish Times*, 21 March 1860. Gen. Off. MS 337, Viceregal Court, vol. 1. Bayly, op. cit., p. 35.

49 Anon., *The King's Visit to Ireland* (Dublin 1821), p. 117. *The Correspondence and Diaries of John Wilson Croker* (ed. Louis J. Jennings), 3 vols (London 1884), 1, pp. 204-5.

50 Gen. Off. MSS 337 (139). Petrie, op. cit., pp. 40-1, 51-2. Fingall, *Seventy Years Young*, p. 62.

51 Larcom MSS. 7504 Memo, 16 Oct. 1871. Hansard third ser., 111, pars 1008-30, 1406-67.

52 *Freeman's Journal*, 20 March 1850. Larcom MSS 7507, Carlisle to Palmerstown, 26 June 1857. *The Times*, 28 March 1858. Hansard third ser. 149, pars 712-82; 346, par. 1334, Spencer to Larcom, 24 Oct.; Larcom to Spencer, 30 Oct. 1871. McDowell, R.B., 'The Irish Executive in the Nineteenth Century' in *Dub. Hist. Rec.* 9, pp. 275-7. *The Gladstone Diaries* (ed. H.C.G. Mathew), 14 vols (Oxford 1982), 7, pp. 514-16.

53 Brynn, op. cit., 156-7. Fitzgerald, *Recollections*, p. 62. *Freeman's Journal*, 18 March 1869, 13 Jan. 1883, 18 March 1885. *Irish Times*, 18 March 1887, 18 March 1890.

54 *Evening Telegraph*, 22 Aug. 1895.

55 MSS Letter Books, Board of Works (NAI) OPW 572/70.

56 Foster, op. cit., p. 424 fn.

CHAPTER EIGHT

1   *Evening Telegraph*, 22 August 1895.
2   O'Mahony, pp. 309-14. McBride, Lawrence W., *The Greening of Dublin Cas-tle* (Washington 1991), p. 3. Colles, Ramsay, *In Castle and Court House* (London 1911), p. 50. *The Graphic*, 7 April, pp. 507, 595; 14 April 1900, p. 531. Annual Register 1900, pp. 251-2.
3   Robinson, *Memories*, pp. 148-9. *Who Was Who 1929-1940* (London 1941), p. 338.
4   *Irish Times*, 5, 11, 18 March 1903.
5   O'Mahony, pp. 318-22. *Daily Chronicle*, 22 July 1903.
6   *The Irish Protestant*, 11 June 1904, p. 375.
7   *The Leader*, 17 Aug. 1901 and generally through editions of 1901-21. Butler, Mary E.L., 'The Irish Gentlewoman: As She is and as She Ought To Be' in *The New Ireland Review*, 15 June 1901, p. 221.
8   Hansard Fourth ser. 174, p. 83.
9   O'Broin, Leon, *The Chief Secretary: Augustine Birrell in Ireland* (London 1969), pp. 124-5. McBride, Lawrence W., *The Greening of Dublin Castle* (Washington 1991), pp. 2-3.
10 Dickinson, p. L., *The Dublin of Yesterday* (London 1929), p. 14.
11 *Dict. Nat. Biog.* 1931-1940, pp. 347-9. *The Leader*, 11 April 1908.
12 Robinson, *Memories*, pp. 224-8. Wynne, Maud, *An Irishman and his Family: Lord Morris and Killanin* (London 1930), p. 208. Pentland, op. cit., p. 161.
13 Aberdeen, Lord and Lady, *We Twa: Reminiscences*, 2 vols (London 1925), 2, pp. 178-180. *Irish Times*, 16 March 1907. Dickinson, op. cit., p. 17
14 *We Twa*, 1, p. 254.
15 Wilkinson, op. cit., pp. 196-7.
16 Robinson, Lennox, *Curtain Up* (London 1942), pp. 82-3. Robinson, *Memories*, p. 228.
17 Bamford, Francis, and Bankes, Viola, *Vicious Circle: the Case of the Missing Irish Crown Jewels* (London 1965), p. 7.
18 Gen. Off. MSS 339, p. 79. Vicars to Dudley, 21 Dec. 1903. Standing Orders: Viceregal Household and Staff (Dublin 1907). *Vicious Circle*, pp. 9-11.
19 Crown Jewels Commission (Ireland): Report and appendix 1908 (Cd. 3906 and Cd. 3936). Rep. pp. i-v.
20 Rep. pp. vi-xi. Mins. evid. pp. 67-78. Wilkinson, Neville R., *To All and Singular* (London 1925), p. 175.
21 *Vicious Circle*, p. 112.
22 Mins. evid., pp. 67-78, 2609-89.
23 *Vicious Circle*, pp. 10, 114.
24 O'Broin, p. 26. *London Mail*, 11 Nov. 1912. *Irish Times*, 5 July 1913.
25 *Vicious Circle*, pp. 11, 159, 168. *Irish Independent*, 15 April 1921.
26 *Freeman's Journal*, 1 April 1903. *Daily Express*, 20 July 1903. *Daily Mail*, 22

July 1903. La Touche, Mrs, *The Letters of a Noble Woman*, ed. Margaret Young (London 1908), pp. 197-8.

27 Robinson, *Memories*, p. 132. *Irish Times*, 28, 29 April 1904. *Irish Independent*, 11 July 1907.

28 Wilkinson, pp. 199-200. *Irish Independent*, 10, 11, 12, 17 July 1911.

29 Asquith, Cynthia, *Diaries 1915-1918* (London 1968), pp. 60-2, 128, 163. Jones, Mark Bence, *Twilight of the Ascendancy* (London 1987), p. 169.

30 *Dict. Nat. Biog.* 1931-1940 (London 1937), pp. 380-1.

31 *Dict. Nat. Biog.* 1922-1930, pp. 319-25. Jones, p. 193. McColgan, John, *British Policy and the Irish Administration 1920-1922*, p. 1

32 Duggan, G.C. (Periscope), 'The Last days of Dublin Castle' in *Blackwoods' Magazine* 212, Aug. 1922, pp. 157, 165-70. Starkie, Enid, *A Lady's Child* (London 1941), p. 139. Jones, op. cit., pp. 215-16.

33 Duggan, op. cit., p. 188.

Sources

ABBREVIATIONS

CSORP	Chief Secretary's Office Registered Papers
Gen. Off.	Genealogical Office
HMC	Historical Manuscripts Commission
JRSAI	Journal of the Royal Society of Antiquaries
NAI	National Archives of Ireland
NLD	National Library, Dublin
PRONI	Public Record Office of Northern Ireland, Belfast

MANUSCRIPT SOURCES

Anglesey, Marquis of, Forms of ceremonial to be observed at the reception and swearing in as lord-lieutenant of Ireland, 1830 (NAI)
Bedford, 4th Duke of, Lord-lieutenancy Papers 1751-61 (PRONI)
Board of Works Papers (NAI)
    Minute Books, 1802-04, 1809-33
    Letter Books, 1817-1900
Bolton Papers (NLD)
Buckingham, Earl of, Memorandum Book, 1777 MS 1471 (NLD)
Buckingham Correspondence, 1780-1830, Joly 39-40 (NLD)
Chief Secretary's Office Registered Papers, 1818-1920 (NAI)

Darnely Papers and Correspondence, 1700-1909 (PRONI)

Forms of ceremonial to be observed at reception and swearing in of the Marquis of Anglesey, lord lieutenant of Ireland, drawn up by W. Bentham, December 1830 (NAI)

Genealogical Office Papers (NLD)

    precedents of receptions, 1806-44

    the book of the viceregal household

    Ulster's office

    the viceregal court (late nineteenth century)

Harrowby Papers (PRONI)

Heron Papers (NLD)

Larcom Papers (NLD)

Leinster Papers (Fitzgerald Correspondence) (NLD)

Palmer, Ellen, Diary, 1847-50 (in possession of Dame Gillian Wagner)

Portland Papers (PRONI)

Richmond Papers (NLD)

Townshend Papers (NAI)

Vernon Barton Papers (NAI)

Notes and letters concerning the life and times of Sir Charles Hawley Vernon, 1766-1823, court chamberlain to the lord lieutenant of Ireland, with a summary by Griselda Vernon Barton, November 1990

The court chamberlain's records of the households of the lords lieutenant of Ireland, 1713-71, rules of precedence etc.

The court chamberlain's records of the households etc., n.d.

Diary of Lord Carlisle's household and successive lords lieutenant, 1781-4

Duties of the gentleman usher to the ladies, n.d.

The forms of the state ceremonies attending the lord lieutenant, c.1798

Westmorland Papers, 1789-1808 (NAI)

Willes Baron John, Miscellaneous Observations on Ireland, 1759-60 (PRONI)

THESIS

Hood, Susan E., *Ulster's Office – The Irish Office of Arms: An Administrative History, 1783-1943*. A thesis presented to University College London, September 1990.

PARLIAMENTARY AND MISCELLANEOUS GOVERNMENT PAPERS

Hansard

Civil Government of Ireland: an account of the salary and allowance of the lord lieutenant of Ireland and chief secretary for each of the last two years, HC

1826-27 (304) 20

Lords-lieutenant and chief secretaries of Ireland since the Union, HC 1826-27 (308) 20

Report from Select Committee on Civil Government Charges, October 1831, HC 1831 (337) 4

Estimates of Miscellaneous Services for the year 1831 (Ireland), August 1831, HC 1831 (177) 31

The Scale of Precedence in Ireland Ulster's Office Dublin 1897

Estimates for Civil Services for the year ending 31 March 1908, HC 1907 (54) 51

Report of the commissioners for inquiring how far the establishment of the Chief Secretary's Office of Ireland may be placed on a more efficient footing, etc., 1852, NAI OP MA 136/17

Viceregal Household and Staff: Standing Orders, Dublin 1907

Crown Jewels Commission (Ireland): Report and Appendix 1908 (cd.3906 and 3936)

King George V: Visit to Ireland 1911: Ceremonial Procedures, Dublin 1911

Offices and addresses of the household and staff of the Earl of Aberdeen etc., Ulster's Office, Dublin Castle, February 1912 (NLD)

SECONDARY SOURCES (MEMOIRS, DIARIES, CORRESPONDENCE)

Abbot, Charles, Lord Colchester, *Diary and Correspondence*, 3 vols, London 1861

Aberdeen, Lord and Lady, *We Twa: Reminiscences*, 2 vols, London 1925

Anglesea, Marquess of, *One Leg: The Life and Letters of Henry William Paget, First Marquis of Anglesea 1768-1854*, London 1961

Asquith, Cynthia, *Diaries 1915-1918*, London 1968

Barrington, Jonah, *Personal Sketches of his Own Times*, London 1832

Barrington, Jonah, *Historic Memoirs of Ireland*, 2 vols, London 1835

Barrington, Jonah, *The Rise and Fall of the Irish Nation*, Dublin 1843

Bathurst, Earl, Report on manuscripts of Earl Bathurst, HMC vol. 129, London 1923

Bedford, John, Fourth Duke of, *Correspondence*, 3 vols, London 1846

Beresford, John, *Correspondence*, 2 vols, London 1854

Buckingham, Earl of, Manuscripts, HMC Fourteenth Report, app., pt. 9, London 1895

Buckingham Papers, Report on MSS of Marquis of Lothian, HMC 1905

Cameron, Charles, *Reminiscences*, Dublin 1913

Carlisle, Earl of, Manuscripts, HMC Fifteenth Report, app., pt. 6, London 1897

Castlereagh, Viscount, *Memoirs and Correspondence* (ed. Charles Vane), 12 vols, London 1850-3

Charlemont, James, First Earl of, Report on manuscripts and correspondence, vol. 1, 1745-83, in HMC Twelfth Report app., pt. 10, London 1891; vol. 2, 1784-99, in HMC Thirteenth Report app., pt. 8, Dublin 1894

Chesterfield, Philip Dormer Stanhope, *Letters of P.D. Stanhope*, 6 vols, London 1932

Chesterfield, Philip Dormer Stanhope, Earl of, *Miscellaneous Works*, 3 vols, Dublin 1777

Cloncurry, Lord Valentine, *Personal Recollections of his Life and Times*, Dublin 1849

Cornwallis, Charles, First Marquis, *Correspondence* (ed. Charles Ross), 3 vols, 2nd ed., London 1859

The Creevey Papers (ed. Herbert Maxwell), 2 vols, London 1904

Croker, John Wilson, *Correspondence and Diaries*, 3 vols, London 1884

Donoughmore, Earl of, Report on Manuscripts, HMC 12 app., pt. 9, London 1891

Dunboyne, Lord, *Butler Family History*, Kilkenny 1966

Egmont, Earl of, *Manuscripts*, vol. 1 (1730-3), HMC 120 London 1920; vol. 2 (1734-8) in HMC 127, London 1923

Emly, Lord, Fourteenth Rep. HMC app., pt.9, London 1895

Ernst-Browning, William, *Memoirs of the Life of William Dormer, Fourth Earl of Chesterfield*, London 1906

Farington, Joseph, *The Farington Diary* (ed. James Grieg), 8 vols, London 1922-8

Fingall, Elizabeth, Countess of, *Seventy Years Young: Memoirs of Elizabeth, Countess of Fingall*, told to Pamela Hinkson, London 1937

Fortescue, J.B., Manuscripts, vol. 1, Thirteenth Report HMC app., pt. 3, London 1892; vol. 2, Fourteenth Report HMC app., pt. 5, London 1894

Frankland-Russell-Astley Manuscripts, Report on, HMC, London 1900

George the Third, *Later Correspondence* (ed. A. Aspinall), 5 vols, London 1861-2

The Gladstone Papers (ed. H.C.G. Mathews), 14 vols, Oxford 1982

Gower, Lord Granville Leveson (first Earl Granville), Private Correspondence 1781-1821, 2 vols, London 1916

Granville, Mary, Mrs Delany, *Autobiography and Correspondence*, 6 vols, London 1861-62

Grattan, Henry, jun., *Memoirs of the Life and Times of Rt. Hon. Henry Grattan*, London 1839

Mr Gregory's Letter Box 1813-1830 (ed. Lady Gregory), London 1898

Greville, Charles C.F., *The Greville Memoirs*, 2nd part, 3 vols., London 1885; 3rd part, 2 vols, London 1887.

Harcourt Papers (ed. W. E. Harcourt), 14 vols, privately printed, 1880 etc.

Hardy, Francis, *Memoirs of the Political and Private Life of James Caulfeild, Earl of Charlemont*, 2nd ed., 2 vols, London 1812

Hare, Theodore J., Manuscripts, HMC Fourteenth Report, app., pt. 9, London 1895

Hervey, Lord John, *Memoirs of Reign of George the Second*, 2 vols, London 1848

Knox, Howard Vicente, Manuscripts, HMC, various collections, vol. 6, London 1906

La Touche, Mrs, *The Letters of a Noble Woman* (ed. Margaret Young), London 1901

Laing Manuscripts, Report on, vol. 2, HMC London 1925

Leeson, Mrs, *Memoirs* (ed. Mary Lyons), Dublin 1995

Leinster, Emily, Duchess of, *Correspondence* (ed. Brian Fitzgerald), 3 vols, Dublin 1949-57

Lennox, Sarah, *The Life and Letters of Lady Sarah Lennox* (eds Countess of Ilchester and Lord Stavordale), 2 vols, London 1901

Lothian, Marquess of, Report on the MSS of Marquess of Lothian, HMC 73 1905

Maxwell, Herbert, *Life and Letters of George William Frederick, fourth Earl of Clarendon*, 2 vols, London 1913

Montague, Lady Mary Worthley, *Letters and Works*, 3 vols, London 1837

O'Brien, R. Barry, *Thomas Drummond: Under-Secretary in Ireland 1835-40: Life and Letters*, London 1889

O'Keeffe, John, *Recollections of the Life of John O'Keeffe*, 2 vols, London 1826

Onslow, Earl of, Manuscripts, HMC Fourteenth Report, app., pt. 9, London 1895

Ormonde, Marquis of, Report on, MSS vol. 2, HMC London 1899

Ormonde, Marquis of, Calendar of the MSS of, HMC, new series 8, 1920

Orrery Papers (ed. Emily Boyle), 2 vols, London 1903

Peel, Robert, *Sir Robert Peel from his Private Papers* (ed. C. S. Parker), 3 vols, London 1899

Pilkington, Letitia, *Memoirs of Mrs Letitia Pilkington 1712-1750*, 3rd ed., London 1928

Robinson, Henry, *Memories: Wise and Otherwise*, London 1923

Rutland, Charles, *Correspondence between William Pitt and Rutland 1781-1787*, London 1890

Rutland, Charles, Duke of, Manuscripts, vol. 3, Fourteenth Rep. , HMC London 1896

Lord Shannon's Letters to his Son Viscount Boyle 1790-1802 (ed. Esther Hewitt), Belfast 1982

Stopford-Sackville, Mrs, Report on MSS, vol. 1, HMC London 1904

Suffolk, Henrietta, Countess of, Letters 1712-1769, 2 vols, London 1824

Victoria, Queen, *Letters* (1837-1861) (eds A.C. Benson and Viscount Esher), 3 vols, London 1911

Victoria, Queen, *Letters* (1886-1901), third series, 3 vols, London 1931

Waldegrave, James, Earl, *Memoirs from 1754-1758*, London 1821

Walpole, Horace, *Memoirs of the Last Ten Years of the Reign of George the Second*, 2 vols, London 1822

Walpole, Horace, *Memoirs of the Reign of King George the Third*, London 1845

Walpole, Horace, *Letters*, vol. 9 (1774-1776), Oxford 1904

Walpole, Horace, *Correspondence with the Countess of Upper Ossory*, 3 vols, Yale 1965

Wellesley, Richard, Marquis, *Memoirs and Correspondence* (ed. Robert R. Pearce), 3 vols, London 1846

Wentworth Papers 1705-1739, Notes by J. J. Cartwright, London 1887

Whately, E. Jane, *Life and Correspondence of Richard Whately*, 2 vols, London 1866

Wortley, Montague, Lady Mary, *Letters and Works* (ed. Lord Wharncliffe), 3 vols, London 1837

Wraxall, Nathaniel William, *Posthumous Memoirs of His Own Times*, 3 vols, London 1818

Wynn, Frances Williams, *Diaries of a Lady of Quality 1797-1844* (ed. A Hayward), London 1864

OTHER SOURCES

A Serenade ... to be presented at Dublin Castle, 28 May 1725, Dublin 1725

Airlie, Mabel, Countess of, *In Whig Society 1775-1818*, London 1921

Airlie, Mabel, *Lady Palmerston and Her Times*, 2 vols, London 1922

Anon., *Baratariana*, Dublin 1777

Anon., 'Lord Clarendon's Policy in Ireland in Dublin', *University Magazine* 37 (1851), pp. 136-57

Anon., *The King's Visit to Ireland*, Dublin 1821

Anon., 'Phases of Social Life', in *DUM*, vol. 65 (1865), pp. 230-40

Anon., *A Detail of Facts Relating to Ireland*, Dublin 1822

Anon., 'Ireland Sixty Years Ago', in *DUM*, vol. 21, pp. 728-44

Anon., *The Vices of Viceroyalty*, Dublin 1850

Anon., *The Mourners: A Sketch from Life*, Dublin 1787

Ballantyne, Archibald, *Lord Carteret: A Political Biography 1690-1763,* London 1887

Bartlett, Thomas, and D.W. Hayton, eds, *Penal Era and Golden Age*, Belfast 1979

Bartlett, Thomas, *Macartney in Ireland 1768-1772*, PRONI, Belfast 1982

Bartlett, Thomas, 'Opposition in Late Eighteenth-Century Ireland: the Case of the Townshend Viceroyalty', in *Dub. Hist. Rec.* 22, pp. 313-30

Bartlett, Thomas, Kevin Dawson and Daire Keogh, *Rebellion: A Television History of 1798*, Dublin 1998

Bayley, William J., *Historical Sketch and Description of Dublin Castle*, Dublin c. 1870

Beattie, John M., *The English Court in the Reign of George I*, Cambridge 1967

Beckett, J.C., *The Anglo-Irish Tradition*, London 1976

Beckett, J.C., *Eighteenth-Century Ireland*, in T.W. Moody and W.E. Vaughan (eds), *A New History of Ireland*, vol. 4

Bence-Jones, Mark, *Twilight of the Ascendancy*, London 1987

Berry, H.F., 'Notes from the Diary of a Dublin Lady in the Reign of George II', in *JRSAI* 8, pp. 141-51

Birrell, Augustine, *Things Past Redress*, London 1937

Boucher, François, *A History of Costumes in the West*, London 1967

Bowen, Elizabeth, *Bowen's Court*, 2nd ed., New York 1964

Bowen, Elizabeth, *The Shelbourne*, London 1951

Brialmont, M., *History of the Life of Arthur, Duke of Wellington*. With additions by G.R. Gleig. 4 vols, London 1858

Briggs, Asa, *The Age of Improvement*, London 1959

Brynn, Edward, *Crown and Castle: British Rule in Ireland 1800-1830*, Dublin 1978

Burke, Bernard, *The Romance of the Aristocracy*, 3 vols, London 1855

Burke, Bernard, *The Rise of Great Families*, London 1873

Burke, Edmund, *Reflections on the Revolution in France*, Dublin 1790

Burns, Robert E., *Irish Parliamentary Politics in the Eighteenth Century*, 2 vols, Washington 1989-90

Butler, Mary E.L., 'The Irish Gentlewoman; as She is and as She ought to be', *New Ireland Review* 15 (1901)

Cannon, John, *Aristocratic Century: the Peerage of Eighteenth-Century England*, London 1984

Carswell, John, *From Revolution to Revolution: England 1688-1776*, London 1973

Carswell, John, *The Old Cause*, London 1954

Cassidy, James P., *Treatise on the Theory and Practice of Dancing*, Dublin 1810

Colles, Ramsay, *In Castle and Court House*, London 1911

A Contest between Marysas and Apollo to be presented, 28 May 1723

Comerford, R.V., *The Land War and the Politics of Distress 1870-1921*, in T.W. Moody and W.E. Vaughan (eds), *A New History of Ireland*, vol. 6

Comerford, R.V., *The Parnell Era 1883-1891*, in T.W. Moody and W.E. Vaughan (eds), *A New History of Ireland*, vol. 6

Connolly, S.J., *Aftermath and Adjustment*, in T.W. Moody and W.E. Vaughan (eds), *A New History of Ireland*, vol. 5

Connolly, S.J., *The Catholic Question 1801-1812*, in T.W. Moody and W.E. Vaughan (eds), *A New History of Ireland*, vol. 5

Corkayne, G. E., *State of the Peerage of Ireland at and Since the Union*, London 1889

Corish, Patrick J., 'Cardinal Cullen and the National Association of Ireland', in *Reactions to Irish Nationalism 1865-1914*, London 1987

Cornforth, John, 'Dublin Castle', in *Country Life*, July–August 1970

Craig, Maurice, *Dublin 1660-1860*, Dublin 1969

Cullen, L.M., *Life in Ireland*, London 1968

Daunt, W.J. O'Neill, *A Life Spent for Ireland*, London 1896

Dickson, David (ed.), *The Gorgeous Mask: Dublin 1700-1850*, Dublin 1987

Dickson, David, *New Foundations: Ireland 1660-1800*, Dublin 1987

Dickinson, P.L., *The Dublin of Yesterday*, London 1929

Doyle, William, *The Old European Order 1660-1800*, 2nd ed., Oxford 1992

Duggan, G.C. (Periscope), 'The Last Days of Dublin Castle', in *Blackwood's Magazine* 212 (1922) pp. 137-90

Dunlevy, Mairead, *Dress in Ireland*, London 1989

Edgeworth, Maria, *Castle Rackrent and The Absentee*, Oxford 1910

Egmont, John Perceval, second Earl of Egmont, *The Question of the Precedency of the Peers of Ireland in England Fairly Stated*, Dublin 1739

Falkiner, C. Litton, 'The Phoenix Park, its Origin and Early History', in *Proc. RIA*, Third ser. 6, Dublin 1900-2

Ferguson, M.C., *Sir Samuel Ferguson in the Ireland of his Day*, 2 vols, London 1896

Fitzgerald, Percy (A Native), *Recollection of Dublin Castle and of Dublin Society*, London 1902

Fitzpatrick, William J., *Lady Morgan: Her Career, Literary and Personal*, Dublin 1860

Fitzpatrick, William J., *The Life, Times and Correspondence of Rev. Dr. Doyle*, 2 vols, Dublin 1880

Foster, R.F., *Modern Ireland 1600-1972*, London 1988

Fraser, Flora, *The Unruly Queen*, London 1996

Freeman, T.W., *Pre-famine Ireland*, Manchester 1957

Froude, James A., *The English in Ireland in the Eighteenth Century*, 3 vols, London 1872-4

Gamble, J., *Sketches of the History, Politics and Manners taken in Dublin and the North of Ireland in the Autumn of 1810*, London 1811

Gash, Norman, *Mr. Secretary Peel: The Life of Sir Robert Peel to 1830*, London 1961

Gatty, Charles Tindall, *Recognita: A Memoir of the Right Hon. George Wyndham*, Naas 1914

Gilbert, J.T., *A History of the City of Dublin*, 3 vols, Dublin 1861

Gilbert, J.T., *History of the Viceroys of Ireland*, Dublin 1865

Gilbert, J.T. and Lady, eds, *Calendar of Ancient Records of Dublin*, 19 vols, Dublin 1889-1944

Gordon, James, *A History of Ireland*, 2 vols, Dublin 1805

Gould, William (ed.), *Lives of the Georgian Age 1714-1837*, London 1978

Greig, James, *The Diaries of a Duchess*, London 1926

Greville, Charles C.F., *Past and Present Policy of England towards Ireland*, London 1845

Gribbon, H.D., *Economic and Social History 1850-1921*, in T.W. Moody and W.E. Vaughan (eds), *A New History of Ireland*, vol. 6

Gwynn, Stephen, and Gertrude Tuckwell, *The Life of Sir Charles W. Dilke*, 2 vols, London 1917

Hammond, John Lawrence, *Gladstone and the Irish*, London 1964

Hammond, Joseph W., *The Hell-Fire Club*, Dublin n.d.

Hastings, Reginald Rawdon, Report on MSS, HMC London 1934

Hatton, Ragnhild, *George the First, Elector and King*, London 1978

Hayward, Abraham, *The Art of Dining*, London 1898

Hill, Jacqueline, *From Patriots to Unionists: Dublin Civic Politics and Irish Protestant Patriotism 1660-1840*, Oxford 1997

Hinde, Wendy, *Catholic Emancipation: A Shake to Men's Minds*, Oxford 1992

Howard, Hugh, *Parliamentary History of Ireland*, HMC Rep. 3, 1872-4, pp. 432-4

Hunt, William (ed.), *The Irish Parliament 1775*, London 1907

Ingram, Thomas Dunbar, *A History of the Legislative Union of Great Britain and Ireland*, London 1888

Ireland's Happiness Completed or a New Poem on His Grace, the Duke of Grafton, Dublin 1723

James, Francis Godwin, *Ireland in the Empire 1688-1800*, Cambridge, Mass., 1973

Johnston, Edith M., *Great Britain and Ireland 1760-1800*, London 1963

Jupp, Peter, *Lord Grenville 1759-1839*, Oxford 1985

Kennedy, Tom (ed.), *Victorian Dublin*, Dublin 1980

Kerr, Donal A., *Peel, Priests and Politics*, Oxford 1982

Lambe, Patrick, *Royal Cooking or the Compleat Court Cook*, 3rd ed., London 1726

Laver, James, *Taste and Fashion from the French Revolution until Today*, London 1937

Lecky, W.E.H., *A History of Ireland in the Eighteenth Century*, 5 vols, London 1912

Le Fanu, J. Sheridan, *The Cock and Anchor*, 3 vols, Dublin 1845

Lever, Charles, *Jack Hinton*, London 1897

Lewis, R., *The Dublin Guide*, Dublin 1787

Lyons, F.S.L., *The Aftermath of Parnell: 1891-1903*, in T.W. Moody and W.E. Vaughan (eds), *A New History of Ireland*, vol. 6

Lyons, F.S.L., *The Watershed 1903-1907*, in T.W. Moody and W.E. Vaughan (eds), *A New History of Ireland*, vol. 6

Lyons, F.S.L., *The Developing Crisis 1907-1914*, in T.W. Moody and W.E. Vaughan (eds), *A New History of Ireland*, vol. 6

McBride, Lawrence W., *The Greening of Dublin Castle*, Washington 1991

MacCaffrey, James, *History of the Catholic Church in the Nineteenth Century (1789-1908)*, 2 vols, Dublin 1909

McColgan, John, *British Policy and the Irish Administration 1920-1922*, London 1983

McCracken, J.L., *The Political Structure 1714-1760*, in T.W. Moody and W.E. Vaughan (eds), *A New History of Ireland*, vol. 4

McCracken, J L., *The Irish Parliament in the Eighteenth Century*, Dundalk 1971

McCracken, J.L., *The Social Structure and Social Life 1714-1760*, in T.W. Moody and W.E. Vaughan (eds), *A New History of Ireland*, vol. 4

McDonagh, Frank, 'The Viceroyalty and Catholic Disabilities', in *Ir. Ecc. Rec.*, Fifth Ser., pp. 373-83

MacDonagh, Michael, *The Viceroy's Post-bag*, London 1904

MacDonagh, Oliver, 'The Politicization of the Irish Catholic Bishops 1800-1850', in *Hist. Journ.* 18, London 1975

MacDonagh, Oliver, *O'Connell: the Life of Daniel O'Connell*, London 1991

McDowell, R.B., *The Irish Administration 1801 -1914*, London 1964

McDowell, R.B., *Ireland in 1800*, in T.W. Moody and W.E. Vaughan (eds), *A New History of Ireland*, vol. 4

McDowell, R.B., 'The Irish Executive in the Nineteenth Century', in *Dub. Hist. Rec.* 9, pp. 264-80

McNeill, Charles, 'Notes on Dublin Castle', in *Jn. Roy. Soc. Ant. Ire.*, Ser. 7, vol. 10, pp. 194-9

Madden, Daniel Owen, *Ireland and its Rulers since 1829*, 3 vols, London 1844

Madden, Daniel Owen, *The Castle and the Country*, 3 vols, Dublin 1850

Maguire, J.B., *Dublin Castle: Historical Background and Guide*, Dublin 1992

Mahaffy, J.P., *Society in Georgian Dublin in Georgian Society Records*, 3, 1911

Malcolmson, A.P.W., *John Foster: The Politics of the Anglo-Irish Ascendancy*, Oxford 1975

Mant, Richard, *History of the Church of Ireland*, London 1840

Martineau, Harriet, *Biographical Sketches*, London 1861

Maxwell, Constantia, *Dublin under the Georges 1714-1830*, London 1936

Maxwell, Constantia, *Country and Town in Ireland under the Georges*, Dublin 1940

Meenan, F.O.C., 'The Medical Consultants of Dublin: A Social and Political Portrait', in *Essays in Honour of J.D.H. Widdess*, Dublin 1978

Melville, Edward, *Sketches of Society in France and Ireland 1805-7*, 2 vols, Dublin 1811

Molloy, J. Fitzgerald, *Court below Stairs*, 4 vols, London 1883

Molloy, J. Fitzgerald, *The Life and Adventures of Peg Woffington*, 2 vols, London 1884

Montgomery, K.L., 'Successful Beauties of the Last Century', in *The New Ireland Review* 5, Dublin 1890

Moore, George, *A Drama in Muslin*, Dublin 1886

Morley, John Viscount, *Recollections*, 2 vols, London 1917

Morris, Esther, 'The Delanys of Delville', in *Dub. Hist. Rec.* 9 (4) pp. 105-16

Munck, Thomas, *Seventeenth-Century Europe: State, Conflict and the Social Order in Europe 1598-1700*, Basingstoke 1990

Murray, Marjorie, 'Entertainment in Eighteenth-Century Dublin', in *Dub. Hist. Rec.* 22 (4), pp. 288-95

Norman, E.R., *The Catholic Church and Ireland in the Age of Rebellion 1899-1873*, London 1965

O'Brien, Gerard, *Anglo-Irish Politics in the Age of Grattan and Pitt*, Dublin 1987

O'Brien, R. Barry, *Dublin Castle and the Irish People*, 2nd ed., London 1912

O'Broin, Leon, *The Chief Secretary: Augustine Birrell in Ireland*, London 1965

O'Carroll, Joseph, 'Towards the Homeless Poor 1725-1775', in *The Gorgeous Mask: Dublin 1700-1850* (ed. David Dickson), Dublin 1987

O'Connell, Maurice R., *Irish Politics and Social Conflict in the Age of American Revolution*, Philadelphia 1965

O'Dwyer, Frederick, 'The Ballroom of Dublin Castle', in *Decantations: A Tribute to Maurice Craig* (ed. Agnes Bernelle), Dublin 1992

O'Dwyer, Frederick, 'Dublin Castle and its State Apartments 1660-1922', in *The Court Historian*, 2, February 1997

O'Mahony, Charles, *The Viceroys of Ireland*, London 1912

Palmer, R.R., *The Age of the Democratic Revolution: A Political History of Europe and America 1760-1800*, 2 vols, London 1959-64

Pemberton, W. Baring, *Carteret: the Brilliant Failure of the Eighteenth Century*, London 1936

Pentland, Marjorie, *A Bonnie Fechter*, London 1952

Percival, John, Second Earl of Egmont, *The Question of the Procedures of the Peers of Ireland in England Fairly Stated*, Dublin 1739

Petrie, Charles, *The Victorians*, London 1960

Puckler-Muskau, Hermann, *Tour in England, Ireland and France in 1828 and 1829*, 2 vols, Birmingham 1832

Riddell, Edwin, *Lives of the Stuart Age 1603-1714*, London 1976

Robins, Joseph, *The Lost Children: A Study of Charity Children in Ireland 1700-1900*, Dublin 1980

Robinson, Lennox, *Curtain Up*, London 1942

Ross, F.E. [F.E.R.], *Historical Reminiscences*, Dublin 1896

Ross, Ian Campbell (ed.), *Public Virtue, Public Love*, Dublin 1986

Sachs, Curt, *World History of the Dance*, London 1938

Sharp, Cecil J., *The Dance: A Historical Survey of Dancing in Europe*, London 1924

Shellabarger, Samuel, *Lord Chesterfield*, London 1935

Simms, J.G., *The Restoration 1660-1685*, in in T.W. Moody and W.E. Vaughan (eds), *A New History of Ireland*, vol. 3

Simms, J.G., *The Establishment of Protestant Ascendancy 1691-1714*, in T.W. Moody and W.E. Vaughan (eds), *A New History of Ireland*, vol. 3

Smith, Robert, *Court Cookery or the Compleat English Cook*, London 1724

Somerville-Large, Peter, *Dublin*, London 1979

Stacpoole, Duke de, *Irish and Other Memories*, London 1922

Stanhope, Earl, *History of England Comprising of the Reign of Queen Anne 1701-1713*, London 1870

Starkie, Enid, *A Lady's Child*, London 1941

Sullivan, T. D., *Recollections of Troubled Times in Irish Politics*, Dublin 1905

Swift, Jonathan, *A Modest Proposal for Preventing the Children of the Poor from being a Burden*, etc., Dublin 1729

Swift, Jonathan, 'A Short Character of his Excellency, the Earl of Wharton', in *Prose Works* 15, London 1901

Swift, Jonathan, *Journal to Stella*, in *Prose Works* 12, London 1897

Swift, Jonathan, *Miscellany of Biographical Pieces, etc.* (ed. Davis Herbert), Oxford 1962

Thackeray, William Makepeace, *Irish Sketch Book of 1842*, London 1908

Tighe, Gregory E., *A Brief Sketch of the Marquess of Anglesey's Administration*, Dublin 1829

Tighe, Gregory E., *Ireland in 1829: the First Year's administration of the Duke of Northumberland*, Dublin 1830

Taylor, W. Cooke, *Life and Times of Sir Robert Peel*, 4 vols, London 1846

Wall, Maureen, 'Government Policy towards Catholics during the Viceroyalty of the Duke of Bedford 1757-1761', in *Catholic Ireland in the Eighteenth Century*, Dublin 1989

Walsh, John Edward, *Ireland One and Hundred and Twenty Years Ago*, Dublin 1911

Warburton, J., J. Whitelaw and R. Walsh, *History of the City of Dublin*, 2 vols, London 1818

White, Terence de Vere, *The Story of the Royal Dublin Society*, Tralee 1953

White, Terence de Vere, *The Anglo-Irish*, London 1972

Wilkinson, Neville R., *To All and Singular*, London 1925

Wood, Herbert, *The Office of Chief Governor of Ireland 1172-1509*, in *Proc RIA*, 36 Sect., pp. 206-38

Wynne, Maud, *An Irishman and his Family: Lord Morris and Killanin*, London 1937

Wyse, Thomas, *Historical Sketch of the Late Catholic Association of Ireland*, 2 vols, London 1829

Young, G.M., *Early Victorian England*, 2 vols, London 1934

DIRECTORIES

Biographia Britannia, London 1784
Burke's Peerage and Baronetage, 106th edition 1999
The Complete Peerage, London 1959
Dictionary of National Biography, 1878–

NEWSPAPERS AND MAGAZINES

Annual Register, 1758-
Blackwood's Magazine, 1817-1922
Dublin Evening Mail, 1823-1922
Dublin Evening Post, 1719, 1732-1875
Dublin Gazette, 1706-1921
Dublin Satirist, 1833-6
Dublin University Magazine, 1833-1922
Faulkner's Dublin Journal, 1726-1825
Express (Dublin), 1832-3
Freeman's Journal, 1763-1924
Gentlemen's Magazine, 1731-1907
Hibernian Magazine (Walker's), 1771-1812
Illustrated Dublin Journal, 1861-2
Illustrated London News, 1842-88

Irish Independent, 1891-1922
Irish Protestant, 1901-15
Irish Times, 1859-1922
The Lady of the House, 1890-1924
The Leader, 1900-22
Paddy Kelly's Budget, 1832-6
Pue's Occurrences, 1704-68
Quarterly Review, 1809-1922
Saunder's News Letter, 1767-1879
The Times, 1815-1922
Whalley's Newsletter, 1714-23

Index